UNIONS AN.

# UNIONS AND LEADERS
# IN GHANA

# A Model of Labor
# and Development

**PAUL S. GRAY**
Department of Sociology, **Boston College**

CONCH MAGAZINE LIMITED (PUBLISHERS)
Owerri    New York    London
1981

Design and Composition by
Conch Typesetting and Graphic Services
Printed in the United States of America by
Celecom Corporation, East Longmeadow, MA


First published 1981

Library of Congress Cataloging in Publication Data

Gray, Paul S   1943-
Unions and leaders in Ghana.
Bibliography: p.
Includes index.
1. Trade-unions—Ghana—History. 2. Ghana—
Economic conditions. 3. Ghana Trades Union
Congress. I. Title
HD6886.G7   331.88'09667   80-18482
ISBN 0-914970-57-7
ISBN 0-914970-58-5 (pbk.)

# Contents

Preface, *ix*

I **Trade Unions and Development, 1**
  The Value of Unions for Poor Countries, 2
    *Unions and Modernization, 3*
    *Critiques of Modernization Theory, 4*
    *The Limits of the Dependency Idea, 5*
    Unions as Institutions, 7
  The Plan of This Book, 9

II **The Legal and Political Environment for Trade Unionism, 11**
  Unions before the Nationalist Struggle, 13
  The Political Connection, 16
  The 1950 Strike, 20
  Divisions and Factions, 23
    *Reunification of the Congress, 25*
    *Summary, 28*
  The "New Structure", 29
    *Origins of the New Structure Idea, 29*
    *Opposition within the TUC, 31*
    *Opposition within the CPP, 33*
    *Parliamentary Debate, 35*
    *The Concordat, 38*
    *1959 and 1960 Amendments, 40*
  Unions in Socialist Ghana, 42
  The Effects of Freedom of Association, 43
  The Effects of Politics, 46
  The Dissolution, September 1971, 49
  Legal and Political Framework in the 1970's, 53

III Patterns of Exchange Between Unions and Society, 55

Government Resources and Policy, 56
  *Two Post-Coup Regimes,* 60
  *The National Redemption Council,* 61
Ties with Private Organizations, 65
  *Employers' Associations,* 65
  *Other Domestic Groups,* 67
  *Foreign Resources,* 68
Effects on Competing Organizations, 70
The *Quid Pro Quo:* Some Brief Observations, 73
  *National Productivity,* 73
  *Socialization of Workers,* 75
Conclusions, 76

IV Industrial Relations: The Continuity of Norms and Rules, 79

Settling Disputes Through Negotiation, 79
  *Before the "New Structure",* 79
  *The Basis for Improving Labor Relations,* 82
  *The New Industrial Relations are Tested,* 87
  *Under the NRC,* 92
  *Summary,* 95
Limiting Issues of Conflict, 96
  *Bargaining: 1959-1966,* 96
  *Bargaining: 1966-1971,* 101
  *Bargaining Since Restoration,* 103
  *Conclusion,* 106
Avoiding Violence, 107
Respect for Opponents' Viability, 111
  *Colonialism,* 111
  *The Nkrumah Years,* 111
  *The Immediate Post-Coup Period,* 112
  *The Progress Party Regime,* 114
  *Since 1972,* 116

V Leadership Skills and Roles, 119

Learning to Lead, 119
  *Education,* 120

*Career Patterns,* 121
Variety of Leadership, 122
   *Early Leadership Roles,* 123
   *The Sekondi "Labor Fighters,"* 124
   *The Primacy of Labor Politicians,* 126
   *The Development of Administrative Roles,* 127
The Legacy of Role Conflict and Ambiguity, 129
   *Branch vs. National Leaders,* 129
   *Administration vs. Bargaining,* 130
   *Limited Democracy,* 131
   *External Pressures,* 132
   *National Leaders of the Future,* 134

## VI  Leadership Norms and Values, 137

Codes of Personal Conduct, 137
   *Status Confirmation,* 137
   *Corruption,* 138
   *Honesty,* 141
Norms Which Reduce Conflict, 142
   *The Impact of Ethnicity,* 143
   *Mutual Dependence* 144
   *Mutual Accountability,* 146
   *Testing Leadership Unity,* 148
   *Responding to Challenges,* 150
   *Leadership Unity and Congress Autonomy,* 152
Leadership Ideology, 153
   *Political Realism,* 153
   *Political Independence and Socialism,* 156
Continuity with the Past, 162
Conclusion, 165

## VII  The Reactions of Workers and a Wider Public, 167

Worker Allegiance to Leaders, 167
   *Ethnicity,* 168
   *Personal Contact with Workers,* 169
   *Demonstrated Courage,* 171
   *Achieving Unionist Objectives,* 173
Commitment of Members to Unions, 177
   *Assimilation of Unionist Attitudes,* 178

*Acceptance of Union Ideology,* 179
Public Opinion of Organized Labor, 181
  *Union Goals and Public Values,* 181
  *The Voice of the People,* 184
  *National Debate on the TUC,* 186
  *Contemporary Opinion of the Unions,* 191
  *Summary,* 193

**VIII   Conclusion, 195**

Findings, 195
TUC Autonomy in the Future, 197
Sociological Implications, 198
The Ghana Model, 200

Appendices, 203

Notes, 209

Bibliography, 219

Index, 227

# Preface

I did not begin my research on Ghanaian trade unionism with the idea that organized labor could rescue this small, developing West African state from its economic difficulties. But neither did I have the pre-conceived notion, today popular in some quarters, that unions are irrelevant to the struggles of Third World peoples to maximize their own freedom. I did believe that many of the causes of the social conflict which accompanies economic development might be isolated by examining the interaction among unions, their leaders, and the environment in which they operate.

If the Ghana Trades Union Congress appears in these pages as a model of institutional growth, this also was not what I initially set out to demonstrate. However, it was impressed upon me by the overwhelming evidence from 14 months in the field. The evolution of trade unions in Ghana became, for me, a case history of how social institutions are formed in the Third World, how they cope with political instability and economic stagnation, and how they contribute to the welfare of their members and nations. The "Ghana model" demonstrates more than the survival of a particular labor movement. It may be an inspiration to those who have created, and who have attempted to lead, many different kinds of organizations. Within the limits imposed by the poverty and economic dependence of their countries, emerging institutions *can* make a difference in the quality of life for millions of people.

This work could not have been carried out without the aid of several groups and individuals. The Comparative Sociology Traineeship Program of the National Institutes of Mental

Health gave financial assistance during my field work in Africa, as well as during the months of my preparation for the field. A generous grant from the Concilium on International and Area Studies at Yale University provided funds for transportation and a supplement to my stipend. I also express thanks to the Institute of African Studies, University of Ghana, Legon, for furnishing me with a base from which to operate when abroad. The African Research Library, Accra, was also most helpful, as was Miss Marjorie Nicholson, of the British Trades Union Congress in London, who kindly allowed me access to the extensive BTUC files on the labor movement in Ghana.

Professors Wendell Bell, David Apter, and Louis Wolf Goodman, of Yale University added to this enterprise with their wise suggestions. Andrew Beveridge, of Columbia University, Rolf Gerritsen and Roger Selley, of the University of Ghana, Jon Kraus, of the State University of New York at Fredonia, Anthony Oberschall, of the University of North Carolina at Chapel Hill, and Joseph Sclafani, of Brown University, each contributed valuable ideas through stimulating discussion of my project when it was in its formative stages.

My acknowledgements would not be complete, however, without mentioning my closest associates in Ghana, naturally, my wife and dear friends, both North American and Ghanaian, but, in particular, many of the leaders of the Ghana Trades Union Congress and its member unions. To these latter individuals, who must of necessity remain anonymous, my greatest debt is owed. Without their cooperation and encouragement this book could not have been written. Indeed, at all stages of the trade union hierarchy, from the topmost leaders to ordinary Ghanaian working men and women, I received the kind of courteous hearing which made this project personally satisfying.

                                                    PAUL S. GRAY
*Chestnut Hill, Massachusetts*
*1980*

## CHAPTER I

# Trade Unions and Development

The French philosopher Montesquieu remarked that social institutions are first created *de novo* by leaders, and that subsequently institutions evolve to the point where they produce leaders themselves. This process is not unusual for Europe and North America. However, it is rare for the developing nations of Africa, Asia, and Latin America, where poverty and the legacy of imperialism make the creation of viable institutions, in politics, education or business, problematic, and where effective leadership is scarce. Hence, this book concerns extraordinary events in an ordinary setting. It is a study of the growth of labor unions in Ghana and their modest, but real, successes. It explains the creation of the Ghana Trades Union Congress (TUC) out of the legal and political environment of colonialism and nationalism, and its survival over the past two decades.

To supplement the historical record, many of the primary data were collected via participant observation of the day to day functioning of the TUC and its constituent unions between August 1972 and November 1973.[1] These data became the basis for an examination of the present-day relations between the unions and their members, as well as the linkages which connect the Congress with Ghanaian society as a whole.

This book is also about the applicability of the Ghanaian example to the understanding of events elsewhere, both empirically and theoretically. As one of the most effective workers' movements of its kind in black Africa, the Ghana TUC may be a practical "model" for other groups of labor unions. But, in a larger sense, what is its significance for development? On this point there is much confusion. Are the unions too weak, as some proponents of "modernization" theory would maintain, or too strong, as some advocates of the "dependency" perspective have claimed? The approach taken in this book is an alternative to these two major theoretical explanations of union growth in poor countries. Unions are not viewed here as flawed copies of their counterparts in western nations, nor as traitors to the ideals of social revolution. Using evidence from Ghana, we suggest that neither conception of unionism is appropriate for Africa, and that Ghana's experience provides heretofore unappreciated lessons for other countries. Before we present our findings, let us examine the sources of the theoretical contradictions and the manner in which this book attempts to resolve them.

## THE VALUE OF UNIONS FOR POOR COUNTRIES

Trade unions are fully legitimate institutions in western society.[2] We are familiar with how they improve members' wages and working conditions and help to smooth industrial relations between workers and management. Less obvious, however, is the value of labor organizations for the developing nations. In Africa the absence of reliable, longitudinal economic data and the relatively brief history of most unions make it difficult to evaluate their performance. In the case of Ghana and several other countries there has been a spirited, if inconclusive, debate concerning whether the improvement in the quality of life for wage labor over the past 35 years has been the result of union efforts, or even whether such improvement has actually occurred.

There have been several useful studies of individual African unions.[3] These have described union structure and leadership, and the relationship between labor and nationalist politics. However, they have been more productive in adding to the historical record than in giving us a precise, theoretical understanding of the role of labor in development.[4] When we study unions in depth, we see the inevitable contradictions which resist elegant systems of explanation: highly skilled, as well as inept, leaders; honest officials and corrupt ones; active and passive workers; and unions which sometimes appear to exercise real clout, but which subsequently act as mere mouthpieces for government.

It is no accident, therefore, that the most influential explanations for the behavior of organized labor in the African context have not been "grounded" in the observation of unions over a lengthy period. Rather, they have been applied to Africa based on general theories of modernization, capitalist economic growth, and Third World dependency. These theories begin with implicit images of trade unions, rather than with their concrete accomplishments and real shortcomings.

*Unions and Modernization*

Until the mid-1960's, the dominant image of emerging labor movements came from liberal analysts of world affairs, who assumed a unilinear, evolutionary path to modernization. According to this view, the highly industrialized economies, urbanization, and intricate division of labor found in the United States and other wealthy countries is the future toward which most of the new states are evolving. Therefore, organizations such as trade unions, which facilitate a smooth transition to a modern social order in western countries, are to be welcomed elsewhere.[5] The changes which unions advocate are desirable and inevitable, to the liberal observer. Labor participation in nationalist struggles should be seen not as dangerous, but as a pluralistic check on dictatorship and as a sign that labor is ready to take its place in nation-building.[6]

Proponents of modernization theory see trade unions as replicas of similar groups which appeared at analagous stages of industrialization in Europe and North America. Thus, it has been suggested that unions may help the worker by cushioning the impact of migration and rapid social change, and that they may imbue the workforce with "labor commitment."[7] Based on this conception of unionism, researchers looked for evidence that organized labor was helping to establish the norms of modern factory routine, promptness, efficiency, and loyalty to a particular job or employer.[8]

This image of unions carries the implication that they are no more a force for revolutionary change in the Third World than in the United States. The subordination of labor to the owners of factories and controllers of capital goes unchallenged. In fact, according to the theory, unions are potentially valuable in part because they might have a beneficial effect on national productivity.

The history of the past 15 years has helped to discredit the approach to the role of organized labor taken by modernization theory. Political instability and no-growth economies are typical in many Third World states, and the record shows that in most cases trade unions have not been permitted to challenge political parties. Neither have they had an appreciable impact on productivity. The attitude of workers *per se* has turned out to be a much less significant reason for the failure of nations to develop than the neo-colonial economic and cultural relationships which have been maintained between former colonies and their wealthy trading partners. Moreover, those unions that did survive often took on functions of political mobilization and became controlled by the state and party bureaucracies. In this respect, they deviated from the pattern of union behavior and growth established in western countries, and from the image of voluntarism. As a result, proponents of modernization theory condemned them as ineffective and circumscribed institutions, without appreciating that divergent paths to development are possible.[9] Plainly, the fact that trade unions have existed in some African countries for 40 years is worthy of our attention. From the perspective of modernization theory, however, it is difficult to see how they are contributing to the states in which they operate, because they are assumed to be only weak approximations of their counterparts in the western, capitalist democracies.

*Critiques of Modernization Theory*

The prescriptive nature of modernization theory, its naive optimism, and its failure to place the appearance of trade unions in the context of neo-colonialism has led to new interpretations of the role of organized labor in development in recent years. According to these critiques, trade unions were at least in part responsible for the collapse of the "development decade" of the 1960's. The argument has been joined by those on the Right as well as on the Left of the political spectrum sho, albeit for opposite reasons, have made similar indictments against Third World unionism. Both have claimed that where unions in Africa are effective in obtaining concessions for their members, they are a wasteful luxury.[10]

The conservative critique accepts the premise of modernization theory that development is possible under the world capitalist order and the tutelage of wealthy countries, but it denies the legitimacy of labor unions in fragile economies. In this view, growth in Gross National Product is essential to modernization. Labor unions serve merely to deprive the business community and government of the capital needed for reinvestment in the economy. Ironically, the radical critique, today the more influential, arrives at the same conclusion about trade unions, although it rejects the idea that increases in GNP or other similar measures are synonymous with true development and independence.[11] According to many on the Left, union members are *de facto* a "labor aristocracy," an unproductive segment of the work force whose gains are made at the expense of the rural masses and the urban poor. This image of trade unions in developing countries depicts them as natural allies of the large firms and multinational corporations which promote the dependency of Third World states.

*The Limits of the Dependency Idea*

The "dependency" critique lays to rest many of the myths of modernization and explains the complacency of many Third World trade unions, as well as the economic failures of developing states. But research into the day to day operation of the Ghana Trades Union Congress provides convincing evidence that, at least in that case, it is based on faulty premises. As we shall see, some of the strongest unions in Ghana are those which have signed collective agreements with foreign-owned enterprises. However, this does not automatically make their members a "labor aristocracy."

It will be demonstrated that Ghanaian unions have not drowned out the aspirations of the urban poor; on the contrary, they have articulated the grievances of the jobless and have ensured their demands a wider audience. This is natural in an African setting where extended family and communalism are still important social norms, and where a wage worker with regular employment is a resource for many other people. Similarly, it will be shown that Ghana's farmers, the supposed competitors of union members, have declined to participate in political alliances advocating the weakening of the labor movement. This is not surprising, either, when one considers that virtually every union member in the country has relatives in the agricultural sector of the economy. These phenomena call into question the existence of a "labor aristocracy" and, hence, the applicability of the dependency critique to the study of unions in other African countries as well.

One cannot deny the subordinate position of Ghana in world markets for her primary products, cocoa, timber and metal ore, nor the impact of decisions made in western capitals on Ghana's economic planning and administration. Actually, growth in trade union membership itself has been negatively influenced by Ghana's dependency, to the extent that capital-intensive projects almost inevitably are preferred to labor-intensive ones, to the potential benefit of multinational business and the detriment of the unions. However, if the existence of a "labor aristocracy" is questionable, then the power of the dependency critique as an explanatory tool is limited. It may explain the poverty of the country as a whole, but not why trade unions took the particular organizational form which they now exhibit, nor how they achieved a measure of power in relation to government. Ghana's subordination in the international arena, as a discrete variable, bears little relationship to the honesty of labor officials, their level of skill, or their reputation with the rank and file or with the public. These are important issues which will not go away, in spite of claims that the significance of African unions is only the extent to which they facilitate or hinder a radical challenge to neo-colonial domination.[12] Ghanaian unions may not be radical, but they are worth trying to understand, nonetheless.

## Unions as Institutions

This book describes and analyzes the process of *institutionalization* which organized labor in Ghana has experienced — in other words, the process by which the attitudes and behavior of labor leaders and their unions have become predictable, expected, and accepted in Ghanaian society. As we discover the reasons for institutionalization, we get to the core reasons for the value of unionism in the African context and reveal more of the latent functions of organized labor than either modernization theory or its dependency critique. For example, unions have survived in part because they satisfy a need for political expression which political parties cannot meet. They have grown because they are more effective in helping to establish a cooperative industrial relations environment than are the governments which have tried to muzzle them. Neither of these trends, evident in Ghana, is adequately addressed, either by theories which see them as weak and ephemeral or by those which depict unions as the minions of world capitalism.

The notion of institutionalization used in this book borrows some concepts from modernization theory as well as Marxian analysis. The modernization idea is of value in sensitizing us to the importation or "transfer" of the labor movement from Britain to Ghana (formerly the Gold Coast). However, the dependency perspective makes us aware of the exploitative context in which this exercise took place. The creation of union structures in Ghana was indeed part of a general process of increasing social differentiation. The form which these structures first took was, of course, affected by norms of traditional group life, but it was primarily the result of the introduction of foreign union models, in part for purposes of colonial domination.

New social roles and clusters of roles appeared, and these had not previously existed in the Gold Coast. As those recruited to fill these roles became union functionaries at various levels, a process of learning occurred in which the recruits recognized their duties and what was expected of them by members and employers. Such socialization, however, included not only the perfection of skills necessary to make progress toward manifest union goals, for example, improving wages, but also the acquisition of those skills needed by leaders to maintain themselves in power. Thus, the new leaders adhered to the pattern of behavior found by Lipset *et al* in American and European unions.[13]

It is at the point where the behavior of early labor leaders became patterned and predictable that we may begin to speak of the institutionalization of the unions. So-called institutional "transfer" produced labor organizations, not genuine institutions. In contrasting the two, Philip Selznick has noted that "the term 'organization' . . . suggests a certain bareness, a lean, no-nonsense system of consciously coordinated activities. It refers to an expendable tool, a rational instrument engineered to do a job." The institution, however, "is more nearly a natural product of social needs and pressures."[14] It is more responsive and adaptive. Its persistence, over time, is accounted for in part by the value of group activity for its members and leaders. It is implicit in previous theoretical treatments of this question that, to the degree that an organization becomes an institution, both the doctrine and purposes of the group will be internalized, and both will become integrated with the life goals of the participants. In addition, it will be perceived that the satisfactions which arise from participation cannot be duplicated by membership in other bodies.[15]

Ample evidence will be presented in this book to indicate that Ghanaian union leaders, at least, have come to value the unions "for their own sake," and not merely as organizations created to perform a specific task. However, this, in itself, would not have ensured the survival of the unions. It has long been recognized that "no institution . . . may be understood in isolation," and that its maintenance and the transmission of its message to new members, or other groups in society, depends on its ties to the larger system of which it is a part.[16] More recently, Melvin Blase noted that "to the extent that an organization succeeds over time in demonstrating the value of its functions and having them accepted by others as important and significant, the organization acquires the status of an 'institution.' "[17]

The impact of an institution upon its environment, its ability to influence economic or political decision making in the larger society, is an indicator of its power. In this work, we define power as a Marxist would; it is not a function of the size of a given group, nor are all institutions equally powerful, in spite of the fact that their members may become attached to, and identify with, their ideas, symbols, rules, and patterns of role relations. Institutions are varying concentrations of power in the service of a set of values and ideals.[18] In the context of underdeveloped, no less than developed contries, unions, as institutions, do grow in response to needs. However, especially in the Third World, where unions have been used as a tool in state building and as a lever for foreign domination, the question of who in society has the authority to define needs is equally important.

In the present treatment, then, the Ghana Trades Union Congress and its 17 affiliated unions will be considered *organizations* which have been in the process of becoming *institutions*. We will show that the Congress is one group in Ghanaian society that has managed, consistently, to exercise power. Internally, the TUC manifests institutional characteristics; it has proven to be relatively long-lasting, with the ability to attract and retain resources and leaders. Externally, it has emerged from political struggles with the capacity to maintain its independence.

## THE PLAN OF THIS BOOK

The remainder of this book is divided as follows: Chapter II explores the political and legal context which permitted the founding of unions in Ghana and which granted them the authority to obtain resources. In Chapter III these resources, membership and income, are assessed, as is the influence of the labor movement upon government decision making. The strength of organized labor is seen as a result of the wide variety of exchanges between unions and the state, the business community, and foreign and domestic voluntary associations. As labor's resource base has grown, so has its ability to negotiate and bargain. Chapter IV examines industrial relations in Ghana, with emphasis on the rules and norms held in common by the Trades Union Congress and its adversaries. The next two chapters are concerned with the leaders of the TUC, the roles they occupy, the skills they have mastered, their codes of conduct, and their attitudes. Then, Chapter VII summarizes the reaction of the rank and file, and the public at large, to the institutional arrangements which are earlier documented. Finally, the Conclusion ties together primary and historical data, commenting on the present-day autonomy of the unions and suggesting that the Ghanaian experience may be helpful as a model for understanding the generic relationship between trade unions and development.

## CHAPTER II

# The Legal and Political Environment for Trade Unionism

When one considers those aspects of the political and legal environment in Ghana which have supported trade unionism or permitted individual unions to come into existence, it is easy to forget how brief the history of modern institutional growth in the country actually is. Until well into the nineteenth century, the colonial mandate was limited to the immediate coastal area, and only a handful of officials and a tiny native elite had been employed in carrying out trade in gold, slaves, and other commodities. When labor unions were legalized in 1941, not even 100 years had passed since the Bond of 1844 had enunciated the British goal of "moulding the customs of the country to the general principles of British law." Labor organizations had been considered fully legitimate for only 16 years before Ghana achieved its independence in 1957. This rapidity of institutional growth against a background of colonialism and underdevelopment must be considered in assessing the effectiveness of its labor movement.

The cash economy after 1900 in the Gold Coast was centered upon the cocoa industry, and until recent years Ghana was the world's major cocoa producer. The value of this crop and her other exports helped produce cash reserves of $800 million at independence.\* Prospects for economic development were as bright as for any African state.

---

\*Official exchange rates for Ghanaian currency appear in Appendix 2.

However, by the time the nation's first president, Kwame Nkrumah, was overthrown in a military coup in 1966, this nest egg had disappeared, and Ghana was burdened with debt. The extent of economic mismanagement in the country during the Nkrumah years has been the subject of much debate.[1] However, the fact is that Ghana, like other Third World countries dependent on the export of raw materials, has found development an elusive goal. Cocoa prices fluctuated disastrously after independence, from 350 pounds sterling per long ton in 1957-58 to a low of 141 pounds in 1964-65. They began a recovery in the late 1960's and reached record high prices in the mid-seventies.[2] But, in spite of this favorable trend, the quality of life for many, perhaps most, Ghanaians has not improved. Inflation, fed by rising fuel costs, was officially estimated to average 23 percent from 1970 to 1976; one unofficial source placed it at over 100 percent for 1977.[3] Moreover, per capita food production decreased, and export figures reflected a stagnating economy, showing an average 3.3 percent decline for the first six years of the 1970's.

These economic realities have had direct impact on the Ghanaian political system. The Nkrumah regime was replaced by the National Liberation Council (NLC), a military government which held power for three years, during which the country's trade deficit was erased.[†] The NLC turned over the government to the civilian regime of Dr. Kofi Busia in 1969. However, by 1971 the debts had begun to increase again, and, faced with the threat of widespread resistance to its unpopular policies, the Busia regime was toppled by a second military coup in January 1972. The officers, led by Colonel Ignatius (Kutu) Acheampong, at first called themselves the National Redemption Council (NRC) and later the Supreme Military Council (SMC). At first, the NRC was welcomed and its members became popular figures, but as the decade progressed, the impatience and dissatisfaction of the public concerning the quality and performance of its leaders grew perceptibly. The SMC became increasingly heavy-

---

[†]The full names of organizations abbreviated in this book are given in Appendix 1.

handed in 1978, particularly in its arrest of those opposing army participation in the government of a proposed Third Republic, provoking a purge of Acheampong and his supporters by Lieutenant General F.W.K. Akuffo. But, in June 1979, a counter-coup led by Lieutenant Jerry Rawlings was successful. In an episode of official bloodletting rare for Ghana, both Acheampong and Akuffo were executed on charges of corruption. A third civilian regime, headed by Hilla Limann, took office in September 1979. Like its predecessors, it is having difficulty fulfilling its targets and promises. The spectre of political instability continues to haunt the country.

In the context of the political and economic events briefly sketched here, trade unions have formed and functioned. For four decades organized labor has been a vital part of Ghanaian history, sometimes actually helping to create the legal and political environment for itself, and sometimes only reacting, along with the rest of the country, to the uncertainties of national leadership and the economy. In our examination of the environment for unionism, we shall see that the labor movement, beginning after World War II, took an active part in the social and political upheavals which moved the British to relinquish control of their colony. However, the unity of Ghanaian labor today, and the absence of rival national trade union centers, is not the legacy of nationalist agitation. Rather, it reflects what happened *after* Africans assumed the power to make laws and public policy.

## UNIONS BEFORE THE NATIONALIST STRUGGLE

Many guilds and artisans' associations existed in the Gold Coast in the nineteenth century. However, they are not properly called "unions" because they were the outgrowth of skills perfected to serve religious and economic needs in the traditional social order, whereas true unions, modern labor organizations, subsequently appeared as the early associations began to adapt to the colonial money economy after 1900, to the growing work force, and to an increasing number of industrial disputes. The weakening of communal and lineage responsbilities among those in urban employment or in mining areas far from home made labor more vulnerable to economic exploitation.

Trade unions, although officially illegal in the colony, were formed when specific grievances were aired in public works, trades, and the civil service. However, they disappeared just as quickly. The government found the escalating labor unrest troublesome in the 1920's and especially during the 1930's, when economic conditions were generally poor, and when illiterate and unskilled workers began to unite and to use the strike weapon for the first time. As early as 1930, Lord Passfield (Sidney Webb) had noted in a dispatch that regulation of wage laborer organizations was of importance, and that colonial governments should act to facilitate the passage of unions into constitutional channels. By the end of the decade, some officials in the Gold Coast had reason to take this advice seriously. Following a cocoa boycott in 1937-38, the Labor Department was formed. Railwaymen soon staged the first truly effective major strike in the history of the country. The workers' low level of subsistence, and the unpredictable nature of the industrial relations process had to be addressed.

The Colonial Development Act (1940) provided that no territory could receive help under the law unless it had in force legislation protecting the rights of trade unions. The result in the Gold Coast was the enactment of the Trade Union Ordinance (1941). Although the colonial government became more positive and activist toward organized labor than ever before, its policy was a combination of liberalism and authoritarianism. The provisions of the 1941 law indicate the unmistakable desire of the British to build up the unions and to use them in order to rationalize labor relations, reduce strikes and absenteeism, and increase efficiency. The Trade Union Ordinance and the Conspiracy and Protection of Property (Trade Disputes) Ordinance allowed for a multiplicity of groups which were weak, poorly financed, and largely ineffective in presenting the cause of labor before government.

In 1942 a Colonial Labor Advisory Committee was created, including members of the British Trades Union Council. As a result, trade union advisors were seconded to the colonial administration. I.G. Jones, a former official of the

Mineworkers' Union in Britain, was recruited to the Gold Coast civil service and headed the Trade Union Section of the Labor Department. Other unionists were absorbed into the department and later, after the war, they began to teach the rudiments of unionism in the Department of Extra-Mural Studies at the newly established University College.

Jones undertook a tour of the country to explain the new labor laws. He reported "considerable suspicion" of Government intentions and a great deal of ignorance concerning the aims and objects of unionism. However, by the end of 1942, four unions had been registered.* Twenty additional organizations had formed and were managing to continue operations by 1946. The initial spurt may be credited to Jones and another former British union official, Oswald Kitching, who was also seconded to the Gold Coast. But these men and the Labor Department could only attempt to guide the larger unions, in sectors most vital to the economy. The "mushrooming" of smaller, company or "house" unions during the period was largely a spontaneous process, encouraged by the changes in the law and the steep rise in the cost of living in the mid-forties.

The impetus for the first national labor center in Ghana came from the Western, Central, and Ashanti regions of the country.† Beginning in 1943, some leading unionists voiced proposals to coordinate the activities of the many house unions which were already formed or in the process of formation. Finally, in 1945, at the Railway Administration Offices in Sekondi, the Gold Coast Trades Union Congress was inaugurated. Approximately 14 unions were represented, although some existing organizations elected not to join. The initial paid up membership of the TUC itself was 5,000. Thus union ranks had grown considerably since the passage of the 1941 ordinance. Between 1945 and 1946, membership was raised to almost 11,000. Unions formed by the employees of several government departments and private enterprises joined the list.

---

*See Appendix 3 for the chronology of union registration.
†See map, Appendix 4.

Thus, before the nationalist movement surfaced in Ghana, the British showed ambivalent support for organized labor. Utilizing the new legislation, the stronger unions, notably those of the railwaymen and miners, were able to demand resources, but the 1941 ordinance did not encourage the formation of effective labor groups, generally. Neither did it prevent the alliance between metropolitan labor organizations and colonial administration from playing an active part in directing the affairs of individual unions.

The Trades Union Congress itself was in an even less advantageous position than its member unions, vis-a-vis government. It was tolerated, and sometimes supported, but it was not given the authority to demand resources of its own, either from workers or from unions. It is reasonable to assume that the Labor Department saw the potential for improved industrial peace which the new body represented, but it must have also been aware that the ability of the organization to influence its constituent groups, especially the more powerful ones, was weak. For this reason, the government continued to rely on Native Authorities — chiefs and religious leaders — to smooth industrial relations.

It is apparent that the British encouraged unions in order to maintain their own input into potentially dangerous organizations and to promote their own economic interests. Actually, this effort was not to succeed.

> The British model . . . failed to take account of the inevitable relationship between the growth of unions and political opposition to British rule.[4]

The rise of politics in Ghana, from 1948 onward, greatly expanded the relevant public which could confer value on the unions' programs. It also made possible, for the first time, the establishment of alliances with domestic centers of power.


## THE POLITICAL CONNECTION

In the nationalist struggle for independence in Ghana, the precise relationship between labor and politics was not planned in advance, nor was it cemented at once. In 1948 the first modern political party in the country, the United Gold Coast Convention (UGCC), began to preach increased expenditures and industrialization. Its watchwords were liberty, freedom, and education. The UGCC wanted eventual independence for the Gold Coast, but its primary aim was to replace British leadership with African doctors, lawyers, professors, and business elites. It would seem, in retrospect, that there was little natural affinity, in ideology or ultimate aims, between organized labor and the UGCC. However, in the beginning,

> nationalism did not demand that unions define their relationship to politics in a precise way . . . .[and] any sort of opposition to colonial rule constituted an acceptable and important contribution to the struggle for independence.[5]

Thus, labor unrest and militancy in 1948 were perceived by the nationalists as support for their efforts.

But the critical problem for the UGCC soon became the maintenance of control over agitation for independence, in which labor played a significant, but not exclusive, role. At first, the party welcomed workers' support, although it remained contemptuous of their leadership. It may have mistakenly regarded the unions' strike activity, as well as worker participation in mass demonstrations protesting economic conditions generally, as evidence of labor's commitment to its platform. Therefore, although the more radically inclined unionists saw the UGCC as being bourgeois-dominated, its ultimate failure to attract labor support in competition with its rival, the Convention People's Party, may be attributed to the UGCC's lack of attention to the movement. Ultimately, it discounted the unions as a significant source of strength.

For their part, the British also misread union motives, attributing the increased labor militancy of the immediate post-war period not to inadequate legislation or genuine grievances, but to the overpoliticization of the unions. In the Labor Department Report for 1947-48, their political activities were mentioned for the first time. In its 1949 report, the department cited the tendency for certain unions to "attach more importance to the attainment of political objectives by

threats of strike action than to the constructive
organization of their own internal economies and the
advancement of their members' interests by patient
negotiation." The strike, in British eyes, had become a
weapon in the nationalist struggle.

Overt TUC involvement with the nationalists surfaced in
the wake of the "Christiansborg riots" in late February, 1948.
A boycott of commercial establishments had been organized
on a countrywide basis, in reaction to high prices. A march led
by ex-servicemen in support of the boycott was fired on by
police, killing two and wounding others. Accra stores were set
afire. The next day demonstrators battered down the gates of
Ussher Fort prison, and some of the inmates were released.
Leaders of the UGCC, in order to"take advantage of the day's
tragic events and use that advantage as a fulcrum or lever for
the liberation of Ghana," sent telegrams abroad asserting that
civil order had broken down and that the Working Committee
of the party was prepared to take over the reins of
government.[6] The government responded by issuing orders
for the arrest of UGCC leaders, including Dr. J.B. Danquah
and Kwame Nkrumah.

Strikes, in response to the police action, closed down public
utilities and transport and spread from Accra to Kumasi.
When the detention of the politicians was announced, the TUC
held an emergency meting of its executive committee in
Sekondi. It realized that no organized body in the country,
including the Joint Provincial Council of Chiefs, would come to
the aid of the detainees, and it resolved to act. Handbills
demanding categorically the release of the six prisoners and
the lifting of a ban on newspapers were printed by the Kumasi
Trades Council and distributed throughout the country. The
tract threatened a general strike if the demands were not met.

The strike, scheduled for March 18, 1948, did not occur. The
Labor Department explained this, in part, by noting that
"there were no signs that the majority of the trade union
members desired their unions to take political action."[7]
Actually, the situation was defused after a meeting between
government and TUC respresentatives from the various
provinces. The colonial secretary, Sir Robert Scott, succeeded
in dividing the TUC delegation by appealing to

"constitutionality" and "legalism."[8] He promised that the detainees would be released when a commission from Britain arrived to inquire into the disturbances. The more militant labor faction, led by General Secretary Frank Woode, expressed dissatisfaction at this argument, but the more moderate group, led by President C.W. Tachie-Menson, sided with the government.

The detainees were eventually released in April when the Watson Commission arrived to make inquiries into the matter. The TUC gave evidence before this body in Sekondi; according to the Labor Department, some of the subjects it broached were "unconnected with the normal functions of trade unions." A.A. Moffatt, president of the Kumasi Trades Council, was arrested and charged with "actions prejudicial to the maintenance of essential services."[9] He was convicted and sentenced without major protest. In what was to be the last concrete offer of help to labor by the UGCC, the party supplied seven lawyers for his defense. But labor's dissatisfaction with this, its first entrance into the political arena, coincided with Kwame Nkrumah's disenchantment with the UGCC. After July 1948, relations between moderates and militants in the party began to disintegrate, even as a new corps of activists seized control of the Trades Union Congress.

Nkrumah, who had served as Danquah's subordinate, announced in 1949 the formation of the Convention People's Party (CPP). Its goal was "self-government now." The CPP appealed to a much wider public than the UGCC did, hastening the pace toward independence and raising the aspirations of Ghanaians of even the lowest levels of income and education. The party was eclectic socialist in ideology, antitradition (except when it suited its own purposes), and antichief. It attracted the dispossessed, the lower middle class, the semi-educated, the underemployed, and all sorts of political opportunists.

The colorful style of Nkrumah, the popularity of his party's platform, and civil disorders directed and exploited by the CPP during 1949-50 led to a rather sudden shift in the devolution of political authority. The British, by 1951, found themselves releasing Nkrumah from jail so that he might head the government. In fact, however, the CPP, in spite of its obvious appeal, was not so well organized as it pretended to be.[10] Nowhere is this better indicated than in its relationship with the labor movement. During 1949 the TUC, wary of British reprisals and thrust into the CPP camp in part by default, embarked on a path which was to leave it disunited and gravely weakened after January 1950. In the heady atmosphere of rhetoric and agitation then prevailing, the CPP, preparing for a critical national election in 1951, did not plan the coordinated working relationship with the TUC that might have prevented the crippling of its labor ally.

## THE 1950 STRIKE

The general strike of January 1950, the second major political activity in which the Congress engaged, was to prove even more disappointing than the activities of 1948. It may be thought that the strike was initiated by the CPP, given that it coincided with the party's "Positive Action" campaign of civil disobedience aimed at achieving independence. But linkages between labor and the CPP were too weak to have made this a possibility. In fact, the origins of the strike were unrelated to politics. For more than one year, the government had refused to consider the grievances of some employees of the Meteorological Department. These workers formed a union headed by H.P. Nyamitei (later a General Secretary of the CPP) and appealed to the TUC for help. A work stoppage began on October 5, 1949, and lasted three months, in spite of TUC efforts to negotiate. The government discharged all of the workers involved in the protest, including those with pensionable positions.

The TUC reacted to these dismissals by threatening a general strike, but the British refused to yield. They did meet with union officials, but as January 1950 approached, the CPP captured the spotlight by negotiating over the issue of calling off the plans for Positive Action. The party attempted to bolster its case by claiming to be able to control the onset of strike activity. Actually, the unions either were not privy to these negotiations or thought them to be hopeless, since they continued to present their own demands directly to the government on the eve of the strike. Perhaps suspecting that the CPP and the British would work out a compromise which would prevent them from obtaining their objectives, the unions even presented their grievances before a meeting of the Joint Provincial Council of Chiefs on January 6. This indicates that the unionists perceived their relationship with both government and party to be so unsatisfactory that they would seek legitimacy for the strike from traditional leaders.

The chiefs refused to sanction the walkout, and the TUC decided the issue for the wavering party by calling a strike. Only after two days had passed did Nkrumah officially declare Positive Action a reality, reiterating his position that the strike should be nonviolent and that certain essential service workers should not participate. Nkrumah asserted that "the response of the people was instantaneous."[11] Actually, the strike was already well under way!

Beginning on January 7, 1950, workers began to withhold services in Accra, and disturbances spread to other major centers. Civil servants were heavily involved, as were commercial employees, but the principal effect of the strike was in the areas of communications and transport. The Labor Department characterized the "general strike" as a "partial cessation of work," noting that at no time did it involve a major percentage of the workers. It pointed out that the Mines Employees Union, at that time the largest and one of the best organized, elected not to join the walkout, and it implied that the failure of the strike could be attributed to the unions' lack of desire to ascertain the views of members on the issue of participation.[12]

The government declared a state of emergency and imposed a curfew. These measures, combined with the efforts of a force of mobile policemen, "limited unrest in the main towns to sporadic outbursts of violence."[13] Positive Action was called off on January 21; by that same date, the government felt confident enough to arrest all of the important CPP and TUC leaders. The army assumed control of Accra, and, almost instantly, the TUC became moribund as the arrest and detention of their officers and mass dismissals of workers caused a rapid loss of interest in the labor movement. Most of the unions remained inactive until the year's end.

The strike had demonstrated the difficulty of injecting politics into what was still, in 1950, a slowly developing and fragile atmosphere for industrial relations. Scabs were introduced, and employers were able to intimidate union officers. At their trials, CPP officials, including Nkrumah, did not make "history-will-absolve-me" speeches. Instead, they appeared to be outbidding each other in professing loyalty to government and constitutional procedures.

It is recognized that the January 1950 general strike left the CPP stronger and the TUC weaker. In spite of its newfound political connections, the TUC was still a collection of predominantly small, weak unions. The party was not able to give it the power which it could not marshal on its own. In particular, the party did not have the authority to confer improved legal status upon the unions, nor could the latter make use of the CPP to improve their relationship to the government.

The British, for their part, did not view the general strike and the disintegration of the labor movement which followed in its wake as the failure of institutional transfer. The causes of the disturbance were seen in the irresponsible actions of some leaders, the atmosphere of "political unrest then existing," the "impending constitutional reform and the growing political consciousness and activity of many elements in the country."[14] They tried to portray the condition of the labor movement in 1950 as an unfortunate, but natural, outgrowth of these conditions. Unionism was depicted as a voluntary activity, the encouragement of which had been a "sound investment." The government, after 1950, maintained that "a strong and responsible Trade Union movement, which can only be created by the experience of voluntary collective bargaining, is of paramount need in the Gold Coast." Union activity was seen as essential to progress toward self-government and to instilling a "spirit of service to the community at large." On the other hand, trade unionism was in its infancy. It was "a child which needs all the advice and guidance which can be given."[15]

Thus, the Labor Department began to reconstitute the TUC. It was reestablished in September 1950 with no funds of its own. Partially glossing over the real anger of some workers at the failure of the strike, and the genuine divisions within the movement itself, the government was indeed able to find a ready corps of leaders and unions that were willing, for the moment, and from various motives, to abide by its conception of what labor organizations should be. In taking action, however, the Labor Department was not "allowing" voluntary, apolitical unionism to flower anew so much as it was replacing the CPP as the patron for some unionists. The government was reviving one arm of a movement which had come apart in a crisis, but government preferences became increasingly irrelevant as independence drew nearer, and it became obvious that help for the unions would come not from the Labor Department, but from Ghanaian politicians.

## DIVISIONS AND FACTIONS

During the critical years 1951 to 1954, the labor movement in Ghana, struggling to overcome the impact of the general strike, literally disintegrated into three factions which were distinguishable according to what relationship between itself and the CPP each faction was willing to tolerate. By 1954, however, a dominant faction was to emerge, one that would secure, after independence in 1957, the legal environment for unions which exists today.

### Moderates and Militants

The year 1951 was to see two elections of importance to the labor movement in Ghana. One was, of course, the national political contest, which the CPP won handily.[16] The other was the TUC election later in the year. Both the British and Kwame Nkrumah were vitally interested in this second election. The British wanted to purge the TUC of its militant leadership, which they associated with the 1950 strike; Nkrumah, while trying to maintain the support of labor as a whole, also wished to avoid angering the British.

Many of the moderate unionists who were being recruited to take over the reins of the TUC during 1950-51, including the executive of the Mineworkers' Union, had remained neutral during the national election. After its victory, the CPP issued

a statement, "Government Policy Toward the Trade Unions."
It was a bland document which avoided any mention of specific
party-TUC ties, and was obviously intended to win back the
support of the moderates. Subsequently leaders of the
Mineworkers and United Africa Company (UAC) Employees
Union, who were wary of Nkrumah and angry at the results of
the 1950 strike, nonetheless endorsed the CPP. It is likely,
however, that their backing came not so much because they
thought that the TUC under the new government would
indeed become "consultative and advisory" (thus preserving
the autonomy of their comparatively well-developed unions),
but because they believed that they would soon be in control of
the TUC itself.

By August 1951, the moderates, Larbi-Odam and Moffatt,
supported and tutored by the British, were able to defeat
militants, Anthony Woode and Pobee Biney, in the congress
election. The reconstituted Gold Coast Trades Union Congress
affiliated with the anti-Communist International Confederation of Free Trade Unions (ICFTU). "But the workers and
leaders in the Western Region would not accept the results of
the election as genuine."[17] Woode and Biney returned to
Sekondi to cultivate their own worker support in a separate
organization called the Ghana Trades Union Congress
(GTUC), as distinguished from the older organization, the
Gold Coast Trades Union Congress. The difficulties in
obtaining legitimacy for the militant wing of labor, difficulties
which were the result of CPP attempts to keep open
communications with all factions, had led to the creation of
two TUC's.

The existence of the twin labor centers became an
embarrassment ot Nkrumah, especially when GTUC officials
began to accuse him of having betrayed the revolution. He
saw that steps would have to be taken to unite the movement.
In preparation for the 1954 election, it was essential to gather
as many organizations as possible behind the party. Nkrumah
said later: "We were in the unfortunate position of having two
Trades Union Congresses in the country. No army can strike
effectively if its forces are divided and fighting against
themselves. Even though each T.U.C. was one hundred per
cent in support of the C.P.P., I insisted that the movement

must be led by only one Congress."[18]

However, Nkrumah could move only carefully against the militants, because he perceived that the party needed the political base of worker support which they gave him. He was in the uncomfortable position of having to sever the connection between his party and those union leaders to whom he was most closely related ideologically and who had been his most vocal labor supporters. His decision to reduce militant influence in the labor movement was perhaps made easier by the fact that all segments of the rank and file had supported him in the 1951 elections, and that the militants had failed to exercise any appreciable impact on the selection of party candidates, as the British had feared they might.

## Reunification of the Congress

The setting for the compromise which was to unite the labor movement in Ghana was the Annual Convention of the Gold Coast Trades Union Congress (GCTUC) in August 1953. Relations between the government and the moderates had improved to the point where they accepted, at the suggestion of the minister for labor, a new voting procedure. Every member union of the GCTUC was to receive two votes, regardless of its size. In addition, an amendment to the Trade Union Ordinance which the CPP pushed through the Legislative Assembly in July permitted non-union members to be officers in the Congress. The new voting procedure and the foregoing amendment were to be the undoing of the moderate leadership.

The compromise which united the movement was made, not between moderates and those militants who had remained within the GCTUC, but between the latter and a third faction, to whom the new rules on voting gave immediate power. These were the so-called CPP "stalwarts," leaders of small unions, some of which had not been affiliated with either rival congress.[19] Nkrumah used the voting power of the "stalwarts" to defeat the moderate candidates at the convention, while, at the same time, the presence of these CPP loyalists diluted the influence of the militants considerably. The outcome of the voting reflected this strategy, in that F.E. Tachie-Menson, the general secretary of the Post Engineering Workers' Union, and John K. Tettegah, of the G.B. Olivant Workers' Union, both "stalwarts," were elected president and assistant general secretary, respectively. The militants Kumah and Turkson-Ocran received the posts of vice-president and general secretary.

Considering the strength of the militants, and the debt which Nkrumah had felt was owed them, the government must have considered the outcome of the convention a success. However, events in the British Empire overseas were soon to affect the composition of the leadership of the labor movement in Ghana, and were to eliminate any remaining feelings of obligation which Nkrumah had toward the Sekondi unionists. In October 1953 in British Guiana, the government had suspended the constitution because of the supposed pro-communist links of Dr. Cheddi Jagan. Nkrumah had reason to feel that the same treatment might be in store for Ghana.

Aside from affiliating their trade union center to the communist World Federation of Trade Unions (WFTU), the militants had sent Anthony Woode on a trip to the countries of the European Communist Bloc. When Woode, in the Legislative Assembly, was debating the 1953 amendment to the Trade Union Ordinance, he had accused the opposition of being afraid of communism.[20] Turkson-Ocran, from his newly elected position in the reunited congress, pressed for affiliation to the WFTU. Although the "stalwarts" had proposed nonalignment, eastern influence was still noticeable. Allegations of communist loyalty, in the opinion of some moderates and "stalwarts," were weakening the bargaining position of some of the union leaders in the Western Region. "Communist literature" mysteriously appeared in Sekondi-Takoradi.

In light of these developments, Nkrumah, not wishing to harm his chances of winning the political kingdom, moved to cut relations with the militants completely in October 1953. Anthony Woode was suspended from the party for having attended a WFTU meeting. The "stalwart" F.E. Tachie-Menson announced that Turkson-Ocran was being removed from his post as general secretary of the Congress for being an alleged communist. He was also expelled from the CPP. TUC offices were transferred from Sekondi to Accra, because of the suspicion that the militants "may capture the headquarters one day."[21]

Reprisals against the militants continued in the following year, when the party refused to renominate Woode and Biney for their seats in the Legislative Assembly. F.E. Tachie-Menson replaced these men in the role of unionist politician; he won a seat on the CPP ticket in 1954. John Tettegah, who had become acting general secretary of the TUC, was confirmed in that position by the TUC convention in September 1954, thanks in part to a new amendment to the law which allowed the appointment of a full-time, paid secretary. He was also appointed to the CPP Central Committee.

In line with the government's attempt to present a respectable image, and in response to the attention which the TUC was now getting from western unions, Tettegah accepted a position on the Executive Board of the ICFTU, to which the Gold Coast TUC reaffiliated. In part, this action appears to have been an attempt to compensate the moderates for the loss of Congress leadership which they had suffered. However, while moderates saw Tettegah as an improvement over Ocran and the militants, their dissatisfaction with "stalwart" control was apparent.

A group of moderates and militants actually staged a *putsch* against Tettegah in 1955, but they were eventually defeated. Expelled from the Congress for engaging in "subversive activities," some of the rebels attempted to win through political alliance the influence which had been denied them within the TUC. The United Africa Company (UAC) Employees Union, the Railwaymen, and the Seamen's and Dockworkers' Union were instrumental in forming the Congress of Free Trade Unions in Sekondi. This group became allied with the opposition party, the Ashanti-based National Liberation Movement (NLM), many of whose leaders had been active in the now defunct UGCC. However, after the stinging defeat of the NLM in 1956, the new trade union center dissolved itself, and most of its constituent unions rejoined the TUC, which in that year adopted the name Ghana

Trades Union Congress.

The militant Sekondi unionists, especially in the railways, had not been able to secure political patrons, but they continued to make trouble for Nkrumah, climaxed by a 1961 strike. Although left-oriented activists ceased to play a major role in the leadership of the Congress, their unions survived as centers of agitation and protest. Their most significant failure in the years after 1954 was not the loss of the confidence of their membership. It was, on the contrary, their loss of influence within the CPP, based on te party's rejection of the political connection they sought. Woode, for example, in goading Nkrumah from the left, had wanted a say in the composition of the party. He wanted it to be an organization based on mass participation, ideologically "pure" enough to reject its bourgeois elements. Nkrumah repudiated this point of view. Increasingly, after 1957, unions were seen not as connecting the party to its mass base by organizing, agitating, or generating power from below, but, instead, as helping the party to govern by direction from the top down, through a process of negotiation and, when this failed, administrative repression.

*Summary*

The events of the period 1950-58 show that Ghana labor, as a whole, repudiated the British position regarding an apolitical labor movement. All three factions — moderates, militants and "stalwarts" — at one time or another actively sought and used political patrons. It was not only the weakness of most unions, but the identity of opposition to continued British rule among unions and the CPP that made this political connection inevitable. Workers had to be free of colonial status, which was almost universally felt to be the greatest factor in their low wages and poor working conditions. Because most unions and the CPP agreed on this point, the party received overwhelming worker support, in spite of some leaders' suspicions and fears concerning Nkrumah.

The confusion generated by the search for patrons exacerbated the weaknesses of the movement. Only after 1956 did most segments discard their hope for British and opposition political support. And only after all but the die-hard militants had agreed upon the CPP as the body with which to cooperate did union membership begin to increase dramatically.

# THE "NEW STRUCTURE"

The "New Structure" of large, national, industrial unions proposed in 1956 and codified in the Industrial Relations Act of 1958 and subsequent amendments, is perhaps the most significant element in the evolution of Ghanaian unions. This institutional framework was not imposed by party or government fiat. It was, indeed, the result of a give-and-take proces, which included frequent interaction between union and party leaders. In some cases, individual actors were co-members in both labor and political organizations.

## Origins of the New Structure Idea

Although the attempted control and domination of the TUC by the CPP may be traced from the date of passage of the Act. it is nonetheless true that "the impetus for the legislation came almost entirely from the labor movement itself."[22] This ironic turn of history has to be explained. The Act has been analyzed extensively by Douglas Rimmer. who pointed out that it should be regarded as an attempt to provide the legal setting in which the search for the union structure most applicable to the Ghanaian environment would take place.[23] This conception of what makes the new law significant forces us. as historical observers. to recognize that the unions themselves. and the party and government officials who first opposed the bill and were later persuaded to support it. did not really know what the net effects of the law would be. However. they came to believe that some "radical" change was necessary.

During the mid-1950's. two British labor advisors had castigated Ghanaian unions for their lack of self-analysis. "It is wise for the trade unions to recognize their own weaknesses. They fall short of representative size and character. They have not set themselves methodically to help the

administration to shape the law in accord with their
experience and needs."[24] But it soon became apparent that a
sizable portion of the movement had understood the
organizational weaknesses of the unions and, rather than
cooperating with the Labor Department in an attempt to
make the 1941 ordinance work, they resolved to propose new
labor legislation in an independent Ghana.

Shortly after assuming office, John Tettegah called for
amalgamation of unions and consolidation with the CPP. The
need for national unions was expressed at the annual congress
in 1954 when a special committee was appointed to study the
subject. This body reported that the TUC was not fulfilling
the expectations of members because of its weak structure;
over 80 functioning unions existed, some with membership of
50 or less. In order to render better service to workers, the
committee recommended "amalgamation of identical affiliated
unions along industrial lines."

Preparation of a bill which would give these changes the
force of law began. Tettegah asked: "Must a labour
organisation seek to accomplish all its objectives with its own
resources, or should it try to insure that Government
legislation becomes an important and possible decisive factor
in securing the workers' position?"[25] With only a suggestion
of the complications involved in establishing such a
relationship with government, he wrote: "Every decade offers
its challenges and opportunities; and this is the challenge of
our new era . . . ."

The Industrial Relations Act, as initially drafted, called for
the consolidation of all existing unions into 16.[26] In 1955, prior
to the 12th Annual Congress of the TUC, only three unions
could be considered national organizations: The Railway
Workers, who claimed responsibility for all railwaymen with
the exception of the engineman; the mineworkers; and the
teachers. After the 12th Congress, the "stalwarts," who had
succeeded in obtaining a resolution authorizing a campaign to
effect amalgamation, engineered the formation of five
additional national bodies. The new groups included workers
in building trades, commercial trades, catering, maritime and
local government employment.

In the following two years, Tettegah accelerated the pace of consolidation. He brought prestige to his project through well-publicized trips abroad to Israel and West Germany, and by gaining the support of British unionists and the ICFTU. Critical, of course, was the backing of the Ghana government and the CPP.

## Opposition within the TUC

As the 14th Annual Congress of 1957 approached, opposition to the New Structure among the militants and heads of some of the smaller unions intensified. The United Party (UP), which had become the opposition to the CPP in the post-independence government, called on workers to reject Tettegah's proposals. The "stalwarts" were firmly enough in control of the TUC secretariat to preclude the possibility that the New Structure would be voted down, but they were forced to compromise over the issue of individual union autonomy. The UAC Employees Union and the Mines Employees Union led the moderates' continued resistance. The latter union feared that it was about to lose its accustomed influence within the TUC, and realized also that the intimate connection between the "stalwarts" and the government would open the way for political interference in its bargaining relationship with the employers' association, the Chamber of Mines. The moderates were joined by the militant Railwaymen.

Protest during 1957-1958 took several forms. Some unions disassociated themselves from the TUC, or remained outside the New Structure until 1959. Others withheld dues. In addition, rumors which were either the result of misunderstanding of the 1957 draft constitution for the New Structure, or the outcome of deliberate misrepresentation, circulated among the constituent unions. It was apparent that some of the larger unions, including two of the few national bodies, the Maritime and Dockworkers and Teachers, were seeking to separate the issue of amalgamation *per se* from the issue of accepting the New Structure under the "stalwarts." However, under government, CPP and ICFTU prodding, they returned to the TUC fold.

The draft constitution was not accepted initially. Tettegah

was at pains to quell fears that unions no longer would be able to negotiate in their own behalf. He strongly denied the rumor that sixpence would be deducted from every worker's weekly pay to be used for the construction of roads and bridges! He tried to argue that the New Structure would not mean the loss of funds by locals and individual unions, although, particularly for the larger bodies, this was not the case. The UAC Workers believed that the TUC would take over their union's buildings and assets; Tettegah also denied this.

The combined weight of the organized opposition to the New Structure and general skepticism about the arrogation of power delayed ratification of the 1957 draft constitution of the Trades Union Congress. A steering committee was appointed to take over the administration of the labor movement until affiliated unions submitted their views and proposals for amendments. Some union officials had to be convinced that "safeguards" were built into both the new TUC constitution and the proposed law. The provision that a member union could appeal directly to government for certification to conduct collective bargaining, if the TUC had failed to act on the union's request for three months, was one of these "safeguards." Tettegah also assured unionists that the principle of compulsory arbitration was only acceptable to the movement on a two-year, trial basis.

In 1958 the draft constitution was finally approved. Interference by the TUC Executive Board in relations between individual unions and management was supposed to occur only when large numbers of workers were involved, including those outside the jurisdiction of the union concerned. It may appear that this provision is a rationale for outright control by the central organization, but as Rimmer suggests, the new constitution was considerably more decentralized than Tettegah had wanted.[27]

The delay in approval of the constitution is evidence for the still-salient, though limited, power of the non-"stalwarts" within the movement. In fact, as late as December, just two days prior to the printing of the new bill for presentation to Parliament, the number of constituent unions was changed from 16, as originally proposed, to 24. This reflected remaining difficulties in satisfying some of the union leaders affected by the amalgamation exercise. However, the likelihood that the New Structure would be approved had encouraged several unions to surrender their individual sovereignty in advance of favorable parliamentary action. Agricultural workers, for example, amalgamated in February 1958, and the Union of Teachers and Educational Institution Workers in July. The Timber and Woodworkers Union was formed in September, three months prior to formal consideration of the bill. The unions, realizing what the bill contained, wanted to be able to make a case before the minister for labor that their bodies were qualified to be certified for collective bargaining.

### Opposition within the CPP

As Tettegah worked within the labor movement to secure the adoption of the new constitution, he had also to convince some of the CPP ministers that the 1958 industrial relations bill should be passed. It appears that his elevation to cabinet rank did not insure that the bill would be looked on favorably; instead, it assured his case a hearing on an equal footing with moderate elements in the party (two CPP members of Parliament were officers of Ghanaian business associations). Although the more ideologically-inclined party functionaries saw in the CPP's "socialist" philosophy an identity of aims with organized labor, this idea was by no means universally accepted, especially before 1960. A minister without portfolio, Mr. Welbeck, expressed the view of the more cautious party leaders when he told unionists:

> I presume that the changes necessary to bring about the reorganization will be voluntary and that it is not your intention to seek government intervention or regulation to introduce these changes by legislative action. The Government would be acting wrongly and exceeding its proper functions if it attempted to impose these changes on individual unions by legislative action.[28]

When Tettegah met with party officials to hammer out the specifics of the bill, he was under pressure from some of the stronger unions to include more provisions for union autonomy. They argued that his chances for establishing the New Structure by law would be greater if the bill could be made more attractive to party moderates. Non-"stalwart" unionists held a concept of industrial relations which was closer to segments of the Ghanaian business community than was Tettegah's. They maintained that allowing for more voluntarism in the movement would give both sides greater freedom to negotiate. In the end, however, Tettegah's position, with few alterations, prevailed, and opposition to the bill within the party was silenced.

It is evident that the principal reason for the party's about-face during the year 1958 was Tettegah's success in persuading Kwame Nkrumah that the Industrial Relations Act was in his, and his party's, interest. Tettegah was able to show, quite convincingly, that employers would not voluntarily cooperate with unions in introducing the check-off of dues, or in permitting union shop. The number of collective agreements signed was small. The failure of voluntary industrial relations to develop in the way in which many unions, particularly those in the private sector, wanted, could do nothing but contribute to frustration, which always had the potential for provoking strikes and hindering productivity. Nkrumah, therefore, realized that to deprive the movement of improved status under law might seriously hinder his plans for national development. Faced during this period with troublesome Ga and Ewe protests, Nkrumah also saw in the TUC a multi-tribal, national movement which could aid in further uniting the country behind him, if the government, by passing the bill, would give it the increased ability to do so These were the principal considerations which caused Kwame Nkrumah to support Tettegah's New Structure and the bill which gave it legal status.

A meeting was called at Nkrumah's residence; in attendance were labor leaders and the recalcitrant, business-minded party leaders. After some discussion, Nkrumah held up the bill and said, "This is my bill; if you will not pass it, I will take the matter to the people in general election." In the parliamentary debate which followed, therefore, Tettegah was able to rely on Nkrumah's support, and on the powerful argument that the bill would improve industrial relations in te country at a time just after independence when many foreign eyes were on Ghana. Business elements, within and outside the party, took some consolation in the fact that, under the new law, the opportunities for staging a legal strike were very limited.

## Parliamentary Debate

Debate on the industrial relations bill, between December 15 and 19, 1958, appears anticlimactic. The United Party M.P.'s who spoke out against the bill, particularly R.R. Amponsah, echoed the concerns of some of the moderates within the labor movement, and those of the British TUC and the ICFTU. But, being greatly outnumbered in Parliament, it was obvious that the UP represented a less salient oposition to portions of the bill than did elements within the TUC and CPP themselves, prior to the bill's appearance. The parliamentary secretary to the Ministry of Labor, A.J. Dowuona-Hammond, rejected every amendment proposed by Amponsah; passage of the bill intact was a foregone conclusion. In fact, it was passed on December 17, 1958, by a vote of 43 to 9. Nonetheless, an analysis of the debate reveals more of the rationale behind CPP support for the law.

Convention People's Party M.P.'s, although voting for the bill *en masse* and uncritically, had good reason to suspect that the defense of the individual freedom of the workers, including the right to strike, expressed so eloquently by Amponsah, was supported partially in the hope that industrial unrest and worker dissatisfcation might bring the CPP down. It was the poor hope of an opposition composed of many of the same elite elements which had been rejected by the voters in previous national elections, and which had failed to cultivate ties with organized labor ten years earlier.

The minister of labor, Ako Adjei, presented the case for the bill. "As the Government are a socialist Government," he said, "it is clear that the needs of labour will be always in the forefront of their policies." He was careful to point out that the impetus for the bill as well as certain specific portions of it were based on the requests of the labor movement, itself. "It is not an idea conceived by the government and imposed on the workers against their will." The parliamentary secretary related that, with regard to ministry control over Congress funds,

> there was a time when many of the unions entertained doubts regarding the integrity of the leaders of the trade unions. As a result of this they appealed to my Ministry to see to it that they were protected . . . one of the greatest fears expressed by the workers themselves is the possibility of collusion amongst the members of the Congress in order to embezzle the funds of the TUC. That is the reason why we are trying to safeguard the interests of the workers so that their hard-earned money will not be misused. [29]

The extensive powers which the minister for labor was to enjoy over the internal administration and finances of the Congress were thus not characterized as an attempt to muzzle or control it. Instead, the government was merely reducing the possibility that the power of the Trades Union Congress could be used contrary to the "interest of the workers."

The fact is, of course, that neither CPP, TUC, nor the opposition had canvassed "the workers" to know what their fears and concerns were, so that the issue of whether or not the workers had demanded the bill, as suggested by the CPP, was not a genuine one. In one rather tragicomic exchange, Amponsah asked the parliamentary secretary, who claimed that the bill was in the workers' "best interest," "Are you a worker?" Without hesitation came the reply, "Yes, I am!"

If one looks beneath the politically-motivated rhetoric on both sides, one may detect a genuine difference of opinion on the issue of protection of workers' rights. Following Nkrumah's dictum that "organization decides everything," the CPP side saw the workers as a corporate group to which the government was giving a legal identity and whose welfare was the concern of the party. The UP member Amponsah, by contrast, regarded the worker as an individual, and not as a member of a group. Plainly, he saw the proposed bill not as an advance, but as a step backward; the amendments which he proposed were designed to include elements of the 1941 ordinance and the Master and Servant Ordinance, which had specified relations between individual workers and their employers. It is difficult to imagine how the opposition could believe that workers would be consistently successful in the redress of individual grievances, when prosecutions under the master-and-servant law were rarely brought under the colonial regime, and when, in any event, the range of employment — especially non-government employment — increased greatly since the 1920's. It is likely, however, that even had Parliament been more evenly divided between the parties so that the imposed organization of the New Structure would not have so obviously rebounded to the benefit of the majority party, the UP would still have opposed it for ideological reasons.

Amponsah, the United Party M.P., was, of course, correct (and prophetic) in noting the ease with which the "interest of the workers" would become identified with the CPP objectives of the moment. Noting that the minister for labor had final approval over rules made by the TUC, he argued: "The Minister can sit in his Ministry and say: 'These rules will not be in the best interest of my party.' He will not say they are not in the best interest of the workers . . . . Therefore he will say: 'I will not approve of those rules.' "

In stating that "if this Bill had existed in 1950 the 'Positive Action' could never have been possible," Amponsah had, indeed, hit upon the single most important reason, in the CPP view, for passing the legislation! The legitimate role of the unions could no longer be agitation, which in 1950 was identified with the nationalist movement, but which in 1958 and after would be identified with upsetting the government's economic plans. The TUC had indeed been accorded certain rights and duties, but in return it would be subject to "supervision to ensure that those powers are not abused. . . . In this way the Government's socialist policy of support for the workers in all their legitimate claims for self-improvement is co-ordinated with the Government's policy of encouraging industrialization and investment in new industries as essential parts of the plan for economic independence."[30] The lengthy grievance and arbitration procedure outlined in the bill was designed to "render the use of strikes and lockouts which . . . hinder the expansion of

industry, largely obsolete," and thus contribute to the success
of economic planning.


## The Concordat

The prevailing western view is that the consolidation of the
Ghanaian unions was accomplished solely for political reasons
and against the wishes of the membership. But this
interpretation fails to distinguish the threat of political control
from the general effort to amalgamate the small and weak
unions which were the British legacy. Considering that after
1953 British advisors themselves were recommending
amalgamation, and that the models for the New Structure
were exclusively western, it is highly unlikely that those who
wished to see a smaller number of stronger unions in the
country were acting purely from political motives. Moveover,
the issue of the "democratic" determination of overall labor
movement policy by individual members is a red herring. It
cannot be seriously contended that plebiscites among a largely
illiterate work force, and in the absence of sufficient, and
unbiased, middle-level leadership to explain the issues to the
workers, could have been successful in Ghana, even if the
upper echelons of the movement had desired them. The real
question is not whether the individual worker approved of the
New Structure, or the 1958 Industrial Relations Act, but
whether the new TUC constitution and legislation improved
the lot of wage labor. In this connection, it will be
demonstrated that both the workers and the CPP regime
benefitted.

The successful implementation of the New Structure and
the labor law was not the result of a scheme or political plot
hatched by John Tettegah and Kwame Nkrumah. Rather, it
was the result of an essentially voluntary "concordat"
between the TUC and the government. The increasing party
control over the affairs of the Congress which became
apparent after 1960 occurred because the unions miscalculated
the leverage which the New Structure would let them
maintain over party and state. To emphasize the identity of
political ambition between CPP leaders and TUC Secretariat
executives is to ignore the limited options open to the labor

movement. Beginning in 1958, a connection was agreed to, but among inherently unequal partners. The Congress was an already-established labor center which itself determined almost all of the provisions of the Industrial Relations Act. However, its "partner," the CPP, was intent on ruling without opposition. The party, because of its ability to pass legislation and enforce it, controlled the political environment for organized labor.

Of course, it was immediately apparent that the unions, in order to participate in the concordat, compromised some of their aims. The government, having established the TUC by law, retained the power, literally, to abolish it by law, to seize its assets and place them with a receiver. The government had set the numbewr of unions and the areas for which they would be responsible after consultation with the TUC, but final authority concerning the acceptance, rejection, or elimination of a union from the list was vested in the ministry. The composition of the list was important, because civil servants, local government employees, and teachers were prohibited from bargaining collectively. This meant that 14 of the 24 unions, initially containing over 44 percent of the organized work force, would be the weaker because they contained civil servants. In theory, the proportion of weaker unions could be raised or lowered by government at will.

Evidence in later chapters will show that, contrary to conventional wisdom, the most significant sacrifice made by the TUC in the concordat was not a loss of its ability to be militant or to act as a pressure group in relation to government. Certainly, the CPP had done what it could to legislate industrial peace and encourage increased productivity. But the greatest disadvantage, from the unions' point of view, was not the curtailment of strike action. It was, instead, the level of administrative control which the Industrial Relations Act permitted government to exercise over the TUC and its unions. In the short run, between 1958 and 1966, this opened the door for CPP manipulation of union program and leadership. In the long run, by 1971, the results of the TUC having been established "by act of Parliament" were even more severe, as a new party and government possessed the power to legislate the congress out of existence.

*1959 and 1960 Amendments*

As the 1958 bill was being considered, Tettegah took aim at
the unionists who resisted it:

"A few selfish leaders now enjoying the favours of
capitalists may try to subvert these revolutionary changes
. . . some of them may still choose to be small kings in their
small domains; but these men of little faith will surely lose
their identity through the overwhelming vote of the working
masses."[31] In fact, it was not the vote of the "masses" which
spelled the end of the resistance to amalgamation, but
government action, in passing the 1959 and 1960 amendments
to the labor law.

It was apparent that the resisters were not living "to regret
their folly," as Tettegah had predicted. In spite of initial
successes and increases in membership, the amalgamation
proceeded at only a moderate pace. Of the 95 unions reported
in 1958, only 50 had amalgamated into the New Structure by
June 1960, according to Labor Department figures. This may
be attributed to a lack of information about the requirements
of the new law, and to some workers' suspicion, especially if
they remained uncovered by collective agreements. However,
the principal reason for the failure to respond to the 1958 Act
was the continued recalcitrance of militant, and some
company, unions, which, because they were not legally bound
to join the TUC, could evade the New Structure. Of course,
the holdouts could not benefit from the guaranteed
recognition and check-off provisions of the Act, but they felt
themselves in a better position to resist interference from the
party and the "stalwart" TUC secretariat.

An amendment to the labor law, passed in 1959, changed
this situation. Now, negotiations could only take place with a
recognized, registered union, and only unions belonging to the
Trades Union Congress could be registered. Another portion
of the amendment required the dissolution of any union not
mentioned in the 1958 law within two months if it did not join
an approved union.

The motivation for the passage of the 1959 amendment was,
in part, political. The CPP was concerned that unions outside
the TUC umbrella might become centers of UP political
activity. However, the 1959 amendment is also properly

regarded as a continuation of the concordat of 1958. The CPP received some advantages, but the TUC obtained government backing to continue the drive for amalgamation which had been one of its prime goals. The 1959 amendment was a decisive weapon in the struggle to defeat the moderate opposition within the movement (as the UAC Workers Union finally capitulated) and to overcome the continuing intransigence of the militant railway workers.

During 1960, the concordat was further cemented with new legislation, the Civil Service Act and additional amendments to the 1958 law. These resulted in gains for both the CPP and the TUC secretariat and, at the time, were welcomed by both.

The government realized that, in spite of the 1959 amendment, opposition to its policies was centered in various departments of the civil service, some of which were not unionized. At first, its position was that union membership for civil servants was to be encouraged, but not made a condition of service. This philosophy left the opposition a foothold, and left untapped a resource of mass mobilization in the form of a large number of non-unionized civil servants. The TUC was only too happy to aid the CPP in this exercise, after the required change in the law. The Civil Service Act of 1960, passed in June, provided the following: "Regulations shall be made for securing that, so far as is practicable and subject to such exceptions (if any) as the public may require, all Civil Servants are members of Trade Unions." Thus, the TUC obtained government cooperation in strengthening unions containing civil servants, historically the weakest in the Congress.

The TUC secretariat, confident of its government backing as evidenced by the reinforcing of the concordat, reduced the number of unions under the New Structure from 24 to 16. Principally on the strength of its special legal status, the TUC appeared, in mid-1960, at the height of its power. However, during the month of August, it became apparent to both the secretariat and the government that the laws passed since 1958 needed even more improvement in order to discourage discontent among some workers and union leaders.

An amendment, hurriedly passed against a background of hostile demonstrations, specified that no worker could remain a non-union member for more than one month when covered by a collective bargaining certificate. Employment of such a worker became an "unfair labor practice." The Secretariat was given the power to discipline member unions by withholding their share of dues collected automatically via "check-off" at the place of employment and remitted directly to the TUC. Again Tettegah had been granted, by law, a power which he could not have persuaded the constituent unions to surrender.


## UNIONS IN SOCIALIST GHANA

In 1960, Ghana proclaimed itself a republic. During the next five years, the program of the Convention People's Party became avowedly socialist, in contrast to its nationalist beginnings. The legal environment for organized labor remained essentially unchanged until 1965. However, the socialist governemnt's attitude toward it became increasingly cynical. The TUC survived a general strike in 1961, but one of the principal effects of the strike was an intensified party effort to control the unions, and the Congress's Secretariat.[32]
. In 1964, party domination of the labor movement was reflected in the appointment of Nkrumah follower Kwaw Ampah as secretary-general of the TUC. One of the first plans he announced was a reduction in the number of unions, from 16 to 10. This exercise was accomplished, under a new Industrial Relations Act, by the forced merging of 11 of the original 16 organizations into 5 new groups. Ampah justified the move by claiming that all of the TUC unions would then be financially stable. In addition to increasing the likelihood of government control over the Congress, the 1965 labor legislation swept away the results of previous negotiation within the TUC over the mandate of several unions to exist.
The new Act resembled its 1958 counterpart. For example, the government retained the right to determine which categories of workers could bargain collectively. But, in a potentially significant departure, the Congress was empowered to make its own rules and was removed from the supervision of the Ministry of Labor. Few trade unionists were deceived by the ostensibly noble intentions of the law,

and the CPP government would have to fall before union autonomy was, in reality, increased. Actually, the 1965 labor legislation only served to bolster the role of the party in deciding the fate of the unions. Far from being a concession to "free labor," it was instead designed to permit further integration of the TUC into the CPP, and to remove it from the influence of a ministry which was distrusted by party officials.

A CPP member of Parliament and minister of labor and social welfare had told the International Labor Organization in December 1964: "We believe in freedom of association but we condemn any form of freedom of association which tends to breed irresponsibility and subversion."[33] In this philosophy enunciating the proper role of trade unions in socialist Ghana, we see the attempted repudiation of the agreement entered into by the unions six years before. For many party leaders, the extent of "irresponsibility and subversion" practiced by the unions was directly proportional to the attempts of the TUC, between 1960-65, to maximize its freedom. For individual unions, if not the Congress itself, the right to life, as part of the concordat, did not need to be respected. It could be abrogated by the party at will.

## THE EFFECTS OF FREEDOM OF ASSOCIATION

Kwame Nkrumah was ousted in a coup in February 1966. For over three years following the takeover, Ghana was ruled by the National Liberation Council (NLC), a military regime which relied heavily on the civil service bureaucracy for support. Great changes took place in the relationship between the government and the TUC; control of administration within the Congress was eliminated, and organized labor was free, for the first time since 1960, to enunciate an independent doctrine. However, some unions which had survived the CPP era, if emasculated, were threatened occasionally under the NLC as well.

Legal authority for the structure of the Congress remained unchanged. The NLC reminded unionists that the suspension of Ghana's constitution by the military did not affect the

administration of the 1965 Industrial Relations Act; it refused
to change the provisions of the law that made legal strikes
almost impossible. However, a major change occurred in the
legal environment for unions containing civil servants. NLC
Decree 134, promulgated on January 31, 1967, allowed
"freedom of association" for government employees; union
membership was no longer compulsory for them. A mass
exodus of civil servants, who now had to sign forms if they still
desired their union dues deducted at source, began
immediately.

Unions composed primarily of government workers were
crippled substantially. For example, the General Agricultural
Workers Union, although it did include some employees in the
private sector, lost about 55 percent of its membership.
However, in spite of the hardships brought about by NLC
Decree 134, all of the constituent unions of the Congress
surivived.

Prior to the coup, the number of unions had been
established at ten by CPP instruction, and unity within the
TUC had been enforced. Now, however, there were no such
restrictions. During 1966 all unions held elections, and many
previously existing grievances and rivalries among union
officials resulted in bids to form additional unions out of the
constituent groups of the Congress. In addition, for the first
time since 1959, new unions appeared outside of the TUC
umbrella.

Splits within existing Congress unions were discouraged by
B.A. Bentum, the secretary-general of the Congress, during
the period, and the number of national unions in the TUC was
kept at 16 during 1966-67. These were, with minor alterations,
the groups specified in the original 1958 legislation. They
included:

> Construction and Building Trades Union
> General Agricultural Workers Union
> General Transport and Petroleum Workers Union
> Ghana Private Road Transport Union
> Health Services Workers Union
> Industrial and Commercial Workers Union
> Local Government Workers Union
> Maritime and Dockworkers Union

Mineworkers Union
National Union of Seamen
Posts and Telecommunications Workers Union
Public Services Workers Union
Railway and Ports Workers Union
Railway Enginemen's Union
Teachers and Educational Workers Union
Timber and Woodworkers Union

Water and electricity workers and a portion of the lorry drivers were denied permission to leave their parent groups in 1967. The seventeenth national union, the Public Utility Workers, separated from the Industrial and Commercial Workers, with the blessings of that union and the Congress, in 1968.

In maintaining this unity, the TUC secretariat showed that it had gained some control over the process by which its own member unions were certified. Under law, all unions had to apply to the government for recognition, but, in practice, during the NLD years, the recommendation of the secretariat concerning the legitimacy of new unions was given great weight. Two unions formed, initially, outside the TUC sought approval of the secretariat prior to certification. This is evidence for the institutionalization of the Congress as *the* national labor center, and is all the more significant because it occurred less than three years after CPP influence had been eliminated completely.

## THE EFFECTS OF POLITICS

The reemergence of democratic politics as Ghana prepared for civilian rule in 1969, and during Dr. Kofi Busia's tenure as prime minister from 1969 to 1972, greatly affected the unions. Although the Congress maintained control over the number of groups under its aegis, the period of Busia's Progress Party (PP) government marked the most significant incidence of splinter unions since the implementation of the New Structure. During the Progress Party's rule, real differences of opinion on trade union issues among leadership and workers resulted in the appearance of the breakaways.

However, critics of the upstart organizations were essentially accurate in their assessment that splinter-group leaders opened the door to the PP, which desired, for reasons of its own, a foothold in the labor movement.

Evidence of direct financial support for the splinter groups is weak; however, it is clear that the Busia regime, unlike the NLC, wanted to reassert the power of government to decide which unions should exist. This legal and moral support probably prolonged the life of the breakaways, and also led to the creation of a rival national union center.

One of the unions comprising the Congress, the Railway and Ports Workers, experienced a serious challenge. The two principal executives of the union had been dismissed by the NLC early in 1969, and charged with not being farsighted or efficient. The union refused to be bullied and asked the TUC to intervene. The TUC reinstated the officers, but, once having come under the shadow of government disfavor, the officers lost the next two union elections. Defeated, they formed a new union, the Railway and Harbor Workers (RHWU), which initially had a membership of 1,000. At this stage, in 1969, there was no indication that the newly elected PP government would support a rival trade union center, so the RHWU applied to the TUC for affiliation.

The Congress did not want to recognize two separate unions for the same class of workers. It went to court to block registration of the new group, and subsequently appointed a committee to look into the unification of the railwaymen prior to its 1970 convention. At this point, however, the government entered the picture, taking away from the TUC the sole authority to determine which unions should be registered. In effect, the PP regime was guaranteeing the survival of the new union. By the middle of 1970, RHWU membership had grown to 3,384. It is significant to note, however, that political ties between the government and the breakaway union were still not solidified, as it could not obtain a collective bargaining certificate.

Initially, the dispute within the Railway and Ports Workers Union was not politically motivated, but the PP was quick to take advantage of the ambitions of leaders and divisions within the rank and file concerning who their leaders should be. In addition, the Railway and Ports Administration may have encouraged the government to come to the aid of the fledgling union because it found that it was easier to deal with its leadership. The general secretary of the RHWU was an active Progress Party supporter, a fact which may have contributed to the new union's rise in the membership, since, during 1970, many junior union officers were in the PP camp. By mid-1971, when the national budget was announced, the RHWU was supporting mandatory deductions from workers' pay and was opposed to automatic dues check-off. Political ties to the union became more direct as the RHWU enunciated its anti-TUC position.

A second major dispute, this one within the Industrial and Commercial Workers Union (ICU), appears also to have been nonpolitical in its beginnings. Early in 1969 A.K. Tevie, a prominent official in the union, decided to capitalize on worker discontent over the monthly dues rate. He formed the Manufacturing, Commercial and Allied Workers Union (MACAWU). His appeal for a 50 percent dues reduction, combined with promises of improved attention to members' complaints which a smaller union supposedly could offer, attracted 800 workers initially. In June 1970, the union reached its maximum of 1,500 members. The union claimed that it was free from outside political manipulation, an assertion which is supported by the evidence, at least until August 1971. It was formed months before the Busia regime came to power and actually experienced the same inconsistent and suspicious attitude of government with which TUC unions had to cope.

Like the other prominent breakaway, MACAWU tried to affiliate itself with the TUC. This request was denied by the Executive Board, nominally because the leader of MACAWU had been defeated in a prior ICU election. The board did not want to establish a precedent of absorbing unions led by dissident leaders who, it appeared, had not secured the support of their immediate constituency. Actually, MACAWU continued in existence until 1972. The appeal of its leadership and platform to an albeit limited number of workers was apparent. However, the TUC secretariat took the position that the union's differences with its parent organization should be settled internally, in order to avoid possible political involvement. A labor commentator in the Congress newspaper wanted to know "whether those workers who have broken away from the I.C.U. think the leaders of their newly formed union will not need money to run it. Are they sure they are not being lulled politically or being used for someone else's purposes?"[34]

In a later instance, following disturbances at Samreboi in March 1971, the TUC disassociated itself from a group of strikers, and warned against an "anonymous," so-called All Workers Association "suddenly appearing as a self-proclaimed spokesman of the workers; these are all the familiar signs of the activity of 'agents provocateurs' — outsiders, attempting to use the workers for some hidden purpose of their own. WE HAVE SEEN THESE SIGNS ALSO IN SOME OF THE RECENT ATTEMPTS OF OUTSIDERS TO CREATE OR SUPPORT SPLINER OR BREAKAWAY GROUPS IN SOME OF OUR NATIONAL UNIONS."[35]

The suspicions of many TUC leaders regarding the Progress Party's intentions appeared more than justified by July 1971. The Congress's opposition to the new national budget was intense, and party attacks on TUC leadership grew more virulent than ever. Against this background of escalating conflict, MACAWU and RHWU announced that they were coming together to form a new national trade union center, the Ghana Confederation of Labor (GCL).

Not since the 1950's had there been more than one national labor organization in Ghana. This fact alone had accounted for the strength of the Ghana TUC in comparison with organizations in other African countries. The new group was inaugurated on August 23, 1971. Less than a week later, the party press claimed that TUC leaders were "shaking." Actually, their trepidation was not caused by the mere existence of the rival center. What worried TUC leadership was the obvious political taint of the new group. Important PP functionaries attended the inauguration ceremonies. The press hailed the arrival of the GCL. Government strategy, plainly, was to make the GCL respectable enough to attract the TUC's unions away.

The separate confederation was a valuable tool in drawing

the TUC into open confrontation. The chairman of the new group toured the country, even as the TUC was conducting a speaking tour of its own to defend its policies. The GCL chairman spoke out against the "ostentation" of TUC leaders and claimed that his unions had been "forced" to leave the parent organization because its policies were not in the interest of the rank and file. "Disgusted workers" were said to be resigning *en masse* from the TUC, not approving of the "collision course" it had set with the government. Branches of the Local Government Workers and the Maritime and Dockworkers were also said to have quit.

The GCL claimed 33,500 members, a greatly inflated figure. Aside from the dissident manufacturing and railway workers, it had some teachers and distillery employees. Government recognition of the latter, in the Cooperative Distillers' Workers Union, was particularly galling to the TUC because they produced *akpeteshie*, illegal gin. The leader of the RHWU became secretary-general of the GCL; its executive secretary was the head of MACAWU. The new group declared itself against strikes as a means of securing redress of worker grievances.


## THE DISSOLUTION, SEPTEMBER 1971

On August 17 the *Ghanaian Times* had predicted an amendment to the labor law to "remove anomalies in the act and bring it in line with the provisions and spirit of the constitution." A few days later, J.H. Mensah, minister of finance, was to tell Parliament that the TUC's demand for doubling the minimum wage was not a realistic basis for negotiation, adding ominously: "There is a certain situation between the government and the labour movement which we should take very serious steps to correct."[36] It was obvious that, having failed to intimidate the TUC by recognizing its rival labor center, the PP regime had decided to make the most significant change in the legal environment for Congress and its unions since 1958.

On September 9, 1971, Act 383, The Industrial Relations (Amendment) Act, was passed in Parliament under a certificate of emergency. The vote was 86 to 21, predictable along party lines. On the previous day, TUC assets had been frozen, its offices and leaders' homes raided. The dissolution was a reality. The new law placed the Congress's assets in the hands of a board of receivers. After determining the liabilities of the organization, the board was to remit to the constituent unions their share of the remaining funds. Receivers were to be paid with Congress monies, and had the right to sell and transfer all property held by the TUC.

The new legislation permitted any group of trade unions to form "any association, federation, confederation or congress . . . for the attainment of their common aims." At the same time, however, the minister for labor and the registrar of trade unions were given increased powers to modify the structure of any union or group of unions. Employees were guaranteed the right to join unions, or to refuse to join, and no employer could prohibit a worker from exercising these rights or discriminate against him for doing so. In effect, the Act reestablished the universal open shop in Ghana, which had ceased to exist since the original amendments to the 1958 law were passed.

Considerable space in the 1971 law was devoted to internal democratic procedures in Ghanaian unions. Voting rules, specifying secret ballot and other guarantees, for example, were spelled out. Failure to comply with these procedures could prevent a union applying for certification from being allowed to operate, and might also be grounds for terminating the certification of already-recognized unions. In other words, the law, which ostensibly protected the rights of individual workers, could easily be used by government punitively, as it legitimized the nonrecognition of unions for a wide variety of causes. In theory, even the most minor infraction might arouse the critical eye of the minister for labor. All existing unions had to reregister within six months and thus subject themselves to government scrutiny.

Existing collective agreements were to be honored under the provisions of the new law, but the minister was given new power to oversee them. In addition, he was able to prohibit any automatic dues check-off which had been freely negotiated between unions and employers if he was satisfied that individual workers had not consented in writing to such deductions. In absence of negotiated check-off, no employer could deduct dues from worker's pay on instructions of the union alone; workers had to agree individually. Dues were to be paid to individual unions, not to a central organization.

Strikes and lockouts, and the threat of such disturbances, could be prohibited absolutely by the government in the "national interest." This provision removed a good portion of the leverage which unions had previously enjoyed in relation to employers. Since strikes, even if they did occur, would almost automatically be subject to a 90-day cooling-off period which might be extended indefinitely, there was less reason for employers to enter into negotiations with unions merely to insure industrial peace.

There was nothing specific in the Act which guaranteed a return to the weak unions of the colonial era, or which permanently proscribed the TUC. On the surface, the new law merely appeared more "liberal" and less coercive than its 1965 predecessor. In fact, of course, Act 383, by upsetting the orderly flow of revenue, could cause irreparable damage. It did not matter that, as Busia pointed out, "any new congress, federation or trade union formed and entered under the new Act would be free, if they wished, to elect as their leaders the former Secretary-General or any othe person."[37] The new leader, be it B.A. Bentum or someone else, would be presiding over an insolvent and politically subservient organization.

The Ghana Confederation of Labor continued in existence as a loose federation for four more months. However, by the time the dissolution was a fact in Ghana, the prestige and popularity of the Progress Party was low enough that some of the breakaway leaders became increasingly nervous about attaching their fortunes to the PP star. The "loose" structure of the GCL, for example, allowed MACAWU to remain neutral toward TUC attempts to resuscitate itself after the September 1971 dissolution. The executive secretary of the GCL, at least, was not firmly convinced that the TUC could be legislated out of existence and did not want to burn his bridges behind him. Although the PP government had obviously welcomed and encouraged his group, he remained skeptical of Busia's ability to maintain friendly relations with organized labor, whether TUC or breakaway unions.

In October, some workers split from their parent group to form the Public Transport Workers Union, but they were unable to obtain a registration certificate from the government. By November, the National Union of Seamen and a branch of the Mineworkers that was dissatisfied with its national leadership were ready to join the GCL. The Seamen adopted a resolution supporting a tax on wages, a part of the government's 1971 budget proposal. But these potential defections, although they impeded a completely united response on the part of the TUC Executive Board toward the banning of the GCL, did not actually occur. The ambition of the GCL leadership and its genuine hopes for the members of its unions were foundering with the crumbling PP regime. In less than two months, a new military government would be in office, one which would not tolerate splinter unions or rival national centers.

The GCL and the breakaways had managed to survive, if briefly, and they undoubtedly gained support, in part, because some leaders and members believed that the PP regime would aid them. In the end, however, they werre disappointed. Breakaways did not benefit from the dissolution; to the contrary, the Progress Party appeared as isolated, ideologically and temperamentally, from the splinter unions as it was from the TUC.


## LEGAL AND POLITICAL FRAMEWORK IN THE 1970's

The Ghana Trades Union Congress was restored when a second military regime, the National Redemption Council (NRC), came to power on January 13, 1972. On February 11, Act 383 was repealed. The legal environment for today's unions in Ghana is, therefore, the 1965 Industrial Relations Act with its subsequent amendments. Like the National Liberation Council in 1966-67, however, the NRC and its successor, the Supreme Military Council, developed policies concerning the legitimacy of individual unions, in spite of their reliance on previous legislation.

It is perhaps ironic that, under the NRC, the legal development that concerned Ghanaian unionists most was not a law which had been changed during PP rule but one which had *not* been changed. The consensus of union executives was that the TUC should owe its existence only to the desire of the member unions to come together, and not to an act of Parliament. When the NRC assumed power, one of the first submissions which the TUC made was for a repeal of the formal, legal status of the body, so that it could not be legislated out of existence. This position indicates that the Congress, in the opinion of most of its leaders, had outgrown the need for the law to be the primary guarantor of its legitimacy. The NRC responded favorably to this initial submission. One union official related that the TUC was given "every assurance" that the law would be modified. However, the government did not fulfill its promise.

Nonetheless, the NRC reasserted the official position taken during 1966-69, that the TUC Executive Board's recommendations regarding certification for constituent unions should be honored. The commissioner for labor required the two major breakaways, RHWU and MACAWU, to rejoin their parent unions. The government also refused to accept a suggestion that the tiny Railway Enginemen's Union be required to join the larger Railway and Ports Workers. The Enginemen had been early members of the TUC, which would have opposed such a move. In additon, although the NRC considered requiring Ghana's largest union, the Industrial and Commercial Workers, to split itself into two separate bodies, it declined to press its demand when the union and the TUC Executive Board resisted.

The Trades Union Congress is today composed of 17 national unions. The right of these unions to exist was formalized under the 1958 Industrial Relations Act, but the legitimacy of organized labor is such that the dissolution of 1971 did not result in the disappearance of the Congress. Busia claimed that, as an appendage of the banned Convention People's Party, the TUC was automatically illegal, and that the failure to abolish it prior to 1971 was merely an "oversight." But, this argument was, in effect, rejected by the NRC and subsequent governments, which did not consider denying recognition to the group despite the continued ban on the CPP.

In 1958, given the opposition to a strong Congress within both the CPP and the labor movement itself, formal legal status was the *sine qua non* of the New Structure. By 1972, however, such a legal environment had actually become a threat to the TUC! The Congress had even assumed authority over the granting of recognition for national unions. This remarkable vitality may be attributed, in part, to its efforts in securing financial and human resources from its environment, a subject to which we now turn.

## CHAPTER III

# Patterns of Exchange between Unions and Society

A specific aim of organized labor is to gain more money and leisure time for workers. A more general, less manifest, need is for unions to be financially solvent, to make regular their supply of membership and income. To accomplish both types of goals, trade unions form working relationships with other bodies whose goals are, at least in part, complementary. In Africa, the state as a major employer, is perhaps the most important of these coparticipants. However, in Ghana a variety of other groups have also aided the Trades Union Congress in securing resources. These have included political parties, voluntary associations, foreign labor centers, and foundations.

The strength of its cooperative ties is indicated, in part, by the ability of the Congress to prevent existing, competing groups from obtaining assets and usurping its unique functions in society. The patterns of interaction which it has established with supporting bodies have, on occasion, been so pervasive as to lead to the denial of legitimacy to other organizations. Governments and outside agencies have coacted with the Congress because they expect that the unions will address the social problems which they feel are most in need of solution. One of these societal needs is the increasing of national productivity, a goal which both business and government share. A related problem is the socialization of workers, so that they may assume the roles required of them. Both sides in the exchange relationship between organized labor and society must be examined in order to determine the extent to which each side's needs have been met.

## GOVERNMENT RESOURCES AND POLICY

For 35 years the Ghana TUC has sought support from the government of the day. Its success has come directly, from *ad hos* negotiations or legislation, and directly, from the appointment of Congress leaders to various boards and committees, either by statute or by administrative decision.

### Before Independence

Government financial assistance to unions was negligible until Kwame Nkrumah and his Convention People's Party assumed responsibility for domestic affairs in 1951. The "mushroom" unions which the enabling ordinances had elicited would have been too unreliable for the colonial government to support directly, and the many house unions were too small in potential influence. But most important was the British ethic of voluntarism, which confined colonial tutelage to administrative advice in a few of the stronger groups. Unions were, nonetheless, instrumental in securing wage increases during the colonial period. Salary commissions made favorable recommendations in 1939, 1941, 1946, and 1949.[1]

After 1951 the CPP took more steps to help the TUC, having fewer illusions about the separation of unions and state. The encouragement of initiative among labor organizations was an important factor in maintaining the loyalty of the worker constituency which the party was courting. Nkrumah reinstated the workers who had been dismissed during the 1950 general strike. In addition, he appointed union officials to review the Lidbury Commission's recommendation for a 20 percent rise in wages and salaries. The 35 percent overall increase granted by the government in 1952 may be attributed to trade union pressure and the exchange relationship between politicians and labor leaders, especially in light of the official wage restraint sentiments then prevailing. Similarly, before 1951, the lowest-paid workers received the highest percentage raises, in contrast to the recommendations of the British. This had been a persistent demand of the unions. But during the 1950's it was apparent that the absence of guaranteed check-off and the creaky negotiating machine for civil service unions were impediments to the ability of labor executives to attract members. Prior to 1956, when the "stalwart," CPP-oriented leadership consolidated its hold on the TUC Secretariat, the government did not place its weight behind the effort to organize the unorganized.

### 1958-1966

The implementation of the New Structure required the initiation of direct and substantial government financial aid to the unions for the first time. During 1956 and 1957, the government paid 12,000 pounds to the TUC.[2] This was a small taste of things to come. John Tettegah proposed that the government grant the Congress a loan to set up the secretariat before automatic dues check-off was instituted. He sought to minimize the TUC's implicit indebtedness to government by emphasizing: "We are not asking for a gift, we are asking for a loan like any other independent organization to be repaid to the government."[3] In fact, however, the loan of 100,000 pounds was never called in. It was to be interest-free; half was to cover the cost of the new TUC hall. The remainder, in two 25,000-pound installments, was "based roughly on the estimated expenditure" of the Congress between 1958 and 1960.

In requesting parliamentary approval for the initial 50,000 pounds, a request which was made on the same day as the Industrial Relations Act was passed, the government maintained that "the trade union movement's record of loyalty and devotion to the cause of national freedom, during the struggle for independence, merits some form of recognition, in the shape of financial assistance." R.R. Amponsah, responding for the opposition, was concerned that Parliament receive some accounting of the manner in which public funds were being spent. He was at pains to distinguish between monies collected via check-off, private organization funds, and the loan.

Kofi Baako, CPP minister of information, summed up the party's attitude succinctly by replying, "Money is money!" Regardless of the source, the party was showing its ability to deliver its part of the concordat. Government revenues available to support the trade unions were at an all-time high.

Cocoa income had risen during the previous decade, and estimated expenditures under the CPP's development program were over seven times as large as the British had envisaged ten years earlier. By 1966, the government had paid over £357,000 sterling ($1,000,000 at the 1966 exchange rate) directly to Congress officials, to finance several TUC-operated business enterprises.

However, the most long-lasting benefit which resulted from the New Structure and the concordat between the TUC and government was the revolution in the TUC's bargaining position vis-a-vis private employers. As one foreign observer noted, ". . . the government has advanced the power of the unions in the country and has legislated a bargaining structure that would have taken the individual unions years to achieve."[4] The new bargaining relationships included the guaranteed check-off for union dues, not as a matter for negotiation, but as an absolute right. Individual workers could, of course, sign a form opting out of the check-off system, but the number of workers electing to refuse to participate was small; and because the union shop was specified as a legitimate matter for negotiation, the number of such shops, and the number of union members, began to grow. Automatic check-off was extended to government employees in the 1959 amendment to the labor law, although they were still prohibited from bargaining collectively.

Allowing for unreliability of statistics, it is nonetheless evident that the amalgamation and guaranteed check-off provisions of the new law resulted in a rapid increase in recorded union membership. From 135,615 in 1958, membership jumped to about 230,000 in the following year.* Since approximately 319,000 workers were recorded in urban wage employment, this meant that the TUC claimed to have organized almost 70 percent of them. While inflated, this percentage is not so unreliable as it might appear, considering that in the wake of independence a variety of public works and public corporation projects, including the harbor at Tema, had absorbed thousands of workers, whose dues were subject to

---

*See Appendix 3.

check-off. By 1960 the unions were ensconced in their new national headquarters, the Hall of Trades Unions. TUC income, at least, appeared to justify the concordat with government. It had risen from 497 pounds in 1958 to over 80,000 pounds in 1960.[5] In the following year, the Congress's income more than doubled, reflecting the compulsory membership of all unions.

At first glance, the unions appear to have been much less effective in improving *workers'* income, especially from 1961 to 1966. In spite of minimum wage hikes of between 18 and 30 percent, the real wage index fell from 118 in 1960 to 64 in 1966 (1939 = 100).[6] The government reported an absence of any active upward pressure on wages during 1963 because of the buoyant supply of labor, and because of the Industrial Relations Act, which "more or less 'controls' the Trade Unions and their wage increase demands."[7] But, although strikes were few, the TUC retained substantial power to influence government. "Given the new collective bargaining machinery, wage demand strikes became less and less useful to indicate union pressure."[8] We need to ask: If the unions were really impotent, why was it necessary to restrain, and eventually to remove, John Tettegah as secretary-general of the Congress?

Concrete monetary gains for workers made prior to the 1966 coup, which are not reflected in the real-wage statistics, included expansion of public projects, which created wage-paying jobs; imposition of price controls; and establishment of employment centers, which reduced the likelihood of unskilled help being hired at wages below the official minimum. Workers were paid for public holidays, and for more days per month; the wage differential between rural and urban areas was abolished; a social security law was enacted. Finally, a great number of social services were provided, including free schooling and hospital care. All of this meant that the lowest paid, in effect, had more money to spend. It is admittedly difficult to trace the direct connection between these benefits and labor agitation, but they were, in fact, identical to well-publicized, prior TUC demands.[9]

It was not through direct financial aid, or even through the Industrial Relations Act, that unionists sought to establish the more important avenues of cooperation with the CPP regime. They believed that, in the long run, regularizing income and membership for the Congress would have to come from unionists' participation in bodies responsbile for establishing national priorities and the making of economic policy. Although some gains were indeed made after 1960, the input into government decision-making was much less than labor desired or expected. The principal reason for this was that the range of overlapping goals between trade unions and political party, which had first prompted direct and indirect assistance, began to shrink.

*Two Post-Coup Regimes*

When the National Liberation Council assumed power in February 1966, it embarked on a policy of economic retrenchment which affected the resource base of the TUC. It closed down or sold to private interests a wide variety of unprofitable state enterprises. This action, together with the elimination of some civil service posts, accounted for a total of 70,492 workers laid off between 1966 and 1969.[10] Union membership and finances suffered accordingly. The TUC lost over 110,000 members between 1965 and 1968, but it is impossible to say precisely what proportion of these were defections from the ranks of civil servants, who were no longer required to be union members. In any event, income dropped from over 386,000 new cedis in 1966 to 248,000 new cedis in 1967.[11]

In spite of these developments, the Congress made a conscientious effort to increase indirect support from government under the NLC. It demanded and received a say in the determination of national economic priorities. In June 1966, the NLC created a political committee to advise the regime. B.A. Bentum, who had been appointed by the NLC to head the Congress, in advance of its 1966 elections, was selected as labor's representative on this committee. The TUC was also represented on the Public Service Structure and Salaries Commission, and a Congress spokesman noted, with some pride, that "for the first time in history [the TUC] had the opportunity of having direct representation on a Commisson charged with the responsibility of enquiring into the salaries and wages and the entire service conditions of the working population."[12] He could have added that such access had not even occurred under the "workers' government" of the CPP.

In response to a "reader's question," a columnist in a TUC publication said: "Yes, trade union leaders should agree to sit on government bodies because they can contribute immensely and be able to influence decisions of government in favor of workers' interests. This minimizes, to a great extent, the degree by which trade unions will have to wrestle with government on policies which are formulated by them without trade union participation."[13] During the NLC period, however, the unionists were to discover that the input they had obtained was no guarantee of favorable government policy.

Under the subsequent civilian government, beginning in 1969, patterns of cooperation were disrupted. The Progress Party government did not reverse the NLC policy of appointing TUC leaders to advisory and consultative bodies, but by June 1971 it had made it clear that it would ignore their submissions. The TUC found itself systematically excluded from national policy deliberations affecting its members. The Busia regime appeared unable to tolerate labor input. Eventually, in the wake of the dissolution, TUC income and membership declined precipitously. One secretariat official estimated the losses at 200,000 members, but this is probably an exaggeration.

## The National Redemption Council

The period under the NRC after January 1972, was marked by a strengthening of direct government assistance. In addition to restoration, the regime enabled the TUC to increase its income and relieved it of the obligation to spend the restored revenues from dues check-off on the reduction of previous debts. It cancelled over $60,000 in house rates owed by the TUC to the Accra-Tema City Council; it authorized about $88,000 as a loan, with a two-year moratorium on repayment, to help the Congress pay salary arrears to its own employees who had been laid off because of the dissolution. Moreover, the TUC was relieved of its obligation to pay back substantial government loans which dated from the Nkrumah period, and which had been dissipated by corrupt and inefficient management. The government also announced that it would implement the findings of a 1967 probe of TUC assets. NRC Decree 111 gave the Congress legal authority to recover misappropriated funds which a commission of enquiry had said were owed to it, a total of over 414,000 cedis ($360,000 at that time). Pressure was applied to some former TUC officers, and almost all of the funds were eventually recovered.

Perhaps the greatest single action which is evidence of the government's financial commitment was the transfer of the ownership of the Hall of Trades Unions to the TUC itself in May 1974. But in addition, the NRC consistently acted to support the welfare functions of the unions. Imported foods, the so-called "essential commodities," were given to the TUC to be sold to workers by the unions, at a time of widespread shortages and high prices. A popular mini-bus service was initiated to transport workers to and from their jobs; many of the vans were given to the Private Road Transport Union on a hire-purchase basis. The same union was allowed to organize a deferred payment plan for its drivers' auto insurance, and the government even helped the union discover which drivers had not paid their dues by checking them when they attempted to renew their operators' licenses!

The regime also contributed to the regularization of membership supply by reinstating many workers who had been discharged prior to 1972. In addition, a government directive helped to stabilize union membership by improving job security. The commissioner for labor prescribed the following: "Employers intending to lay-off ten or more workers at a time should notify the Commissioner . . . in writing . . . stating the circmstances leading to the lay-off; . . . such lay-off shall not be effected until the Commissioner's permission has been granted."[14] The directive went on to say that employers could not violate the intent of the order by discharging workers one by one. Although both government and the private sector did, in fact, lay off some workers during the period under review, this order prevented anything like the wholesale redundancy exercises which took place under the NLC in 1967-68.

Several government projects which had been abandoned after the 1966 coup were reinstated, including prefabricated concrete, cement, brick, and chemical manufacturing, and gold refining. These measures opened up new jobs, as did the export bonus paid to international merchants. Various low-cost housing schemes aided the construction trades. In addition, the government began a program of subsidizing rural industries, expanding agricultural and fishery products (under Operation Feed Yourself), and revitalizing state farms. These measures somewhat reduced unemployment in rural areas and allowed for unionization of more rural workers. By 1977, the number of workers affiliated with the Congress eclipsed the record set in 1965.

Indirect support of unions, through appointment of their leaders to consultative and policy-making bodies, was expanded under Ghana's second military regime. Below is a partial list of boards, commissions, and committees on which TUC representatives served, under the auspices of the government.

Ad Hoc Committee on Housing
Agricultural Commodities Prices Review Committee
Ashanti Goldfields Corporation
Bank of Ghana
Educational Advisory Committee
Food Production Corporation
Korle Bu Hospital Committee
Logistics Committee
National Advisory Committee
National Apprenticeship Council
National Committee for Rehabilitation
National Road Safety Committee
Public Accounts Committee
Salary Review Committee
Seamen's Welfare Board
Social Security Advisory Board
State Construction Corporation
Tax Review Commission
Tema Development Corporation

Aside from formal appointments, the NRC also asked labor officials to consult with them on an informal basis concerning proposed changes in legislation and in local government organization.

The consensus of union officials was that communications between the Congress and the NRC were effective in setting out the positions of each. This opinion was based, in part, on the multiplicity of personal relationships established through TUC participation in the groups cited above. It was said that the commissioner for labor devoted two full days each week to TUC affairs, and that the highest levels of government, including the chairman of the NRC, were informed of TUC positions on important questions on a regular basis. Certainly, the substantial wage increases granted in 1973-74 (described in detail in Chapter IV below) and the additional raises given in 1977 are evidence that the military regime was listening.

But, although channels of labor input into the establishment of national priorities were maintained, they were at times ineffective. Many of the boards could not take a decision unless union representatives were present, but the unionists could easily be outvoted. Moreover, representation on commissions established by government was not automatic for the TUC; the power to include unionists remained in the hands of the government. The Congress was indeed part of the Salary Review Committee; it demanded, and received, additional representation on that body. But it was barred from the Prices and Income Board, which had the power to set and enforce wage and price controls.

Government proposals for increasing cooperation with the TUC have been characterized by a balance between promises and warnings. The delivey of resources has occasionally carried the threat of control, or the actual exercise of control. It occurred to some unionists, for example, that the establishment of an NRC office in the Hall of Trades Unions enhanced the ability of the regime to monitor union affairs as much as it improved communications with labor. The office was later closed by mutual consent.

Organized labor has experienced some failures since 1972. The monies collected from workers under the National Development Levies of 1961 and 1971 have not been returned; the social security scheme has not been converted to a retirement plan, as the TUC has demanded, and most of its payments are still death benefits; the government has not implemented an equitable price control program. Perhaps the major unattained labor goal is effecting a redistribution of income in Ghana. Government wage increases have not improved the relative position of the unskilled, lowest-paid worker. The movement's struggle to accomplish its manifest goals is, perhaps, never-ending. On the other hand, its membership base is strong, and its financial integrity is at an all-time high.

## TIES WITH PRIVATE ORGANIZATIONS

*Employers' Associations*

Prior to 1966 there was little development of independent relations between unions and domestic, non-governmental groups performing complementary functions. Under the CPP, it would have been difficult to propose such collaboration in contravention of party policy, and almost all groups in Ghana were subjected to infiltration and co-optation of leadership by the CPP. An important exception to this last generalization was private associations of employers. These associations were a natural outgrowth of the system of industrial relations which had emerged following the legalization of the unions, and, by 1960, they had developed patterns of exchange with Congress leaders.

The paucity of employers' associations in Ghana prior to 1958 may be attributed to the retarded growth of the private sector, generally, and the historic domination of public employment. In a milieu characterized by labor surplus and relatively weak unions, little pressure could be placed on the employers. It is significant that the earliest permanent employers' group, the Chamber of Mines, appeared in an industry with a strong union. As the number of private businesses and public corporations increased during the 1950's the chamber was joined by federations of employeers in timber, ports, and construction. By 1958 a Forest Producers' Association, which attracted about 200 members, accounting for one-third of the export trade in wood products, and a

Ghana National Contractors' Federation had made their appearance.[15]

The formation of an employers' group which could act as an umbrella for all types of enterprises, and particularly manufacturing industries, was not possible before 1956. The Ghanaian Federation of Industries, inaugurated in that year, attracted only 60 members. But one outcome of the implementation of the New Structure was the formation of a larger and more permanent organization. The Ghana Employers' Association (GEA) was founded on January 13, 1959, less than one month after the Industrial Relations bill was passed. Initially, it contained 50 members, but 109 were registered by its first anniversary.[16]

While the new labor law did not, of course, require the establishment of an employers' group, the formation of the GEA may be viewed as evidence of recognition by the better-established enterprises, particularly those financed from abroad, that employer unity was desirable in the face of the automatic status granted the unions. The GEA, originally, was composed of foreign employers in Ghana who considered the association a needed defense against the possibility that the CPP would use the unions as weapons against them. However, the reality of the New Structure also encouraged Ghanaian employers to band together. The first such organization was the Bakery Owners' Association, which appeared after the Caterers' and Meatcutters' Union struck in 1959 to protest lack of recognition under the Industrial Relations Act.

Collective bargaining was the major activity which brought the GEA and TUC together prior to 1966. But, after the NLC coup, the range of contacts increased. By then, the GEA contained Ghanaian enterprises. It was, for the first time, able to enter into contracts with labor completely removed from national politics. The Congress and the GEA met to discuss problems of development and further ways of cooperating with each other. In subsequent years, through their combined efforts, they both secured representation on the Social Security Advisory Board. They also collaborated in suggesting to government that changes be made in the 1965 Industrial Relations Act.

The Labor Advisory Council (LAC), a body specified in both the 1958 and 1965 labor laws, became an important forum for exchanges between employers and unions. The council contains seven management representatives and seven unionists — TUC secretariat officials and union executives. The minister for labor must approve the appointment of members and the council's agenda. The body met sporadically during the CPP period, primarily to advise the Labor Department, and it was dormant during 1966-67. However, from 1968 through 1971, it gathered regularly.

The GEA and TUC used the council to debate matters of substance. For example, in 1969 the government proposed the establishment of a labor court. Some leaders in business and the unions were wary of the plan, feeling that there was not enough labor law in Ghana, or precedent, on which the decisions of the court could be based. The Congress and the employers succeeded in making the Labor Advisory Council the venue for the discussion of the implications of setting up a labor court. The government was not able to satisfy the objections which both parties raised. After the NRC coup, the council, again, was not convened by the government, but this did not affect the continuation of cooperative relations between the employers' association and the unions. The GEA now contains over 300 employers.

## Other Domestic Groups

After 1966, contacts were also established with a variety of other organizations. The TUC joined with the Ghana Bar Association and the Legon Society for National Affairs in making daily comments regarding NLC policies. The National Union of Ghana Students sought, and obtained, the cooperation of the Congress in making its demands for changes in the student loan scheme. The Busia government opposed the establishment of these alliances, but it could not prevent them.

After dissolution and restoration, a number of other groups sought connection with the Congress; these included students and the Ghana National Association of Teachers. By 1973, the

TUC executive board had not approved formal affiliation with these bodies, but they continue to liaise informally.

In contrast to these profitable exchanges between the Congress and a variety of voluntary organizations, collaboration with nonincumbent political parties has been unproductive. Some prominent unionists supported the National Liberation Movement and its successor, the United Party, between 1956 and 1961, but these flirtations did not give the unions any special advantage. In fact, they resulted in attempts to manipulate the unions. The opposition under the Progress Party, the Justice Party, maintained a pro-labor posture. In the fall of 1971, a Justice Party labor spokesman declared that Busia's Progress Party was "hysterical," and that it was determined to kill the TUC and split the workers' movement.[17] But, ironically, the existence of a parliamentary opposition, an important element in a national democratic environment, did not increase official toleration for unions as pressure groups. The similarity between TUC and Justice Party positions was not attributed to a coincidence of opposition to government policy, but to a subversive plot. In Ghana, nonincumbent parties have not had enough to offer the TUC to enter into durable alliances with it or to play a positive role in the attainment of institutional status for the unions.

*Foreign Resources*

The International Confederation of Free Trade Unions, supported by the Western bloc countries, has rendered financial and technical assistance to Ghanaian unions. Beginning in 1953, it operated a headquarters in Accra, which was then used by the moderate wing of the labor movement. In a relatively short time, however, it came to the support of the "stalwart," CPP-oriented, Congress secretariat. John Tettegah appealed to this international body to help him "forge the instruments of our political, economic, and social liberation."[18] He received organizational aid in implementing the New Structure, particularly in the drafting of the new legislation, and some money.

The links with the ICFTU were broken after 1959 and have never been officially reestablished. Nonetheless, the TUC has

continued to draw support from the International Trade
Secretariats (ITS's), which are loosely connected with the
ICFTU. These have maintained a posture of avoiding the
conflicts between eastern and western labor centers, because
the aid they provide is of a practical nature, and of no explicit
ideological orientation. The assistance of the ITS's has come in
the areas of bargaining, provision of health and safety
services, labor administration, and worker education. Of the
17 International Trade Secretariats, eight are currently
cooperating with TUC unions. Some unions, because of their
industrial nature, have established ties with more than one
ITS. Only three of the 17 functioning unions in Ghana have no
such relationship. Some of the Ghanaian union heads have
served on the boards of the ITS to which their union is joined.
Although the international bodies do not fund Ghanaian
unions for their general operation, they have, on occasion,
waived the dues required for associating.

The TUC is also linked to the International Labor
Organization (ILO), based in Geneva. Its delegations visit
Ghana periodically, although the exchanges between the TUC
and this group are primarily informational. Membership in the
ILO can contribute to the recognition of unions in less
developed areas by their adversaries, because the
organization calls for tripartite representation from business,
government, and labor. However, in Ghana, the ILO
connection has been more than "window-dressing." The
Congress took the case of locked-out shipyard workers to the
ILO for adjudication, at considerable embarrassment to the
NLC and, later, the Progress Party governments. The fact
that foreign intervention was sought, because of the
unresponsiveness of local officials, is credited by most
unionists for the eventual rehiring of the workers.

African trade union centers have played a minor part in the
institutionalization of the Ghanaian unions. The All African
Trade Union Federation (AATUF), backed by Kwame
Nkrumah and led by John Tettegah, received funding from
Eastern Bloc countries, but its major programs were
activated outside Ghana. With the exception of AATUF
involvement, the Ghana TUC has scrupulously avoided linking

itself with African labor centers for most of its history. Only in 1973 did it join the Organization of African Trade Union Unity (OATUU), an arm of the Organization of African Unity. The headquarters of the OATUU were established in Accra, a situation which, ironically, benefitted the TUC, in spite of the weakness, and lack of specific program, of the international body. Several unionists credited the moderation of NRC labor policy to the location of the offices of the OATUU in Ghana.

Assistance from individual, national labor centers, including the AFL-CIO (United States) and British TUC, as well as Soviet and Eastern European unions, is well publicized. The American labor center aided in setting up a clinic, and combined with the Friedrich Ebert Foundation of West Germany in a workers' housing scheme. This particular foreign connection was strong enough that, when the board of receivers under the dissolution threatened to seize the houses as part of TUC assets, the Americans and Germans were able to prevent it. A Workers' Housing Society was formed to administer the scheme.

The West Germans' attentiveness to the TUC is the most visible of any foreign government in Ghana. They maintain a full-time attaché to coordinate the German activities aiding labor. The Konrad Adenauer Foundation is also active in the country, helping to set up workers' cooperative credit unions. Many of these links were originally created when Willy Brandt, then foreign minister of West Germany, visited Ghana and was asked by the TUC to help reestablish relations with German unions. However, the subsequent cooperation has not precluded contacts with East Germany or other communist countries. Although their profile is lower, they regularly invite Ghanaian unionists to attend courses and seminars.


## EFFECTS ON COMPETING ORGANIZATIONS

Patterns of exchange between TUC and government, or complementary groups, have become so expected and predictable that rival labor organizations have frequently found making alliances of their own to be difficult or impossible. Indeed, throughout most of its history, Congress has not had to compete with other, national labor centers. The Confederation of Free Trade Unions (1956) was stymied by its failure to obtain enabling legislation, and it never had the opportunity to develop the inter-organizational ties that would have helped it to become viable. Similarly, it is plain that the government allowed the TUC's most serious rival, the Ghana Confederation of Labor (1971), to form merely as an act of political expediency. This group, too, disappeared as it attempted, unsuccessfully, to secure official support.

There is, however, another group which has competed with the congress for membership and income. This is the Junior Civil Servants Association (JCSA), which includes employees in government ministries and departments. A 1959 amendment to the Industrial Relations Act had inhibited the formation of such an association by stating that government employees had to be represented by approved unions unless they earned in excess of 660 pounds a year. In 1967, however, NLC Decree 134 changed this situation, giving civil servants the option of belonging to any group, including an association.

In 1968 the JCSA was founded. The TUC had not been consulted in the granting of legal sanction to the association. It is thought that the civil servants prevailed upon the NLC to proclaim Decree 134, in return for which the active cooperation of government workers in administering the affairs of the country was promised. However, legitimacy is weaker for the association than for the TUC, because its existence is only allowed, not guaranteed. The government, as employer, is not compelled to recognize it in negotiations. Moreover, like other TUC rivals, the association has failed to establish effective routines for acquiring members and funds. It claims that, at the height of its strength, prior to September 1971, it contained 15,000 members; today the number of dues-paying members is much lower. The NLC and subsequent governments have been inconsistent, at best, in cooperating with the JCSA.

In 1967, the TUC became dissatisfied with the anti-inflationary recommendations of a government survey

(The Mills-Odoi Report) as they affected its civil service members, and tried to block their implementation. The NLC would not agree to this, but it did postpone implementation when the JCSA presented its grievances. The association showed that it had established some leverage with government when it succeeded in forcing a review of the Mills-Odoi findings (the Mensah Review). However, when the Mensah findings were delayed, the association threatened a strike. Its position was weak enough that the NLC actually banned the association, and only restored it when it declared its "loyalty."[19] However, no threats were directed at TUC unions which had said that they also would strike; instead, the Congress won a promise that the Mensah Review would be released.

The JCSA's major failure, and the most important reason for the weakness of the association, has been the government's denial of automatic dues check-off for its members, which would have the effect of stabilizing its income. Its inability to obtain check-off also contributes to the viability of TUC unions containing a majority of civil servants, which do enjoy this privilege. However, in spite of the superior strength which TUC affiliates have shown, the association continues to justify its existence as a separate entity on the grounds that leaders of civil service unions are "unnecessary middlemen" between workers and government. This position is reinforced by an ideology which stresses individual job security, rather than strength in unity. Based on this comparison, it is apparent that the JCSA, although viable as an *organization*, is not an institution, nor is it likely to become one.

The TUC has not had to adopt a posture of overt hostility to its association rival. Although it has criticized the lack of militancy of the latter, and the association's position on modifying, rather than completely revising, the General Orders, or civil service regulations, under which employees operate, the TUC has been able to rely on its own patterns of exchange with government to keep its competition in check. In spite of the loss of union members suffered under NLC Decree 134, the Congress characterized the legal change as "democratic and good."[20] It takes the position that a union, as distinct from an association, will, in the long run, be able to provide more services to workers and will, therefore, have more appeal to them.

When criticism was voiced in the press that another association, the Senior Civil Servants Association, had been behaving like a union, the secretary-general of the TUC remarked that its alleged behavior was no reason to ban it. Had the association, in fact, been assuming the functions of a union, he noted, the registrar of trade unions would have informed the government accordingly. The TUC was indicating that it could count on its established connections to prevent the usurpation of its unique functions.


## THE *QUID PRO QUO:* SOME BRIEF OBSERVATIONS

For the most part, this chapter has documented what government and complementary organizations have done for the unions. However, if we are correct and, indeed, an exchange mechanism is operating, we need to specify what the Trades Union Congress offers in return. We suggest that all these contributions continue to flow because of the perception of government and private groups that the unions are contributing to the solution of some major social problems in Ghana.

### National Productivity

One important societal need has been to increase national productivity. It is not possible to correlate the scope of union programs with the rise and fall in gross national product, but we can take the incidence of strikes and "man-days lost" as direct threats to productive potential. Insofar as unions have been able to discourage strikes, influence their brevity once initiated, or serve as a mechanism for government control of strike behavior, organized labor may be said to be aiding the effort to increase production.

Appendix 3 contains data on the number of work stoppages and man-days lost for each year from 1945 through 1976. Even if we omit the years 1962 through 1965, when union autonomy was at a low point and strikes were rigidly suppressed, we still note as few as two, and no more than 83 work stoppages per year. Only in 1951, when the movement had been intimidated by the failure of the 1950 general strike, could unions not take credit for the relative calm. In every other year, against a background of increasing union membership, the number of strikes is remarkably consistent and, in fact, surprisingly low, given the rising worker expectations prior to independence and the unstable economic conditions after 1965. Similarly, the lengthy strikes in the mines, reflected in the data for 1948 and 1956, and the 1961 general strike, spurred by militant railwaymen in Sekondi, stand out as atypical. It is apparent that the vast majority of work stoppages have lasted less than one day.

To illustrate these points, we may note that between 1967 and 1969 a wide variety of industries were affected by labor militancy. Mineworkers, dockers, railwaymen, lorry and taxi drivers, university workers, bank, sugar estate, and local government employees all participated in labor disputes. The union official responsible for the General Transport and Petroleum Workers in the Western Region reported that during 1968 no fewer than 100 disputes in that area alone were brought to his attention. The General Agricultural Workers Union reported, between 1968 and 1970, ten demonstrations and protests involving about 13,600 workers, and six "sit-downs" or "go-slows" affecting 10,500 men. In addition, 735 industrial grievances were processed by the union during this period. By contrast, there were only three actual strikes among agricultural workers, involving no more than 6,000 men.[21]

It may be appreciated that these are only two of seventeen unions, and that the individual grievances, in these unions and others, could themselves have been the cause of strikes. Beyond the large number of grievances filed, unions had other motivations to strike; for example, work stoppages could have been used by local union officials to focus attention on more general complaints. In light of all these reasons to strike, it is significant that the number of actual strikes was not greater.

We may legitimately infer that the unions' moderating influence on industrial relations accounted for this regularity. When relations with the government were at their worst, in 1971, the total number of strikes increased, but only to 71. Some of these were in fact a protest against the dissolution itself. In other cases, union officials, aware of the deteriorating situation, were less inclined than usual to impose sanctions on their more militant branch leaders.

If our interpretation of these data is correct, the TUC's relatively cordial relations with the Ghana Employers' Association may be explained. Several businessmen reported that, although illegal strikes did occur, Ghana has compared favorably with other, less developed countries in which they considered operating. The opinion was also expressed that, although the productivity of the Ghanaian worker was lower than that of his British counterpart, the threat of strikes was much lower in Ghana! Most businessmen did not regard the legal difficulties in staging a strike as being the exclusive reason for the comparative industrial peace. Indeed, particularly among GEA members, the TUC was given a share of credit.

The number of work stoppages for the years 1972-74, just after the NRC assumed power, is lower than in any period since the enforced industrial peace of 1962-65. The figures for 1975-77 indicate a continuing moderate trend. In no case have TUC officials formally condoned strikes as was the case between 1966 and 1971. In fact, when wildcat strikes occurred in 1977 in the production and service sectors of the economy, primarily among professionals and nurses, the TUC opposed them.[22] These data help to explain why, since 1972, resources have been granted to the Congress in unprecedented amounts, considering that unions are now independent of government.

*Socialization of Workers*

A second *quid pro quo* is that the unions have helped to explain to workers what the government, and their employers, expect of them. One of the obligations which the Congress assumed, in return for the financial security given

by the 1958 concordat, was to educate workers concerning not
only their rights, but their duties and responsibilities as well.
The Convention People's Party never did eliminate agitation
and protest as a union tactic, but during the Nkrumah years
the TUC did communicate to workers the rationale behind
many government decisions affecting them.

High labor turnover and the tendency for workers to
migrate between urban factories and rural farms are often
cited as evidence for the failure of the Ghanaian to assimilate
the "work ethic." Victor Allen expresses a view, shared by
many observers, that, on entering the labor force, the African
many have no understanding of "the motivating forces of
individualism and accumulation." Industrial responsibility,
initiative, incentive, and discipline are not comprehended,
"for these do not figure in traditional African lives."[23]

Of course, unions cannot force workers to keep their jobs,
but they can encourage labor commitment by specifying, in
collective agreements, benefits to be granted workers with
long tenure. These contracts and less formal negotiations in
which the fairness of "established practices" of employers is
debated, serve a socializing function of workers. It is in the
unions' interest to reach a consensus with management
concerning production standards, punctuality, and other
indicators of labor commitment. Indeed, unions may be more
effective than employers in instilling discipline when they
voluntarily adhere to bargaining agreements.[24] The fact that
unions containing civil servants have been allowed to form and
to deduct dues from workers' pay shows that the government,
as an employer, is as aware of their socializing function as is
the private sector.


## CONCLUSIONS

In the last section we examined a portion of the evidence for
the assertion that, in cooperation with or independently of
government, the TUC has been able to address two important
social needs in Ghana — preventing strikes and socializing
workers. These efforts, although they have not been

completely successful, have been exercised consistently and predictably. Evidence for the institutional status of the unions is seen in the survival of the Congress after the demise of the CPP, the regime with which it liaised more directly, and which succeeded in reducing its autonomy furthest. This survival indicates that its efforts to solve social problems were valued more than the party which nurtured it, by elements of the Ghanaian business community, and by the coup-makers, who evidently believed that the unions were equipped to aid in legitimizing the military. Although an intimate financial connection with the CPP has been documented above, it is clear that the vulnerability of organized labor has decreased greatly since 1966, as a variety of complementary groups have been allowed to operate independently.

The direct and indirect government support obtained by the TUC, as well as the aid rendered by domestic and foreign sources, reinforce the position that organized labor has become a permanent force in Ghanaian national life. The Busia government, which ignored labor to a greater degree than other regimes, and which dissolved the TUC, found itself deposed three months later. It was able to interrupt the flow of money and members into the TUC, but only for a short period. One of the reasons for this is that, for two decades, patterns of functional exchange between the unions, on the one hand, and government and voluntary groups, on the other, had been learned and practiced.

Although direct and indirect forms of government assistance, taken together, were more evident than at any other period in the history of organized labor, the unions are today also more able to resist co-optation. The establishment of a working relationship has not weakened the boundaries between unions and government as it did during the Nkrumah period when it was said, "The CPP and TUC are one." Indeed, a significant effect of this contact, in addition to the regularization of the unions' human and material resources, has been to increase outsiders' awareness concerning the distinctive norms and rules by which organized labor establishes its policy positions. This is a subject treated in the next chapter.

## CHAPTER IV

# Industrial Relations:
# The Continuity of Norms and Rules

Labor organizations participate in common activities with their adversaries, business and government. As unions become institutionalized, the principles which govern their own behavior are also adopted by the other contending parties; a continuity appears between the norms and rules of the institution and those of other groups. The impetus for this process is the desire for conflict regulation, if not resolution. This desire on the part of the government, the unions, and the business community in Ghan is documented in this chapter through an examination of the manner in which labor relations in the country have evolved. The discussion is organized according to a set of specific norms and rules on which unions, as institutions, and their co-participants have come to agree.[1] These include:
1) settling disputes through negotiation
2) limiting the number of questions on which conflict may legitimately arise
3) avoiding violence
4) respecting the viability of one's opponents.

## SETTLING DISPUTES THROUGH NEGOTIATION

*Before the "New Structure"*

In Ghana, during the nineteenth and early twentieth centuries, disputes between workers and management or government were considered illegitimate. Primitive and coercive methods of consensus-building in industrial relations were employed. "Whether he liked it or not, the 'native' was part of a European capitalist system, and by gentle persuasion he was to be convinced that this obliged him to work for the good of himself and the whole system."[2] Such "gentle persuasion" included forced labor, little or no pay, long hours, and wretched conditions. There was little understanding of the concept of "contract" of employment, and the rationale for work was, in many cases, the Europeans' alone. Workers were able to form illegal unions, and some disputes were settled to their satisfaction. However, the norm of speedy and orderly adjudication of grievances was not shared by the disputants.

The 1941 ordinances made possible the establishment of sustained working relations between recognized unions and employers, but there was no automatic change for the better in industrial relations. Employers refused to initiate negotiations, or allowed disputes stemming from grievances to drag on. The Mineworkers, one of the more active and responsible early unions, found that management "looked down on the union as an intruder — a mere upstart with a deplorable membership." After more than two years of fitful negotiating, the miners threatened a strike in 1946, but management appeared "unconcerned" and "indignant."[3]

Nonetheless, prior to 1950, strikes over the issue of union recognition were successful in a number of firms, and joint negotiating machinery began to appear, in which some regular discussion of worker grievances occurred. A committee set up to hear the complaints of the Railwaymen's, Posts, and Public Workers union reported that the group "had prepared their case with great care and argued it was pertinacity, and we found there to be substance in many of the representations".[4]

Even this limited activity is remarkable, because the colonial government, in its position as employer, advisor to unions, and wage-setter, dominated the environment for industrial relations. The British realized that neither employers nor unions had yet internalized the value of settling disputes promptly, and, in addition, it was often in the interest of government to prevent any disagreement from being aired. The advice given to the early unions in Ghana called for a "friendly" feeling between unions and management. One pamphlet read: "Trade unions are formed to try to make sure that workers and employers understand one another." Workers with grievances, it said, should be aware that industry is very important to them. "If the employers are unable to keep their business going, the workers will have no work . . . the worker will become poor because there will be no money to pay him."[5]

But the British influenced unions' attitude toward the settlement of disputes not only with government propaganda, but also in their position as a major employer. This domination limited union expectations and caused the unions, during the 1950's, to await the recommendations of wage boards, even when they might have won more on their own. The over-reliance on salary reviews also encouraged unions in a wide variety of industries to make identical and automatic demands, without enough appreciation for the variation in different enterprises.

Efforts directed toward individual negotiations were retarded, with unions preferring to apply pressure to government — first the British, and subsequently the CPP. The result was a lack of expertise in dealing with disputes in the private sector. When these disagreements appeared unresolvable, unions tended to rely on government intervention. This meant that there was little motivation to follow or practice established grievance procedures. Unions did not engage in a coordinated effort to improve the conditions of employment. Disputes were, instead, sporadic, and unplanned.

By the mid-1950's, this situation caused some labor leaders, managers, and Labor Department officials to feel that they were failing. The British had encouraged trade unionism, but in their concern for the colonial economy and the orderly transition to self-government, they had actually contributed to the unsatisfactory industrial relations in the country. Conciliation, while practiced occasionally, gained little acceptance. The government, in a vain attempt to encourage business and labor to arrive at their own agreements, made very little use of its powers of arbitration. The private sector was not motivated to establish its own norms of speedy resolution of disputes, because it viewed government as its pacesetter and protector. Businesses were exhorted to sign collective agreements and to enter into negotiations over grievances, but they almost invariably declined, preferring to follow the yardstick of civil service wages and working conditions.

The result of these trends was that, even on the eve of independence, hostility between unions and employers was continual; the contending parties did not respect one another. Aping the practices of the former colonial businessmen, many indigenous managers regarded labor as a commodity, and they felt that their "duty" to the workers was somehow fulfilled if they merely paid them wages. In general, there was an absence of "established practices" on the part of all employes in their dealings with workers; such dealings remained capricious and unreliable, from the standpoints of both unions and government.

## The Basis for Improving Labor Relations

This failure to establish mutual norms supporting conflict resolution, prior to 1958, was one of the major reasons for the promulgation of the Industrial Relations Act by the Trades Union Congress, and the eventual acceptance of the Act by the CPP in 1958. The new law specified, in detail, negotiating machinery which was to be created by unions and management, as well as the responsibilities of the government in cases of conciliation and arbitration.

The formal, legal environment for grievance handling in Ghana has remained substantially unchanged since 1959. All employers whose businesses contain workers belonging to certified unions are required to meet with union representatives in a standing negotiating committee.[6] If a dispute is unresolvable, the matter is to be referred to the

Labor Department for conciliation and, within two weeks, arbitration. Awards of arbitration tribunals must be approved by the minister responsible for labor. A strike is legally possible, but only in the unlikely event that neither party wishes to arbitrate, and the minister agrees that the dispute is not to be arbitrated.

The same law also specifies unfair labor practices; alleged offenses under this section are not properly subject to conciliation or arbitration, but are referred to a special tribunal for settlement. At present, unfair labor practices include:

> discrimination against an employee because he is a union member;
>
> seeking to induce an employee not to join a union;
>
> taking part, as an employer, in the formation of a union;
>
> failure to permit a full-time union officer to confer with member employees;
>
> activities by an employee intended to cause "a serious interference" with the business of his employer;
>
> union recruiting on employer's premises without permission;
>
> conferences between union officials and members, on the employer's premises, without permission.

It was reported that many employers initially saw the 1958 Act as a government attempt to control the militancy of the unions.[7] Indeed, some businessmen—especially foreign employers—did not dread arbitration, should negotiations under the new law fail, because they thought they had a good chance to win their case. However, other employers, perhaps a majority of the non-expatriates, viewed the legislation as coercive. It would take a decade or more of practicing the negotiation procedures specified in the Act before patterns of genuine cooperation would appear between the unions and some of these "unenlightened" businessmen.

Under the CPP, it soon became apparent that the party was to be intimately involved in the process of dispute settlement, although the legislation had not assigned any role to it. Managers were compelled, on occasion, to grant their workers time off so that party officials might deliver lectures on socialism or "Nkrumahism." Employers reported that bribes were exhorted from them, which, if unpaid, would lead to the TUC's making an issue of "imaginery" grievances and staging a walkout. The government was known to be giving token stipends to striking workers in cases where the strike was being used to put political pressure on employers.

The party's use of unions to intimidate businessmen who were its political enemies gave organized labor a great deal of power in the private sector, out of proportion to what was, initially, its relatively low level of sophistication in grievance handling. Expatriate employers and the larger firms acceded to union demands because they perceived, correctly, that the party was capable of forcing them out of business, and because they could afford to pay the bribes and provide the improved working conditions which the party and unions expected. However, in spite of the fact that settlement of disputes in favor of labor was often enforced by the party, B.C. Roberts, characterized as a "hostile observer" of Ghana's industrial scene, reported that the unions' relations with expatriate employers had developed well.[8] As early as 1964, he concluded that the TUC and the Employers' Association "have agreed on important advances on the scope of collective bargaining and joint consultations." What accounted for this relatively cordial atmosphere, against a background of party coercion?

To answer this question, we must first distinguish between the compulsory aspects of the 1958 Industrial Relations Act and the isolated and arbitrary interference of the CPP. Both the legislation and the behavior of the party may have been obnoxious to many employers. But the law remained consistent during the period; the 1965 labor law did not alter negotiating procedures. Therefore, while many businessmen were doubtless relieved that, beginning in 1966, the CPP was no longer a factor in industrial relations, mechanisms for the settlement of disputes had, nonetheless, been established during the Nkrumah years. Patterns of behavior in compliance with the law had been learned and practiced. The "advances" mentioned by Roberts reflect this process.

Second, although employers were compelled, under law, to eliminate past practices which they had thought desirable prior to 1959, other provisions of the 1958 Act were conducive to the reduction of industrial conflict. The guaranteed check-off helped to promote cordial worker-management relations by eliminating dues collection exercises, a perennial source of tension in the workplace. The control which government maintained over certification of unions for bargaining relieved employers of the obligation to deal with rival unions, each claiming to represent their workers. Similarly, workers were protected, by law, from employers' choosing to recognize one union and refusing to bargain with another.

In western countries, "residual hostilities" left over from the struggle to organize workers are a major cause of continuing mutual suspicion between unions and management.[9] It may be argued that, in Ghana, the likelihood of such hostility was less than in other countries, because labor's struggle had been more with government than with business. The CPP, rather than the TUC, was blamed by employers for the power enjoyed by the unions prior to 1966.

It has ben indicated above that in spite of the automatic strength granted to unions in bargaining, beginning in 1959, their prior experience in negotiating was limited. Both labor and management were thus thrust into a learning situation, in which the difficulties common to both gave each some understanding of the other's problems. In 1959, for example, the Labor Department published a model constitution for a standing joint negotiating committee. It is likely that neither side had ever seen one before, and the practical difficulties involved in setting up the committee, as required by law, made cooperation desirable.

A major influence on evolving industrial relations during the Nkrumah years, aside from the legally-prescribed avenues for settling disputes, was the informal behavior being learned by union functionaries. Unionists discovered that there was an "ideal type" of grievance-handling procedure, from shop floor to the TUC secretariat, which it was in their interest to follow. These procedures were not codified either in labor law or the TUC constitution, nor were they always followed exactly the same way, but they became the model for resolution of conflict between unions and management. They could be practiced in the majority of labor disputes, where outside political interference was not a factor in industrial relations.

Under these informal norms of grievance handling, a worker does what management tells him, unless the activity is unsafe or dangerous. If the employee thinks he has been treated unfairly, he may file a grievance with his imeediate supervisor. If the grievance is not redressed, the worker may ask his union branch secretary, or another local official, to intercede in his behalf. Legitimate grievances are based on:

> violation or misrepresentation of the collective agreement;
> violation of labor laws and regulations;
> violation of "customs" and past practice;
> obvious physical and/or mental abuse of a worker.

Branch leaders who support grievances arising from other causes run the risk of being unable to obtain support from their unions. In addition, employers who believe that local officials are too ready to take up the cause of workers with an illegitimate grievance may be unwilling to listen to them when more serious infractions occur.

One principle underlying these norms of dispute settlement is that the worker, or his union, must take advantage of the lowest available level of adjudication. The further up the hierarchy a dispute travels, the more intransigent an employer may become. In addition, if a dispute is taken off the shop floor, settlement is inevitably delayed, so it is in the interest of both management and labor to resolve conflict at a low level, so that discontent does not fester. If, after presenting their case, the branch officials do not obtain satisfaction, an industrial relations officer from the union meets with the head of the department in which the offense is alleged to have occurred.[10] In cases where the middle-level union and business representatives cannot reach agreement, the general secretary of the national union, or his deputy, may meet with the standing negotiation committee. Failing to reach a compromise at this level, the disputants take the case to outside conciliators or arbitrators.

These informal norms of conflict resolution adopted by the unions, within a complementary legal environment, laid the foundation for a productive industrial relations atmosphere between 1959 and 1966, in spite of the blatant political manipulation for which the CPP was responsible.

## The New Industrial Relations Are Tested

Under the NLC regime, between 1966 and 1969, unions appeared more confident of their ability to negotiate than ever before. The Congress had become committed to the idea that independent bargaining, rather than alliance with outside patrons, was the most direct and reliable method of obtaining its goals and those of the nation. In relations with management the TUC maintained that "fair, speedy settlement of grievances benefits both sides because happy workers produce more."[11] B.A. Bentum, the secretary-general of the Congress, resigned from an incomes commission after it placed an arbitrary ceiling of five percent on wage increases. His objection to this policy went beyond the loss of income to workers. He saw it as a threat to free collective bargaining, recognizing that the more prosperous businesses could afford to pay larger increases, and that they were willing to negotiate them.

As for the public sector, unions were certified to represent civil servants, but under law there were still no negotiating committees for them. This situation led to much confusion and delay of settlements between civil servants and the government, and a call by the TUC for streamlined procedures. By 1968 formal machinery had broken down completely in some ministries, in part because of hostility toward unions among senior civil servants, and because of the rivalry between the unions and the associations. *Ad hoc* departmental negotiating teams were created, but they were not very effective.

Many employers gave evidence, during this period, that they neither understood nor wished to adopt the negotiating norms and rules by which the unions were operating. Some of them believed that the Congress had been a mere tool of the CPP, and they underestimated the unions' ability to force compliance with the law now that the party had disappeared. In addition, the government, although officially "nonpolitical," had to compromise with organized labor on occasion, a fact which exasperated those employers who had assumed that the NLC would support them just as the CPP had supported the unions. After 1966, therefore, there was an increase in victimization, lockouts, and resistance to negotiations. Some employers failed to implement agreements which had been signed. Worker complaints over arbitrary dismissals, suspensions, and unpaid bonuses were ignored, and a number of firms failed to contribute to social security, workmen's compensation, and medical care schemes.

These violations of norms may be explained by noting that the employers who bullied workers may have been reacting to the way they were, themselves, bullied by some unionists under the Nkrumah regime. Moreover, in some cases managers disregarded the spirit of agreements by enforcing discipline procedures which were technically allowed, but which encouraged worker resentment. Formal negotiating machinery, under law, was still too awkward; employers took advantage of this and refused to meet with union representatives. In addition, delays occurred between the recommendations of arbitrators and government's approval of the final settlements, during which employers refused to modify their practices.

The NLC recognized the already-existing "proper channels" for settling disputes and expressed faith in them. In addition, it authorized new machinery for resolving industrial conflict, centering on regional and district committees of administration. But it is apparent that industrial peace dependend not only on formal rules and structures, but on compromise concerning the interpretation of rules. Norms supporting rapid settlement of disputes were not yet shared among some businessmen and civil servants, but between 1966 and 1969 the military leaders' posture toward organized labor was also inconsistent and sometimes hostile. The NLC, accustomed to giving and receiving formal orders within a military hierarchy, had a limited understanding of what it could do to maintain a productive environment for industrial relations.

The Progress Party regime, from 1969 to 1971, reacted even more strongly than the NLC to what it perceived as an insufficient commitment of labor and management to settling disputes. However, the PP was likely to blame the TUC and its leadership, rather than the business community, for industrial unrest. The PP's lack of sympathy with the cause of labor, and its isolation from leading unionists, led to suspicion of the Congress even when the latter merely supported the process of orderly negotiations. To reduce the influence and prestige of the unions, the Busia government sometimes appeared to be sabotaging the very negotiations in which it was committed to participate.

During this period, the unions stated repeatedly that they were dissatisfied with aspects of the labor law with regard to settlement of disputes, but, in the spirit of compromise, they agreed "to accept these and work within them as our contribution to the national task of reconstruction."[12] However, attempts at compromise failed, as the government would not change the grievance procedure. Instead, using bombastic and sarcastic rhetoric, it attempted to provoke in labor a hostile attitude toward existing negotiation practices. The TUC's 1970 demand for a one hundred percent increase in the minimum wage was dismissed as an "absolutely useless proposition" and not a subject for realistic negotiation. The settlement of disputes was frequently delayed or stymied by difficulties in communication between the contenders. By mid-1971, as the following examples show, relations between the regime and organized labor had reached a low point. It is easy to lose sight of the steadily increasing similarity of norms between unions and the private sector, in the face of several highly publicized battles with government, culminating in the dissolution of the Congress.

Four hundred workers struck the Tema Shipyard and Drydock Corporation in June 1971, their principal grievance being a delay in the signing of a 1969 collective agreement. Dr. Bruce-Konuah, the PP minister of labor, claimed to have

given the TUC an ultimatum that workers would be
discharged unless they returned to their jobs; the TUC denied
knowledge of it. A meeting was arranged between the
ministers of labor and transport and the Maritime and
Dockworkers Union, as well as TUC secretariat officials.
Bruce-Konuah did not appear at the set time. He claimed to
have been at Tema on his own, trying to persuade strikers to
resume work. Workers, according to the union, agreed to do
so after meeting with their leaders, but, it was claimed, the
minister allowed the lockout of the strikers to stand and
ordered recruitment of new workers.

Under pressure from the union, the ministry admitted that
there had been a communications snag, but all that the cabinet
and the prime minister would grant was that the
ex-employees should be considered alongside new recruits in
hiring. Based on this treatment, Bruce-Konuah noted that the
newspapers had been "incorrect" when they reported that he
had fired the workers! The secretary-general of the TUC met
with the minister shortly after the strike ended, pledging
industrial peace, but grave mutual suspicion prevailed. In
spite of the obvious willingness of labor to talk, the official
position that most of the workers' grievances had already
been settled before the strike began did not really leave much
room for discussion.

In July 1971 there were more work stoppages, which
indicated a further breakdown in relations between the
government and the unions. Railway Enginemen struck, and
the regime's response to their demands for a new promotions
system, improved salary structure, and tax-exempt overtime
pay was to issue ultimata that the workers were to be
dismissed if they continued to strike. The union claimed it was
"not bothered" by the pressure, but the Congress pleaded
with the government to negotiate with the Enginemen instead
of threatening them. A working committee of the TUC
Executive Board agreed that, in both the shipyard and the
railroad disturbances, strikes would have been avoided had
management used existing machinery for resolving disputes,
instead of trying to intimidate the unions with bluffs.

The TUC leadership decided to send a delegation to present

their views on the 1972 budget to the government, but they received no reply to their request for a meeting. It was widely believed that some of the more important party leaders allowed the breakdown in communications to occur in order to justify the dissolution. The regime had deliberately interrupted the flow of communications essential to negotiations in another instance, when it concealed from the Congress the favorable recommendations of a pay research unit, set up to weigh the justice of worker grievances.

In August, a PP official called for the abolition of guaranteed check-off of union dues, sayig that it was a "communist idea." B.A. Bentum branded the statement "ridiculous and unfortunate," but it was clearly calculated to have an adverse effect on negotiations with employers. Unionists bemoaned the fact that, in order to fend off government attacks, they were required to spend less time negotiating than they would have liked. The lack of respect for the negotiation process shown by the Busia regime served as a cue for some private sector firms. Moreover, the regime encouraged some employers to take a "hard line" against the unions.

A political scientist's study of union-management relations during the Busia period noted many complaints concerning the unions' behavior.[13] Some firms reported difficulty in disciplining their workers because, as they saw it, threats of job action by the unions inevitably ensued. Workers, it was alleged, could "sleep on the job and sabotage the production process, with almost every assurance that they would go undisciplined." Unions were accused of using intimidating tactics, and of begging, in order to get managers to ignore employees' inefficiency. Some employers also cited continuing political influence in some unions, although they recognized that this was contrary to official TUC policy. There is no indication, in these data, of the means of sample selection, so it is probable that these views do not represent a majority of Ghanaian businessmen. But it is interesting to note that the respondents, while highly critical of some TUC unions, also expressed the desire for a more orderly negotiation proces.

In fact, the norm of settling disputes, which had survived

the increased industrial unrest under the NLC, continued to be confirmed by those employers who had no explicit political connection with the Busia regime. Joint standing negotiating committees, even within public corporations, met regularly. Employers, through the Ghana Employers' Association, carried out, for the first time, independent mediation of disputes with the Industrial Relations Department of the TUC, in lieu of using government conciliation. Moreover, arbitration under Labor Department auspices continued unabated during 1969-71. The government followed the practice of appointing both labor and management representatives on the arbitration teams, an option not required by law.

*Under the NRC*

Colonel Ignatius Acheampong, head of state and chairman of the National Redemption Council, was no stranger to labor affairs. He had been chairman of the National Liberation Council Committee of Administration in the Western Region, locale of many disturbances in the railways and mines. In this capacity, he had noted in 1967 that the main duty of the TUC was to protect workers from the arbitrary acts of employers and to help improve their conditions of service through collective agreements. His NRC government, beginning in 1972, made several decisions which aided the unions in attaining these goals.

The NRC commissioner for labor called for a 20-year "industrial truce." Workers who ignored existing grievance machinery were criticized, and leading unionists were warned to follow it.[14] But such rhetoric did not denote a special hostility to labor. One difference between the Busia regime and the NRC was that the latter did not hesitate to castigate managers when they appeared to be resisting orderly negotiations or the implementation of agreements already signed. Thus, the commissioner also noted that "many employers, often faced with legitimate demands by workers, take refuge by stating that productivty has been low. This has indeed become a stock excuse . . . I think . . . the time has come for a responsible approach to the whole issue."[15] In another instance, the commissioner for transport threatened to oust the executive of the Railway and Ports Authority if it continued to delay the impelementation of a pay research unit report favorable to the union. This same authority was also forced to meet with the Railway Enginemen, although it had previously refused to do so.

The commissioner of labor told the Ghana Employers' Association that, during 1972, "no labor dispute was found so intractable as to be referred to arbitration; indeed most matters were resolved at the conciliatory level." Labor Department officials reported no interruption in patterns of adjudication which had been established under previous regimes. One conciliation officer, who had participated in several dozen cases, indicated that all of them had been settled to the satisfactiion of both parties. Occasionally, by meeting with each side separately, the officer was able to secure even higher wages or better working conditions than the union had demanded.

Relations between the Labor Department and the TUC had been strained, occasionally, by the legacy of the colonial period, during which the TUC had been regarded as hostile. The department attempted to improve relations by explaining that conciliation officers are not judges, although they may propose that either side modify its stand if, in their opinion, it is unreasonable or unrealistic.[16] They see their main duty in providing facilities for the orderly presentation of the position of both sides. In spite of some differences of opinion between unionists and Labor Department officials since 1972, the Congress recognized the valuable role of the government in conciliation, particularly in disputes involving employees of public corporations. In addition, the NRC indicated its readiness to establish permanent consultative machinery for civil servants, in answer to the TUC's request. The unions hoped to participate in consultations as part of an executive body whose decisions would be binding.[17]

Perhaps the most serious industrial relations problem faced by the NRC was the effect of inflation controls on negotiations. A severe disagreement between the regime and the unions over the duties of the Prices and Incomes Board arose in 1973. The board was established "to formulate an appropriate incomes and prices policy" and to recommend "measures that might be required for the regulation of wages and salaries, interests, profits, dividends, rents and prices . . . ." It was explicitly stated that the functions of the board were not restricted to incomes regulated by collective agreements, but the most widely publicized and controversial activity of the board was its ability to nullify negotiated ʰracts which violated its guidelines for wage increases.

By June 1973 a great backlog of agreements, already signed by maangement and labor, had yet to be approved. A TUC official wrote to the commissioner for labor, explaining that the "lukewarm attitude" of the board was causing frustration among workers and lowering their morale. The government-owned press editorialized that the board must speed up its work "in tempo with the revolution," and hinted at conflict between the board and the commissioner.[18] Government began to apply pressure on its creation, and the logjam of agreements began to clear, to the satisfaction of the TUC.

It was not merely the delays in implementing agreements that troubled the Congress. In spite of assurances from the head of the Prices and Incomes Board that freedom to negotiate was not being infringed upon, it did establish a two and one-half percent ceiling on wage increases. The unions considered this an abridgement of their rights, on grounds similar to their opposition to the 1969 Incomes Commission. Subsequently, the TUC's criticism was greatly reduced when the board, as a matter of routine, began to allow wage increases in excess of its own guidelines.

Members of the Ghana Employers' Association were as upset with the delays caused by the Prices and Incomes Board as the Congress was. The association considered it a "serious omission" that GEA and TUC representation on the board was not allowed. Several employers praised the TUC publicly for its "maturity" in wage negotiations.[19] However, the GEA is not a legal entity in negotiations, and serves only to advise member businesses as to their rights and duties, under law. In spite of its increased stature during the NRC period it could not force compliance from its members.

A number of recalcitrant employers, who are inexperienced in dealing with labor or hostile toward the unions, continue to follow procedures which upset orderly settlement of disputes. A major complaint of the unions is that negotiations are often conducted with management representatives who are not empowered by their superiors to approve the final agreements. A few employers also continue to intimidate workers into violating agreements. However, more typical among GEA members is acceptance of the working relationship between the TUC and their organization. In at least one case, salary increases have been paid, on the recommendation of the association, in advance of agreement on working conditions. Expatriate employers, in particular, use the offices of the GEA to minimize conflict between themselves and the unions.

During the NRC regime, the Congress appeared confident of the government's respect for the negotiation process and did not hesitate to criticize businessmen who, for political and economic reasons, refused to cooperate. "The time for union representatives hand-holding with management is over," said one unionist at a training seminar. Industrial unrest, according to the Congress, may only be reduced when grievances are settled promptly. The evidence does suggest that government supports this view and that the majority of employers do, as well.

*Summary*

The stable, formal legal environment and the increasingly consistent, informally-sanctioned patterns of grievance handling within the unions have had the effect of improving and increasing the number of relationships among the disputants since 1959. Most employers, initially, believed that the labor legislation was coercive, and the CPP did introduce an additional element of compulsion into industrial relations. But, over the past 20 years, grievance handling procedures have become relatively predictable, and this has caused management to value them. Most employers, appreciating the unions' compliance with the law and the attempts of the TUC to induce workers to follow the chain of command in seeking to

redress their grievances, have been willing to avoid lockouts
and to support the standing negotiating committees. These
trends have been especially noticeable since 1971, because the
effect of national political rivalries on industrial relations has
been greatly reduced.

## LIMITING ISSUES OF CONFLICT

The parties signing a collective agreement seek to regulate
conflict between them by reducing the number of items which
may be the source of legitimate disagreement during the life
of the pact. Thus, the evolution of these agreements in Ghana
has been an important factor in increasing the continuity of
the norms to which unions and management subscribe.[20]
Before 1959 the main impediments to the signing of collective
agreements in Ghana were the weakness of most unions and
the predominance of public sector employment. The
Mineworkers was a notable exception, a virile union which
concluded agreements on a regular basis with a major private
sector industry. Aside from these contracts and a handful of
others, there was little regular bargaining activity before the
New Structure, and this only when the government
persuaded management to meet with or to accept the decision
of an arbitrator. It is true that the British, as compared to the
French in Africa, had allowed more independence in
bargaining. But few Ghanaian unions possessed the clout, on
their own, to force negotiations. In 1956 the *Labour
Department Report* stated that "voluntary collective
bargaining is now generally accepted in industry." This was
more wishful thinking than an accurate description. In fact,
the 1958 legislation included bargaining guarantees, in part
because TUC leaders recognized that their unions would
remain weak, in spite of automatic dues check-off, if
employers could avoid the negotiating table.

### Bargaining: 1959-1966

In spite of the provisions of the Industrial Relations Act, its
effects were not immediate. Only six agreements were

concluded between April 1959 and June 1960. The number of agreements in force depended on three principal factors. The strength of a particular union was important, because its degree of unity and ability to pressure management often determined the initial willingness to negotiate. Unions without a staff large enough to conduct regular negotiations, or to oversee agreements, could not be expected to conclude an increasing number of contracts. In addition, only seven of the 16 TUC unions were certified to bargain; the remainder contained civil servants.

A second consideration was the willingness of the government to enforce the law, without which the number of agreements might have remained small. As it turned out, the regime was motivated to support early bargaining efforts. Agreements with foreign firms were encouraged, because they did not have an appreciable impact on the national economy, but certain domestic enterprises were also the target of union bargaining activity, with government backing.

Section 20 of the law allowed for "extension" of collective agreements, by administrative action, to workplaces where employees do "the same kind of work" as those already covered by agreement, but whose employers were reluctant to negotiate. The commissioner for labor was required to give due notice to employers to be covered by extension orders, and the latter were asked to communicate their objections, which government was free to ignore. The Ministry for Labor pointed out that the advantage of extension orders was that "they are convenient for both employers and unions, since they save considerable time in fresh negotiations and make it possible for working conditions in homogenous units of commerce and industry to be covered by single collective agreement."[21] In fact, issuing the orders, or threatening to do so, became a convenient method of cowing political enemies of the CPP who had business interests.

A third factor affecting the number of agreements signed was the attitude of employers. Some Ghanaian businessmen took advantage of inconsistent law enforcement and the weakness of several of the New Structure unions in order to ignore the specified bargaining procedures. Political friendships were often effective in reducing union pressure to negotiate, but the extension orders handicapped most of the local firms to which they were applied, regardless of the politics of the proprietor.

It is clear that employer support for collective bargaining was primarily from foreign-owned enterprises which could afford to pay relatively higher wages as a result of the new agreements. In addition, few Ghanaian businessmen operated with profit margins substantial enough that they could remit monthly dues to the TUC without depriving themselves of capital needed to run their enterprises on a day-to-day basis. By contrast, most of the foreign firms were sensitive about their "image." The agreements that most resembled American and European contracts were signed with these firms.

Unions may exercise bargaining power far beyond their true economic strength when they deal with expatriate enterprises. And, as we have seen, the Ghanaian unions, through the CPP, were also quite successful in securing negotiations with smaller, local firms. However, the increase in the number of agreements signed prior to 1966 did not necessarily reflect genuine agreement among the parties. Frequently, if labor's demands were refused to management, the unionists would return to the TUC hall and telephone the minister for labor, who would intercede in their behalf. This behavior was not conducive to developing mutual norms of conflict regulation. Where government influence was blatant, the necessity for unions to compromise in limiting the number of questions around which conflict could legitimately arise was reduced. The absence of normative continuity was also reflected in the failure to renew some agreements after they had expired.

Table 1 summarizes the evolution of bargaining in Ghana:

Table 1. *Collective Agreements in Ghana, 1959-77\**

| Year | new agreements signed | bargaining certificates issued | total agreements in force | approx. % of union members covered |
|------|------|------|------|------|
| 1959-60 | 3 | n.d. | 21 | n.d. |
| 1960-61 | 7 | 200 | 28 | n.d. |
| 1961-62 | 13 | 393 | 41 | n.d. |
| 1962-63 | 6 | 75 | n.d. | n.d. |
| 1963-64 | 11 | 72 | n.d. | n.d. |
| 1965-67 | 17 | 837 | n.d. | n.d. |
| 1967-68 | 18 | 461 | n.d. | n.d. |
| 1969-70 | 40 | 247 | 121 | 48 |
| 1973 | 10 | 75 | 148 | 55 |
| 1974 | 59 | 74 | n.d. | n.d. |
| 1975 | 59 | 59 | n.d. | n.d. |
| 1976 | 66 | 57 | n.d. | n.d. |
| 1977 | 57 | 30 | 180 | 65 |

\*Sources: Labor Department Reports, for the years through 1969; for 1970, "Report on the Activities of the T.U.C. ((Ghana)) to the 3rd Biennial Congress Held at the Advanced Training College—Winneba, 31st July-2nd August, 1970" (mimeo); for subsequent years, author's data.

After an initial spurt in the number of certificates issued, there is a modest, steady increase in contracts actually concluded during the Nkrumah years, 1960 to 1966. This indicates that the process was hardly automatic. In the great majority of cases, the government did not intervene, but merely authorized the unions to bargain.

The form, if not the exact content of the agreements, was borrowed from western sources. Because the more intricate pacts signed with large, expatriate enterprises set the standard for smaller firms, even the first contracts did cover a wide variety of issues. Each of the subject headings, reproduced below, is an area of regulated conflict, at least for the life of the contract.

| | |
|---|---|
| scope of agreement | salaries and wages |
| interpretation of agreement | increments |
| amendments | overtime |
| recognition of the union | hazardous duty |
| maintenance of union membership | allowances |
| union notice board | tools |
| union meetings | grievance procedure |
| standing negotiation committee | acting appointments |
| duties of employees | frustrated work |
| rates and standards of employment | pay day |
| medical care | paid vacation |
| welfare | maternity leave |
| housing | sick leave |
| education and training | holidays |
| retirement benefits | absence from work |
| employment procedures | redundancy procedures |
| apprenticeship | supervision |
| promotions | warnings |
| hours of work | dismissals |
| transportation to work | termination |

Most of these items were contained in agreements signed as early as 1961.[22]

*Bargaining: 1966-1971*

Table 1 indicates a great increase in the number of certificates issued, and the number of agreements signed, after 1966. These totals reflect the renewed vigor of unions generally in the wake of the coup, and less government interference. In addition, the practice of granting extension orders routinely was continued; unions in manufacturing, construction, and timber industries were leaders in taking advantage of this provision of the labor law. Another reason for the growth of bargaining after 1966 was a change in the status of employees of public corporations. These workers had been prohibited, by Cabinet decision, from bargaining collectively during 1963-65. However, unions began to demand bargaining rights for these employees and, following the NLC takeover, they were allowed to sign contracts.

Moreover, the Ghana Employers' Association began to encourage the signing of "group agreements," individual contracts between a single union and a variety of similar or related industries.[23] Typically, a group agreement covers working conditions for several firms and leaves the wage negotiations to the separate parties involved. Therefore, in assessing the rise in the number of contracts after 1966, the existence of group agreements should be noted, since the number signed does not, in itself, indicate the number of workers covered. Total agreements in force doubled during the period between 1965 and 1970; and it is reasonable to assume that the figures for new agreements signed actually conceal even more growth in the strength of bargaining.

As the number of contracts multiplied, more unionists gained first-hand knowledge of negotiating procedures and tactics. In addition, TUC education programs trained neophyte bargainers. Although the independence of the unions was problematic under Nkrumah, by 1966 several of them had developed a cadre of personnel who could teach bargaining skills, based on their own experience. Apprentice bargainers were taught, as they are today, that the collective agreement is essential to keep the employer from deciding what wages and benefits are to be paid. The chief task in negotiations is said to be indentifying the discretionary powers of management, and limiting these, as much as possible, within the agreement. It is to be expected that the first pact signed with a particular employer will, perhaps, not be a very good one from the union's point of view, but the purpose of renewing talks is to cover any loopholes left over from the previous contract. Therefore, as agreements expire and are renegotiated, bargainers learn more of what to expect from employers, and more about how to obtain benefits for the members. This process, really one of education as much as king refinements in the contracts, continues almost daily in Ghana, and is extended to additional branch union officers as their firms come under the provisions of new agreements.

We have already noted the mutual hostility which characerized relations between the government and the Congress during 1969-71, culminating in the dissolution. It is therefore significant that in the Busia period the number of certificates issued and agreements in force continued to climb. We may explain this, in part, by first noting that conflict regulating contacts between private employers and unions were strong and could not be abrogated by the regime. Second, the government itself also appeared to recognize that collective bargaining was valuable. Unions vigorously made wage demands in 1971, believing that official figures on the cost of living were 30 to 50 percent too low. Nonetheless, in that year four governmental unions were issued bargaining certificates for the first time. In addition, the practice of issuing extension orders continued. In one case, the terms of an agreement between the Construction and Building Trades Workers and two contractors' associations were extended to no fewer than 86 firms. This occurred only four months prior to the dissolution.

Finally, and ironically, Progress Party hostility to organized labor may have contributed to the growth of bargaining in Ghana. By June 1971, J.H. Mensah, minister of finance, was stating publicly that there was little reason for workers to join unions, because even nonmembers benefitted from collective agreements. The government attempted to reduce the attractiveness of membership by extending bargaining to whole classes of workers, whether members or not. Although this policy was intended to underscore Mensah's contention that unions were unnecessary, it actually boosted the prestige of the Congress, with whom workers identified efforts to increase the scope of bargaining.

## Bargaining Since Restoration

Between May 1972, when the Congress began to function after restoration, and December of that year, member unions applied for 69 collective bargaining certificates. The continuation of orderly negotiation and signing of agreements is remarkable. The dissolution, although it upset the unions' routines of resource acquisition, did not disturb the mutual expectation of bargaining activity. Indeed, the figures for the following year indicate an increase, both in the number of contracts and in the percentage of union members covered, as compared to 1970.

Table 2 shows bargaining achievements by union as of 1973, when the TUC may be said to have overcome the negative effects of the dissolution.

Table 2. *Bargaining in Ghana, by Union, to July 1973*

| union | approximate membership 6/73 | number of agreements signed (at least) | % of members covered by agreements |
|-------|------------------|------------------|------------------|
| Industrial and Commercial Workers | 80,000 | 80 | 80% |
| Construction and Building Trades | 39,000 | 5 | 70% |
| Mineworkers | 23,500 | 2 | 100% |
| Maritime and Dockworkers | 20,000 | 7 | 90% |
| General Agricultural Workers | 40,000 | 6 | 35% |
| Public Utility Workers | 12,200 | 4 | 100% |
| Timber and Woodworkers | 16,000 | 13 | 75% |

Table 2. (Continued)

| union | approximate membership 6/73 | number of agreements signed (at least) | % of members covered by agreements |
|---|---|---|---|
| Teachers and Educational Workers | 14,100 | 7 | 50% |
| Public Services Workers | 16,000 | 1 | 25% |
| General Transport and Petroleum Workers | 5,000 | 18 | 80% |
| Health Services Workers | 9,000 | 4 | 20% |
| National Union of Seamen | 3,120 | 1 | 20% |
| Private Road Transport | 25,000 | 2 | 1% |
| Posts and Telecommunications Workers | 7,422 | 0 | |
| Local Government Workers | 19,000 | 0 | |
| Railway and Ports Workers | 10,500 | 0 | |
| Railway Enginemen | 816 | 0 | |
| TOTALS | 340,658 | 148 | 55% |

The larger, stronger, and more experienced unions, *e.g.*, Maritime and Dockworkers, Timber and Woodworkers, and ICU, had concluded highly favorable agreements, providing the following benefits, among others:

    severance pay for dismissal
    automatic salary increments
    two weeks' leave per year for unskilled labor
    free medical care
    maternity leave with pay
    transportation to and from work
    guaranteed accelerated promotions
    pay bonuses up to 50 percent of salary.

In 1974, the Railway and Ports Authority became a public corporation, and pacts were signed with both the Railway Enginemen and the Railway and Ports Workers. The percentage of union members covered by contracts then rose to almost 60. By 1975, the Posts and Telecommunications Workers were also dealing with a corporation, and by the end of 1977 all 17 unions had concluded at least one agreement. The number of new certificates issued and pacts signed remained buoyant; total agreements in force reached an all-time high.

The NRC government, as we have pointed out, supported attempts to increase the number of contracts signed. However, the creation of the Prices and Incomes Board in late 1972 may be seen as a strategy to check the power of the unions to obtain wage increases, which were averaging about 30 percent and had ranged to 85 percent. But the board was unable to hold the line. *Collective bargaining has advanced in Ghana to the point where the government is no longer the pacesetter for wages and working conditions*, an historic development reversing a trend initiated under British rule. It is true that over 70 percent of Ghanaian wage earners in the nonagricultural sector work for the government in some capacity, but many of these work for public boards and corporations whose personnel, production and bargaining policies are determined independently. Because negotiating machinery, under bargaining certification, is more regular, flexible, and responsive to the economy than the recommendations of wage boards, the initiative in setting standards has passed to the unions.

As early as 1968 the Mills-Odoi Commission noted that civil service wages for comparable work were lower than in the private sector, but that wages in the public corporations were much higher. A 1971 study by the University of Ghana confirmed that these anomalies were increasing, except that it placed the private sector above the public corporations in paying real wage increases.[24] The signing of additional collective agreements since 1972 has further exacerbated the inequities in Ghanaian wage structure.

The ineffectiveness of the Prices and Incomes Board and the unions' aggressive bargaining led to the establishment of the

Salary Review Committee in August 1973. As it announced the formation of the committee, the government also granted an immediate seven and one-half percent interim pay increase to all civil servants making less than 100 cedis ($877.00) per year. In effect, the wage increase guideline established by the Prices and Incomes Board was a dead letter. In February 1974, the Salary Review Committee recommended an additional increase of up to 20 percent for civil servants, which was accepted by the NRC. The added wage bill for government was over 16 million cedis (about 14 million dollars) annually. The committee's final report called for further boosts in pay, allowances and pensions. The cost of all increments was estimated at over 40,200,000 cedis ($35,000,000) per year. The government issued a white paper in which it accepted these recommendations. However, it went further, raising the maximum tax-exempt income, and increasing the minimum wage to 92.5 percent over the August 1973 interim award.

Government acceptance of the recommendations of the committee in order to reduce the anomalies between negotiated collective agreements and civil service pay scales was seen by the unions as a great victory. The contractual relationships between unions and private employers have had a profound impact on national wage structure.

## Conclusion

It may be thought that the unions which have signed large numbers of agreements have, since 1966, wrested influence over national wage policy from an unwilling government. It is true that aggressive bargaining presented the NLC, PP, and NRC regimes with limited options. However, as we have seen, the government also manifested a desire to aid the Congress's bargaining efforts. This cooperation was recognition of the conflict-regulating role of labor contracts. The TUC was not horrified at the NRC's call for a 20-year industrial truce so long as the truce did not impinge on its right to bargain. Indeed, A.M. Issifu, secretary-general of the Congress, was willing to risk alienating workers in the private sector when he openly encouraged the Salary Review Committee to confine its concern to the civil service. He realized, even if some union members did not, that bargaining would lead to even more wage increases for workers, in the long run.

Of course, the right to bargain is guaranteed under law, but we have seen that the relationships which have been nurtured by the bargaining process are more powerful than the law; negotiations continued even during the months of the dissolution. The British observer, J.L. Roper, was most accurate in stating, prior to the enactment of the New Structure, that "the bargaining strength of the unions and the nature of the agreements they can win for themselves will be more important than any Ordinance passed."[25]

## AVOIDING VIOLENCE

At a preliminary stage in the evolution of relations between unions and management, there is a tendency for both sides to view the strike as "the ultimate test of survival." This feeling injects a high degree of emotion into disputes and increases the likelihood that violence will occur, or continue unchecked. However, once unions become more secure financially, and once bargaining has become accepted, "both sides come to view industrial disputes and strikes as a continuation of the bargaining process."[26] The likelihood of violence is greatly reduced.

In Ghana the degree of industrial peace has indeed increased as mutual insecurity has diminished over the years. Unions now desire to avoid violence, as do private employers and government. However, in addition, there are strong cultural sanctions in Ghana against the use of force against the person. In a country where violent crimes are rare, it is difficult to assess the impact of agreement on negotiating norms as a discrete factor in reducing violent industrial relations. The relative absence of violence has aided the institutionalization of the unions by keeping unpredictable behavior of workers and law enforcement agencies to a minimum. Violence often has unforeseen consequences which are likely to disrupt the flow of resources into the unions, or to inspire negative public opinion.

The British attempted to discourage work stoppages with propaganda in the 1940s. Their position was that "trade unions are really formed to avoid strikes whenever possible."[27] But, it was the disruption of the economy, rather than the actual occurrence of violence, which concerned them. After a fifteen-day strike by railwaymen in 1947, the Labor Department could report that "no disorderly incidents occurred," in part because of the "discipline and good humour of the strikers." Similarly, 33,000 miners representing all 16 mines in Ghana stopped work for 35 days without loss of life or injury. In fact, no fatalities or casualties as the result of strike activity were reported between 1940 and 1948. Between 1947 and 1950 there were 118 strikes in the country, none of which produced as much violence as the 1948 riots (in which two protesters had been killed and several more wounded).

During the Nkrumah period, the major violent conflict was the 1961 strike, which began with a wildcat walkout among railway workers in Sekondi-Takoradi and spread rapidly to other urban areas. Between eight and ten thousand workers were involved, for up to three weeks in Sekondi, but only two days in Accra. The strike was marked by intimidation and threats on both sides and sporadic police intervention. However, it ended when Nkrumah indicated that he would use the military to force a return to work. Although the strike aroused bitter feelings, there is much evidence that some of the violence which accompanied it was inspired by opposition politicians in order to the embarrass the CPP regime.

In its duration and rancor, the 1961 strike is unique in Ghana's labor history, but between 1961 and 1966 disturbances were few, and violent confrontations with police did not occur. This relatively peaceful environment for industrial relations has been explained by the assertion that economic conditions in Ghana were really better than the statistics suggest. It has also been claimed that the Ghanaian is "cheerful" in the face of adversity.[28] It may be argued, instead, that norms of avoiding conflict had already been established, as the unions were becoming institutionalized in the 1960's. Violent tactics were little-used by Ghanaian workers because arbitration and bargaining, or the hope of establishing such a relationship with employers, were preferred to the alternative. The 1961 strike did not set a precedent for the use of force in industrial relations because it was an extension of political debate and the union's lobbying efforts, rather than a desperate attempt to preserve unionism.

We have noted that after 1966 the number of grievances and labor disputes greatly increased. However, violence marked only two stoppages of work under the NLC, both in the mines. The disturbances at Prestea in May 1968 resulted in a police-worker confrontation, rare in Ghana, and violent loss of life, even more rare. In March 1969, miners at Obuasi struck; general rioting occurred and looting was reported. Several workers were killed and policemen continued to fire into a crowd after it had turned and run.

The roots of both violent outbreaks were found to be similar. Working conditions were poor; the local union did not enjoy the confidence of some workers; existing grievance procedures were not followed, either by management or by government departments. However, the immediate precipitating causes of the riots were found to be false promises made to workers and lack of training or advance preparation by police.[29]

The trade unions reacted to the loss of life immediately and critically. Although General Afrifa of the NLC spoke of the need for improved negotiating machinery, the unions were disappointed when no labor representative was appointed to the commissions which investigated the shootings. The NLC, underestimating the emotional impact of the occurrence of violence, also did not appoint any member of high judicial rank.

The Busia regime had assumed power by the time the inquiry into the Obuasi affair was concluded. So unusual had been the loss of life that the government, in spite of its differences with the TUC during 1971, agreed with the union that management had precipitated the strike by failing to live up to its promises. It blamed itself for the poor communications between the various ministries involved in the dispute, and it stated that the police would be disciplined and that the individual who had killed a bystander was to be prosecuted.

Almost simultaneously with the publication of the Obuasi white paper, however, another incident involving loss of life took place, this time in the timber industry at Samreboi. The TUC condemned the "brutal act of the police in shooting and killing people instead of adopting the known civilized methods in dispersing a mob."[30] No loss of life occurred as the result of labor disturbances during the following five years.

In western countries the conduct of legal strikes has become predictable; organized labor has learned to control irrational, emotional outbursts. By contrast, in Ghana, official strikes called by national union leadership are illegal, and there have been only a handful of these since 1958. However, the predominance of local, wildcat strikes has not precluded the deliberate use of labor agitation in channeling threats of violence to productive ends for the unions. It is recognized that the prospect of the use of force, or even a brief work stoppage, may be enough to encourage the settlement of a dispute. A training manual for local leaders notes that the threat of a strike may be even more effective than the strike itself: "A Branch Secretary cannot declare a strike over a grievance. It would be illegal. But if the workers have told him that they will go on strike if no settlement is reached, it is only fair if he tells Management so. The threat of a strike naturally will get Management to reconsider its position. . ."[31]

Where threats do not achieve the desired goal, the wildcat strike is a logical alternative, and it has been actively discouraged by Ghanaian unionists only when an unpredictable response by management or government is feared. These stoppages appear unplanned and "leaderless," but the reverse is frequently the case. In fact, wildcat strikes are often an effective mechanism by which a poor union, being unable to sustain a long walkout, may exercise force short of violence. Although wildcat strikes are illegal in Ghana they have become ritualized. Once initiated, they follow a relatively predictable pattern: demands are made, a short work stoppage occurs, national union officers intervene, and negotiations are resumed or begun in the great majority of cases.

## RESPECT FOR OPPONENTS' VIABILITY

*Colonialism*

In the report of the Labor Department for 1938-39 it was predicted that European employers would learn to appreciate the African's "good manners, his innate cheerfulness, and the broad grin." It is not surprising that the respect of the business community for unions was inhibited by such stereotyping and the paternalistic colonial mentality. The Ghana Chamber of Mines, for example, resisted Mineworkers' attempts to bargain collectively for almost four years, from 1944 to 1947. The chamber only agreed to arbitration following government intervention during a 35-day strike involving 33,000 workers. In its presentation to the arbitrator, management noted contemptuously that "no gold mine has been established by the Africans living here; if they had, then the African would be entitled to say who would manage their property."[32] Many of the early, "mushroom" unions were founded in protest of maltreatment of black workers by white employers. Allegations of racism fostered mutual suspicion which persisted after disputes were resolved. We have noted that the British were ambivalent toward unionism in Ghana, although they had passed enabling legislation. The rejection of the unions' equation of colonialism with racism was, in part, responsible for the failure of the British to aid organized labor more directly and substantially.

*The Nkrumah Years*

Many unionists believed the CPP when it promised them a close, working relationship with national policy makers, prcisely because racial differences between the latter and organized labor had been eliminated when Ghana gained independence. Furthermore, most observers agree that the prospect of direct influence on the party led some labor leaders, including John Tettegah, to discount the provisions of the 1958 labor law which limited the independence of the unions. However, it became apparent after 1960 that the CPP, although it was neither paternalistic nor racist, maintained goals which conflicted with those of the unions. The perceived identity of aims and ideology between some unionists and party leaders had been based on a common set of aspirations for their country. But voluntary support for the party was predicated on the anticipated impact of the TUC program upon party program.

Economic problems, caused in part by the precipitous decline in the price of cocoa, prevented the needs of workers from receiving top priority. In order to remain in power, the CPP took steps to insure that the unions would be unable to oppose it. As this occurred, from 1961 to 1966, the unions were used increasingly as a tool for social control, rather than as a channel for the articulation of workers' economic grievances.

The unions had entered into a concordat with the CPP because of a desire to increase their financial strength and membership. The party had approved these plans, initially, to increase productivity and reduce industrial unrest. However, as early as August 1961, the same TUC which had been granted high status under the New Structure was being pictured as a Frankenstein's monster, "striking fear into both the Government and private employers." Officials of the TUC were accused of forgetting that the party was supreme, and that their positions were obtained as a result of CPP efforts in their behalf. Similarly, "the strong position in which they now find themselves in their negotiations with the Private Employer class would have been virtually nonexistent . . ." were it not for CPP support.[33]

After 1964, an official identity of party and union norms was enforced through repressive means. The monolithic Congress structure merely enabled the government to absorb the TUC more easily. As the minister for labor noted, "It is easy for some people to believe that the system of trade union organization and industrial practice which is based entirely on the principle of voluntarism offers the best possible advantages for any new nation. The Government does not subscribe to this view."[34]

## The Immediate post-Coup Period

We have pointed out, above, that the norm of settling disputes through negotiation was not completely assimilated by employers under the NLC, between 1966 and 1969. In addition, a number of managers in both the public and private sectors evinced a lack of respect for the unions and less than full support for their viability. A chief labor officer told one researcher: "The planners are concerned with rational economic targets and the workers with economics of the stomach — and note that anything that affects the stomach causes spontaneous reaction."[35] The Congress was aware of its enemies within the civil service and noted that NLC Decree 134 "in fact was not aimed at dissolving the trade union movement [but] its application, as understood by certain individuals, was towards that end." The unions criticized employers "who look upon trade unions and their leaders with contempt."[36]

Perhaps naively, the NLC refused to believe that some of its allies in administering the affairs of state were enlisting its aid in the partial dismemberment of the labor movement. Under the "technocracy capitalism" practiced by the military regime, there was freedom of association, but also insensitivity to the concerns of groups, such as labor, that were not a part of the governing alliance. The TUC's call for representation on policy-making bodies was agreed to, in part because the NLC wanted to maintain contact with unionists and their ideas, but also because it continued to fear CPP influence over organized labor and sought to reward leaders who would combat it.

The norms of freedom of association and toleration for diversity in national life were shared by the unions. However, the reliance of the military on "experts" in the development of economic policy was to prevent the strengthening of relations between the Congress and the regime. B.A. Bentum and his assoiciates, who were asked to serve on various commissions and boards, found themselves facing highly trained and credentialled opponents, including advisors from the International Monetary Fund. The civil servants' and foreign advisors' formal qualifications and university degrees, which the unionists lacked, were helpful in persuading the NLC to adopt recommendations which differed markedly from the labor leaders'. For example, the government accepted the position of the Mills-Odoi Commission that wage increases which the unions were demanding were unwarranted because "the sequence of events does . . . dramatically demonstrate the futility of trying to improve living standards by wage increases . . . not related to . . . national productivity."[37]

In spite of the problems in achieving common norms for the TUC and NLC, the unions did not feel that they had been singled out for special, harsh treatment. Much of labor's hostility was deflected away from the soldiers, toward the senior civil service. The stringent economic measures did not reduce the freedom of TUC unions to conduct their own affairs. It was during the subsequent regime, however, that attempts were made to eliminate the Congress's criticism of the government. Many of the bureaucratic allies of the NLC came to power themselves, so that what had been a failure to achieve normative consensus prior to 1969 became, in addition, a direct threat to government from 1969 to 1971.

## The Progress Party Regime

B.A. Bentum, in a speech attended by Progress Party Prime Minister Busia at the Hall of Trades Unions in August 1970, implied that Busia was receiving bad advice from so-called "experts" who had encouraged him to ignore the unions. In a masterpiece of rhetoric, he then noted: "As long as the trade union movement and the government have the same principles, the same philosophy, and the same ideals there is no reason why the two could not work in harmony for the good and prosperity of the country." But the PP regime, which had been unsuccessful in its attempt to unseat Bentum at the 1970 Winneba Congress, subsequently began to bypass the authority of the TUC's secretary-general. It questioned his legitimacy and that of other elected labor leaders. In so doing it showed not only a lack of respect for the viability of its opponents, but its opposition to the principles by which the unions regulated their own affairs.

For example, J.H. Mensah, the minster of finance, indicated a basic misunderstanding of TUC administrative norms when he expected the secretary-general to "order" constituent unions not to strike. The minister took the position that, since his government had given "concessions" to the Maritime and Dockworkers, Secretary-General Bentum should have brought pressure to bear on miners and factory workers. Whether Bentum possesed the power to control member unions in this fashion is arguable, but, in any case, the government was unable to influence rule-making within the Congress. In another instance, Mensah appeared, uninvited, at a meeting of the Executive Board of the Congress. Arrogantly, he told the unionists to spell out what was bothering them. The board objected and suggested that it be given time to prepare an orderly presentation. The minister retreated in a huff.

Because of its failure to understand the norms governing inter-union behavior and the relationship between the secretariat and member unions, the regime believed TUC leadership to be unreliable. As early as July 1970, J.H. Mensah, at a PP rally, claimed that Bentum did not enjoy the confidence of the government. He added, probably more in hope than from accurate intelligence, that the secretary-general had lost the confidence of union members, as well. By mid-1971, the regime appeared to have adopted a policy designed to discredit Bentum. At a press conference, the minister for labor impugned Bentum's integrity by leaving the impression that correspondence concerning the minimum wage, which Bentum had publicized, had not, in fact, taken place. On another occasion, as the Bentum was meeting with the Ministry of Labor to settle a strike, the Ministry of Transport was sending letters of commendation to 120 union members who refused to participate, as well as a cash bonus.[38]

By August, Bentum's right to hold office was being openly challenged as the government press unleashed a barrage of vilification against him personally and against his organization: "People are itching to know how financially strong the T.U.C. is."[39] Rumors were spread that Bentum's salary was 14,000 new cedis per year (it was actually 4,000 new cedis) and that unnamed "foreign sources" were supplying the TUC with funds. The Congress reacted to these attacks by sending all of the union general secretaries on a speaking tour of each of the regions of the country. The TUC viewed the tour as educative, informing its membership of the manner in which their leader had been treated, and supporting Bentum's economic positions based on the unions' review of the state of the economy.

When asked to name the immediate, precipitating cause of the dissolution, most union officials mentioned the speaking tour and the government's reaction to it. The evidence suggests, however, that it was not merely the content of the

speeches which aroused suspicion and anger. The speaking
tour was considered an illegitimate and politically-motivated
attempt to topple the regime because it underscored the
absence of normative continuity between the Congress and
the government. The TUC was reasserting its right to
establish and maintain its own codes of conduct and to elect
and support leadership of its own choosing.

*Since 1972*

Under the NRC, respect for the viability of the TUC as an
opponent in industrial relations was strengthened.
Government rhetoric and action were not uncritical of labor,
on occasion. However, what was unusual about NRC
administration of labor affairs was its relative consistency in
fulfilling promises and making good on threats. In weighing
the potential harm on the basis of government warnings, and
potential benefits on the basis of promises, the Congress knew
that it would not always come out ahead, but the behavior of
government, as an adversary, was more predictable than had
been the case in past years. Organized labor is now viewed by
the government as an essential partner, with business, in
maintaining a cordial industrial relations environment. To this
end, the Congress has been given material and financial aid,
but not so much as to make it appear weak or unstable. In
addition, government has not hesitated to defend some labor
positions before the business community.

The leadership of the Ghana Employers' Association has
also subscribed to the view that the TUC should remain a
viable opponent. The acting chairman, at the Twelfth Annual
General Meeting in 1972, noted that the association was
"aware of the advantages employers derive from negotiations
and consultations with a strong organized labor movement."
The GEA supported the congress's efforts to discourage
splinter unions which, the association noted, "ferment
inter-union rivalry, resulting in chaos and disruption of
harmonious labor management relations." It was expected
that workers would have disagreements with employers from
time to time over interpretation of contracts, but these were
not resented or rejected, automatically. They had become
part of the game and accepted. For its part, the Congress

reciprocated the confidence which the association evinced by leaving it to the employers to present the case of both labor and management, on concluded agreements, to government, e.g., before the Prices and Incomes Board.

Of course, many employers with whom the unions negotiate are not members of the association, and some firms within the association remain skeptical concerning the value of collective bargaining. However, it is significant to note that, in negotiations, even several firms hostile to labor justify their failure to meet union demands by citing union contracts which have been concluded previously with other businesses at lower rates of pay. Pay scales and conditions of service to which a union has already agreed are now accepted as standards for industry.

In its participation on the various commissions and statutory bodies to which union representatives were appointed from 1972 to 1979, the TUC encountered less resistance to its proposals than under the NLC or Busia regimes. One reason for this is that the military did not make an overt alliance with the civil service in the determination of national policy, nor was it so influenced by formal qualifications and professional degrees as were its predecessors. The Congress was able to avoid presenting "minority reports" at the conclusion of deliberations because it received, for the most part and by its own estimate, a fair hearing. The consultative bodies now serve the real conflict-regulating function of making each of the participating groups aware of the demands of the others, of limited government resources, and of the impact of their demands on other groups. A GEA official reported that such continuous exposure to the positions of management and labor had led to an understanding of the problems common to both sides, as well as those which are unique to each.

Additional evidence of mutual respect among labor, business and government is the avoidance of blanket condemnation of the other parties. Certain "irresponsible personalities" or radical elements within each group have come to be the primary objects of criticism. A leading unionist, for example, characterized a former NRC commissioner for labor as a "buffoon," but the friction between the commissioner and the Congress did not provoke NRC retaliation, and may even have been a factor in his removal. Nor do the occasional attacks to which the Congress has been subjected automatically cause alarm. The acting secretary-general stated:

> We and Government are like the two superpowers, U.S.A. and Soviet Russia. We have our basic differences, but we can never clash head on because we realize that we shall annihilate ourselves.[40]

## CHAPTER V

# Leadership Skills and Roles

We have thus far established that, as unionism in Ghana has taken root, patterns of functional exchange with the environment and predictable industrial relations have evolved. These processes have enabled the present union heads and TUC secretariat officials to learn the technical and organizational skills which are necessary for institutional success. This chapter explores the acquisition of skills and role taking among the labor elite. Some role conflict and ambiguity are present today. These are the result of historical circumstances peculiar to Ghana and, more generally, the competing demands placed on labor executives in developng countries.

## LEARNING TO LEAD

General secretaries of Ghanaian unions have perfected leadership skills by coming up through the ranks; all, so far, have been workers and lower-level officers prior to assuming their present positions. This is in marked contrast to the experience of most other African union leaders, who were either outsiders with clerical skills who had not themselves been union members, or so-called "labor entrepreneurs," who have drifted from country to country without being well-grounded in the labor history of any one nation. The time required to advance gradually within the movement has resulted in a mean age of 47 for Ghanaian general secretaries.

The youngest is 36; the oldest, 61. As a group, they are mature, by African labor standards.

*Education*

Current Ghanaian union heads have an average of ten and one-half years of formal education. Six of the 17 have the equivalent of a high-school diploma, seven have had some high school, and four attended only primary school. These figures are, however, quite misleading, because all of the men have attended additional trade union courses. Some leaders reported taking extramural classes at the University College of the Gold Coast as early as 1946. These courses were held in Accra and Kumasi on a regular basis, as well as in special Easter and New Year's sessions. The ICFTU also trained and advised leaders, locally, curing the 1950's, until the TUC disaffiliated. By 1958, Workers' Colleges at Accra and Takoradi were established by the Peoples' Educational Association. Two of the present general secretaries graduated as "labor cadets," and several others attended seminars. The Workers' Colleges were designed to prepare leaders for their responsibilities under the New Structure.

Aside from education within Ghana, all top officials have traveled abroad for courses ranging in duration from one week to several months. It is not usual for a general secretary or national chairman to have made three or four visits to britain or America.[1] All of the union heads have been to Eastern Bloc nations as well as Western, although invitations from communist countries have been declined from time to time. It is, admittedly, easy to overestimate the impact of the junkets on the improvement of leaders' technical and organizational skills. Some of the time abroad is spent performing ceremonial duties and covering topics not directly germane to union administration. However, most of the trips last more than one month. At the very least, foreign travel, if it does not provide time for actual study, does acquaint leaders with problems in other countries and with ideas for the solution of similar problems at home. It also helps them to establish valuable personal contacts which are the basis for future technical assistance.

*Career Patterns*

All of the present general secretaries became active in union affairs while still in their twenties. Some reported having older brothers or uncles who were officers before them. Most of them assumed a lower level position as a branch officer within a few years after joining the work force. The oldest of the leaders held a position in 1946; the youngest did not become involved until 1966, but all were union members before the 1966 coup. The great majority held some office before the New Structure took effect in 1958. The 17 leaders have spent an average of 24 years actively involved in labor affairs. There is a remarkable continuity in their career patterns. Only three of the secretaries, two of whom went to Nigeria following the 1961 strike, broke their individual affiliation with the TUC once they had joined a union.

This consistency is all the more significant considering that 16 of the 17 were recruited to their first union office during the Nkrumah period. The change of government in 1966 did not end their careers; in fact, it was of benefit to them. They, as junior officers, merely replaced their superiors. Only one of the general secretaries held that office prior to the ouster of Nkrumah. The top leaders have now been in office for an average of eleven years.

Lengthy tenure of office has a profound effect on the attainment of instututional status for unions. Regular turnover of officers, and the existence of a "loyal opposition," are rare. And continuity of program and ideology, which is essential to the positive valuation of the group by members and society, is dependent primarily on continuity of leadership. In Ghana, most New Structure general secretaries remained in office for six years, until those loyal to John Tettegah were forced out. Between 1964 and 1966, instability was at its peak as the result first of party purges and then of the NLC coup. By 1967, however, tenure has restabilized. Over the next seven years, eight of the 17 unions retained the same leader; six unions experienced only one change of general secretary. The turnover rate for national chairmen was similarly low. Six groups kept their chairmen throughout the period, and six experienced only one change. Only five unions replaced both their general secretary and chairman, and, in three groups, both officers remained the same. The senior officers of the TUC secretariat also maintained their positions. These patterns were established in spite of attempts to politicize the unions during the 1969 election and the 1971 dissolution.

To account for this record of longevity, we may note that union bureaucracy, "with its formal organization and division of functions among the members, makes it possible for a minority to achieve the interests of the association with the majority participating very little or not at all."[2] In the Ghanaian case, the likelihood of oligarchic control is increased because there is a greater education gap between leaders and led than in western trade unions. Thus, the number of aspirants to office is even more severely limited because there are minimum standards for leadership (e.g., literacy) which many members cannot meet. In addition, turnover of members may mitigate sustained opposition to a leader. In Ghana instability of the membership base is magnified because workers cease to be members when they are unemployed and thus do not have dues deducted from their pay.

## VARIETIES OF LEADERSHIP

As the structure of the Congress has become more complex and bureaucratized, and as the political milieu for labor activity has changed, union leaders have learned to play a variety of roles.[3] These include:

1) The commander of a fighting organization — the "general" who inspires and demands unity, maintains a militant posture, devises strike tactics, etc.

2) The political leader — who enjoys legitimacy conferred by the members or outside authorities, and uses his skill to influence national policy in favor of labor.

3) The administrator of a fraternal society — who supervises his office staff and coordinates welfare and services for members.

4) The bargainer — whose strategy is based on knowledge of what employers can pay, and the value of labor to their enterprises.

Formal training, as it has been outlined above, may aid the leaders in conceptualizing these different, and sometimes contradictory roles, but most of their learning has come from practice, and from trial and error. The various historical stages through which the TUC has passed have been marked by the rewarding or discouraging of differing leadership roles. However, as a group, labor leadership in Ghana has shown each of the foregoing constellations of behavior.

*Early Leadership Roles*

Pioneer Ghanaian unionists fit the pattern described by Victor Allen, in which there is "little or no division of labor; men perform composite tasks and are not chosen on the basis of their fitness for the tasks."[4] As a result, many leaders were not competent to deal with either membership or employers. The small, poorly-organized house unions were typically short-lived or hopelessly ineffective. Some of their leaders "were as ignorant as the rank and file membership, or if anything, held positions in unions by reason of their brawn."[5] Because the unions were too poor to provide welfare services and were not accepted by employers in bargaining, there was little chance for leaders to practice administrative behavior. Political skills were of limited use in a colonial environment characterized by the "command model" of decision-making. Similarly, leadership based merely on physical strength or the mastery of a few parliamentary tricks was not legitimated.

An account of the beginnings of a union within a small commercial firm run by Indians inciates the absence of role models for labor leaders in the private sector in the immediate post-war period. The man who eventually became the head of the union was a secondary school graduate who was an accountant in the firm. He had no background in unionism: "I did not know what a union was." But, as an accountant, he was in a position to see that the firm was making great profits, especially in comparison with the wages paid. Therefore, he helped to start the Indian Employees' Union. There was no pay for union leadership. Dues had to be collected by hand,

and the activities of the union were confined mostly to Accra.
Victimization was rampant. "As soon as an employer found
out there were union members working for him, he sacked
them ," the leader said later. He had started his union "by
instinct," but when he read an advertisement that the Labor
Department was offering help in union organization, he went
to see a British advisor. He has "been a unionist ever since."

The labor leaders' acquisition of political skills was
accelerated in 1948. The rise of domestic politics meant that
party organization provided role models for the unionists.
Most leaders chose to emulate the populist, Nkrumah, rather
than the cautious and aloof politicians of the United Gold Coast
Convention. Strikes during 1948-49 were legitimated by the
nationalist movement. In those days, as one foreign labor
official later said, "many unionists wanted to prove how good
they were by going on strike as soon as they got an office, a
file, and a pencil." With some justification, the Labor
Department cited, as the cause of industrial unrest,
"unscrupulous demogogues" who engendered the belief
among all workers that they were entitled to "back pay,"
retroactive salary awards which applied only to
ex-servicemen and other select groups. The prestige of office
and the exhilarating experience of exercising power were the
rewards for which these leaders worked. Yet to come were
the financial benefits and the explicit political connections
with the CPP government.

### The Sekondi "Labor Fighters"

Increasing militancy of leaders and emphasis on their role as
"commanders of fighting organizations" resulted from the
legalization of unions in an environment where many
employers refuled to recognize them. By August 1948, a
change in TUC leadership reflected this phenomenon.
Anthony Woode became general secretary, with Pobee Biney
his deputy. Both men had been active in the 1948 strikes.
Woode, then only 22 years old, had made his reputation in the
movement when he organized the Oil Storage Workers in
Takoradi and signed a collective agreement with management
in 1947. Biney was the leader of the Railway Enginemen.
These and other leaders from Sekondi — E.C. Turkson-Ocran

and Isaac Kumah, for example — repudiated the moderate position of Charles Tachie-Menson, the TUC's first president, who was then forced to resign. The new leadership was younger, more ready to strike, and more intimately connected with the nationalist movement than was the older, more acquiescent group. The militant posture led directly to the ill-fated "positive action" campaign and the dismemberment of the labor movement in 1950.

We have noted that three factions crystalized among the labor leadership in Ghana between 1950 and 1956: the militants, the moderates and "stalwarts." These may be distinguished not only according to their patrons in the political arena, but also according to the leadership roles which were emphasized by each. The "stalwarts" were politicians; the moderates sought to consolidate their positon as administrators; the militants adopted the posture of "fighting generals" of the labor movement.

The reaction of most workers to the events of January 1950 may have been defeat or fear, but the mood in Sekondi was angry. Workers' resentment was increased by the detention of Biney and Woode. The Gold Coast Unemployed Association was founded, nominally to recover lost jobs, but within a year it was to become the nucleus of opposition to British-inspired "apolitical" unionism. Its officers toured the major industrial centers and opened branches throughout southern Ghana, although their major strength was in the west. After the 1951 TUC election in which the moderates were victorious, the association became the rival trade union center, the Ghana Trades Union Congress. At its first annual conference in 1952, Anthony Woode became president. The leaders of this group considered themselves Marxists.

It has been maintained that the Sekondi-based GTUC was merely a front for the CCP and received no genuine working class support.[6] The evidence, however, suggests that its founders, Woode and Biney, were indeed accepted as leaders by the majority of workers in their own backyard; the fact that they had been rejected by the British-influenced Gold Coast TUC only added to their credentials. Besides, between 1952 and 1953, the GTUC was a source of embarrassment to the CPP, which hardly controlled it. Woode and Biney took a

much stronger position than did the moderates on both wage
and political matters, warned of the dangers of foreign capital
controlling the Volta Dam project, and pushed for immediate
independence. They denounced corruption, derided the cult of
Nkrumah personality, and ridiculed the syncophants who had
begun to cling to the leader.

## The Primacy of Labor Politicians

Chapter I described the compromise engineered by
Nkrumah at the 1953 TUC election, which had the effect of
elevating to power John Tettegah, the "stalwart." Following
the election, the militants were stripped of their influence
within the TUC secretariat; Ocran, Biney and Woode were
expelled from the CCP. As "commanders of a fighting labor
organization" they possessed more charisma than has since
been seen in Ghana unions, "a power quite dissociated from
their ability to organize and administer."[7] But as politicians
they had failed. At this point in the institutionalization of labor
leadership within the Congress, administrative and political
roles, legitimated by the CPP, had become dominant.

In turn, the moderates, leaders of larger and more
financially-secure unions, also found their position declining to
the benefit of the "stalwarts," between 1953 and 1956. This
was so, in spite of their superior administrative experience.
They were discredited because of their use of the British as
patrons, but more inportant, they found themselves greatly
outnumbered by opportunistic labor leaders who had joined
the ranks of the "stalwarts" following the CPP's election
victories. As proposals for the New Structure were aired in
1955-56, it became obvious that it was the "stalwarts" who
would be the administrative leaders of the TUC. Their acumen
as politicians had placed them in line for the labor cadetships,
(that is, junior leader traineeships) and foreign training
necessary to fill the new, salaried leadership posts which were
created.

We have pointed out that the opposition of the moderates
and militants to the New Structure was bound for defeat. The
opposition spokesman in Parliament cited the stalwart
unionists as those "who once claimed to be verandah-boys but
who are now castle kings."[8] But there was little which could

be done to halt the "stalwart" takeover once the CCP had been convinced that the New Structure was desirable.

The Tettegah-led "stalwart" forces appear to have surprised some within the other two factions with the suddenness of their influence on the Congress. A change in the voting rules did aid their rapid advance. However, although they were opportunistic, they were the leaders of real unions. Their organizations were, indeed, mostly small and weak, but this was ot unusual for Ghana. The stalwarts' one distinguishing feature was their greater sensitivity to the prevailing political winds.

John Tettegah himself had a legitimate labor background. He had begun work in 1949 as a stenographer after graduation from secretarial school. During 1949-51 he served as a branch secretary in the G.B. Olivant Employees Union, a small "house union" in a foreign-owned mercantile firm. This union affiliated to the moderate Gold Coast TUC. Between 1951 and 1953 he was a member of the General Council of the GCTUC, and, at the age of 23, was elected assistant general secretary. The great notoriety which he was to receive, and his intimate identification with Nkrumah and the CPP up to 1964, should not disguise the fact that his beginnings in the movement fit the pattern of many of today's general-secretaries.

## The Development of Administrative Roles

Of course, the unity of the labor movement after 1958, in part imposed by law, was crucial to its evolution as an institution. What may be overlooked, however, is that the emergence of the three factions described above, rival trade union centers, and shifting political alliances also contributed to the process. Growth in the number of unions, which united in various combinations in an attempt to gain tactical advantage, provided a general increased number of leaders with opportunities to exercise power and to learn and practice executive and organizational skills. It is apparent from the accounts of inter-union intrigue that a generation of officers had mastered the machinations of parliamentary debate, learned to cope with rowdy or recalcitrant audiences, and developed the ability to display discretion by compromise.

Contact with party officials, sometimes sought, sometimes unwilling, increased these leaders' awareness of the connection between the game they were learning and the larger stakes involved in winning national elections and attaining independence. A by-product of the foreign ties made with Ghanaian unions during this period was to make the local men aware of their position through international comparisons of wages and living standards.

Another significant factor in the strengthening of union leadership is the existence of legally-prescribed criteria for top union officials. General secretaries and treasurers were required to be literate, to have worked in industry for six years, to have been a member of a national union during that time, and to have been an employee of a particular establishment, as well as a member of its branch union, for at least two years. The British had intended to reduce the likelihood of political manipulation in unions by preventing the rise to power of counterfeit unionists who were political hacks. The law did not prevent political unionism, of course, but it has remained on the books to date and has discouraged both uneducated aspirants to office and outside agitators. In attempting to influence the TUC between 1954 and 1964 the CPP did not have to flout this law. There were enough unionists who met its criteria, and who also were "politicians."

After 1958, the forced and voluntary consolidation into 16 national unions resulted in spectacular membership increases, with some unions quadrupling in size within two years. Thus, New Structure leaders were compelled to devote more attention to their administrative roles. As the Nkrumah years passed, administration became the dominant concern of many officials. In the next chapter, we shall examine the reasons for the decline in importance of the politician's role, which had been essential in the 1950's. Intrigue and dissension within the CPP itself rendered some leaders' political connections more liabilities than assets between 1962 and 1965.

Reduced emphasis on the union leader's role as commander of a fighting organization, required by the CPP and the "stalwarts," reflects more than the rivalry between Accra and Sekondi, or Nkrumahism and Marxism. It is still in evidence today. None of the present general secretaries is a firebrand general, although, to be successful, a modicum of tactical expertise is required. By 1960, top officials were managers of, rather than creators of, discontent. They had become agents in the institutional channeling of animosity. As Everett Hughes has noted, the agitators must give way to the negotiators.[9] Certainly, the reaction of the general secretaries to the 1961 strike indicated that by then, the TUC was an established group whose officers actually feared agitation.

## THE LEGACY OF ROLE CONFLICT
## AND AMBIGUITY

If, over the past fourteen years, senior labor leaders have devoted more attention to perfecting their roles as administrators than to their roles as "labor fighters" or politicians, this should not be taken as evidence that role conflict or role ambiguity has disappeared within the Ghanaian labor movement. Various roles may be occupied simultaneously by an able and resourceful leader, but the tensions inherent in the exercise of multiple roles, which were apparent in the Nkrumah period, remain.

### Branch vs. National Leaders

Leadership has been much less stable, and less institutionalized, at lower levels in the heirarchy. The agitator's role, which has become counterproductive for general secretaries, is still being practiced by many branch officers. The 1961 strike, in which middle-level leaders refused to obey their superiors' orders to return to work, is the most blatant example of the conflict between agitators and administrators in Ghanaian labor history, but it is by no means the only one, nor the most recent one. Compared to the top officials, branch leaders are less experienced, they are less secure in their positions, and almost all are unpaid. Their behavior today, therefore, appears as a mirror image of the senior officers' during the 1940's and 1950's. The temptation to act as a "fighting general" is frequently overwhelming.

Strain within the hierarchy has been especially acute when workers have been persuaded to abandon militant tactics in advance of a hoped-for favorable decision from employers, but the latter, or government, have then ignored the law. In frustration, national leaders may issue tongue-in-cheek prohibitions against militant tactics, but this is only a short-term solution. B.A. Bentum, during his tenure as the TUC's secretary-general, complained that he was earning the image of a "strike-breaker," because, in the final analysis, his administrative and political roles were more salient than that of "fighting general."

## Administration vs. Bargaining

Ideally, the roles of office manager and negotiator should complement each other. The more favorable contracts are consummated, the larger and more reliable is the union's income from membership dues. The larger the income, the more welfare functions the union can perform and the more subordinates may be hired to help the general secretary. Similarly, the greater efficiency of the group and the more services it provides, the more attractive it should be to its membership, and the leadership may, therefore, be more effective as a spokesman for them. In practice, however, this ideal blending of roles is achieved in only one or two of the 17 national unions. Dues are set so low that even an aggressive bargainer with a gradually expanding membership cannot pay for enough staff, nor provide enough services. All leaders expressed the desire to expand their administration, but only two had concrete plans for securing a dues increase.

Leaders of smaller unions take personal responsibility for conducting bargaining, having no money to pay experienced negotiators. Thus, inevitably, they cannot practice the role of office administrator as much as they would like. Because they can afford only low-salaried clerks as assistants, the office work-load accumulates. In most unions, bargaining and dealing with industrial unrest take precedence over office management. Even in the largest unions, there is little time for leaders to obtain expertise in more specific welfare functions, such as the running of workers' business enterprises or the training of the rank and file to participate in management of private companies.

*Limited Democracy*

There is an inevitable tension between being an efficient administrator and encouraging support and participation from the workers. The more a general secretary remains in his office, or at the bargaining table, the less time he has to rally the membership. This is one of the reasons why decentralization of decision-making is so rare in trade unions.

In Ghana, and elsewhere in Africa, the first generation of unionists was able to resolve this tension by being autocratic. The small size of their organizations and the absence of sophisticated lower level leaders lessened the need for regular participation and consultation. Among the second generation of Ghanaian officials, however, conflict between admintive and internal political roles is more acute and more difficult to resolve. All general secretaries have had to pay increased attention to the legitimation of their decisions by local officers because their unions are now larger and could not function without branch organizations. Some unions contain hundreds of local officers who have little administrative power themselves, but who are the only officials many workers ever see.

A few general secretaries delegate administrative duties to subordinates and devote most of their time to cultivating contacts with the rank and file. But most leaders, lacking such reliable and skilled deputies, resolve the role conflict by dealing with a restricted political clientele, a white-collar constituency of junior officers and workers. After the restoration of the TUC in 1972, each of the 17 national unions held extraordinary conferences for the election of leaders, although they were not legally required to do so. Officials were unanimous in the view that they should have a new mandate in light of the change of government. The great majority of officers were confident that they would be reelected. In fact, only one general secretary was subsequently removed by the delegates, and another was removed by the National Redemption Council, without significant Congress protest.

The industrial structure of Ghanaian unionism reduces the burden of general secretaries' political roles. All unions have always contained both blue- and white-collar workers. It is the latter category which has produced the vast majority of labor officials in Ghana at all levels, and all but one of the present union leaders. In fact, a major reason for the pattern already described, in which secretaries have come up through the ranks, is the absence of purely blue-collar, craft organizations. Outsiders and foreigners might have served these groups as officers, were it not for the available supply of clerical workers in all unions. Leaders with education and training in white collar positions are separated from blue collar members by choice and necessity. It is easier, and often more productive, to communicate with each other or with the clerical grades, rather than with groups of illiterates. It is also difficult to recruit illiterates to serve on branch committees, and only a few unions officially encourage it.

Leaders cannot instill a sense of collective responsibility among the rank and file when so many decisions are made for workers, rather than by them. Some of the general secretaries speak of "disciplining" their men: "You can't let workers run loose." This attitude is the result of the gulf between white-collar leaders and blue-collar workers. It acts as a self-fulfilling prophecy. To assume that illiterates cannot act responsibly in administering their own affairs, even at the branch level, is to encourate the apathy and passivity about which complaints are so often voiced. It is not surprising that, as the result of this conflict between leadership roles, a workshop on "Problems Facing Organized Labour" in 1973 cited the "lack of total involvement of the rank and file," a "problem of accountability in the leadership" and the "lack of an effective two-way communication."

*External Pressures*

Finally, there has been a continuing conflict between the leadership's administrative roles and that portion of the political role which relates not to the membership, but to the outside environment. It is not bureaucratic red tape which has hampered the fulfillment of administrative responsibilities, so much as political interference. To protect itself against manipulation, the Congress, from 1958 to 1964 and again from 1966 to 1971, relied on individual unionists, particularly the secretary-generals, Tettegah and Bentum, to run interference. Both men not only experienced personal role conflict — administrator versus politician — but their attention to national politics resulted in the enervation of administrative capacity among the general secretaries.

As Tettegah began to lose favor with the CPP in 1962, his effectiveness as a labor administrator was crippled. His supporters among the leadership also became marked men; several were eventually removed. Anti-Tettegah elements, which had previously respected his power within the movement but had been skeptical of his politics, coalesced in opposition. All leaders were compelled to pay more attention to political contacts, both within the Convention People's Party and without, because the protective shield which Tettegah had provided was shattered. Bentum, for example, made contact with a future member of the NLC, Chief Inspector Harlley. Several middle-level leaders reported "laying low," trying to avoid being squeezed between the factions within the CPP by lessening their own political involvement, but not to the point where they would be purged. Some men of obvious administrative ability refused to serve their unions as elected officials because they feared being victimized by the politicians.

After 1966, Bentum's attention to national politics was handsomely rewarded. He was the only former CPP official to retain a top post within the TUC, and not coincidentally, to be appointed to the NLC's National Advisory Committee. Bentum's role as administrator was made easier by the fact that all but one of the general secretaries had been purged after the coup in an exercise largely directed by himself. Some new leaders, although elected by union members, believed that he had played a part in their advancement.

Bentum protected the general secretaries consistently, by serving as their spokesman, and by absorbing much of the criticism directed against them by the NLC and PP regimes. However, there were rumblings of opposition, both before and after the dissolution of the Congress, saying that he had used the TUC to advance his own political stock. From his position as guarantor of the administrative roles of his cohorts, it was tempting for him to become more the national political figure than the unions' chief administrator. He complained that union leadership should not be left to one man and urged branch leaders to participate.[10] But, like Tettegah before him, he dominated administratively by virtue of his external political role-taking.

Compared with his predecessor, the present secretary-general, A.M. Issifu, appears as a less dramatic figure, less likely to dominate newspaper headlines and more willing to subordinate himself to the achievements of the TUC and its member unions. The Congress has benefitted from this change of leadership style. Because less power is exercised at the very top, the general secretaries have become more effective administrators, having more opportunity to practice what they have learned. It is a mark of maturity for the Congress as an institution that the Executive Board, composed of the leaqders of all 17 unions, can now accept responsibility for the fulfillment of the political leadership ris-a-vis the environment. However, should this environment become more hostile than it is at present, this particular leadership role conflict may reappear.

## National Leaders of the Future

National union officers today encourage workers to become leaders by setting examples. Every participant at a seminar is told that he is a potential industrial relations officer, general secretary, and secretary-general. Even A.M. Issifu, it is pointed out, has come up through the ranks. It is undoubtedly difficult for many of the recruits, at the inception of their training, to believe that their own advancement is really possible. The current generation of national leaders is well entrenched, yet they are young enough to control the movement for many years to come. Recruits who do become convinced that a career in their union or the TUC is worthwhile will have to wait seveal years before obtaining a salaried position. The great majority of those who commit themselves will remain at a low level of responsibility, although as unions grow and staffs increase in size, some new positions will become available.

Yet, unionism should be an increasingly attractive vocation in the future. A generation of Ghanaians, particularly the highly educated, harbored hopes of raising their status, going into business and becoming wealthy. But today, opportunities have narrowed. Secondary school leavers cannot find work, and many graduates are prevented from attending universities because of the severely limited number of places. These developments already have strengthened recruitment by the Congress at its base, the branches.

As an institution changes and matures, its opportunities for attracting and retaining different kinds of personnel change. Organized labor has preserved its integrity and has established a system of promotion and advancement that universalistic emphasizes standards of leadership. Therefore, it is in a position to offer an increasingly attractive career alternative to educated Ghanaians who, twenty years ago, would not have considered it.

## CHAPTER VI

# Leadership Norms and Values

Senior union leaders in Ghana share many problems. They attempt to cope with financial adversity, to run a bureaucracy, and to escape government manipulation. Moreover, they must do all this while trying to establish relationships with the rank and file and junior officers so that they may keep their posts, and with the business community so that they may win concessions. These common experiences have evoked a unified set of norms and values to which leaders adhere — standards of honesty efficiency, mutual dependence and accountability. The effect of these shared attitudes and behaviors is to minimize conflict and rivalry among labor executives. General agreement on what constitutes trade union ideology is both a reason for, and a reflection of, the extent of cooperation and good faith among them.

## CODES OF PERSONAL CONDUCT

### Status Confirmation

The long tenure typical of union heads provides them with the opportunity to confirm a new position in Ghanaian society. For almost all the present general secretaries, assuming office represented a status rise. Their fathers' occupations varied from "unskilled laborer, railway worker, and farmer to an accountant, the only one not of low status."[1] By contrast, they, as general secretaries, earn roughly $3,500 per year, placing them in the upper ten percent of Ghanaian wage earners. Most live in middle-class neighborhoods. The union provides a car and driver, travel allowances, and the opportunity to further one's education.

In spite of these undeniable advantages, however, most of the officers see themselves essentially as "self-made men," who are not paid enough, given their experience and training. Foreign-owned firms in Ghana, for example, pay over twice what the unions can afford for executive talent. Because union salaries are comparatively low, a career in industry, particularly in personnel departments, has been attractive to both senior and middle-level leaders. Sometimes, firms use promotion into management as a technique to eliminate skilled local negotiators. But the number of high-salaried positions in the private sector has always been small, and the prospects for a union leader seeking them have worsened in recent years as the number of applicants with extensive formal education has increased. This trend is reflected in the fact that none of the general secretaries who left their positions between 1966 and 1973 was recruited away by industry. All would have continued as officers in the union, if allowed to do so. A few of them accepted positions in the TUC secretariat.

Studies of African trade unions have noted that leaders view their organizations as a "stepping stone" to even higher status and more money. While this generalization is exaggerated, there is some evidence that it is at least partially confirmed in the Ghanaian case. Several former heads of the Congress and individual unions now serve as executives in state corporations and private firms. But few of these men held union office after 1966, and as many, or more, are now unemployed. The commitment of the second generation of leaders to their unions may be explained, in part, by their awareness of the career patterns of their predecessors. Their occupational mobility is restricted. The union today is not a "stepping stone," but is itself the primary means of confirming the officers' middle class status.

## Corruption

What has been the relationship between tenure of office, upward mobility, and dishonest and self-serving behavior? A survey of TUC history confirms that the view that corruption and attention to personal aggrandizement have been most evident not among officers of long tenure, but among those who perceived their positions to be insecure. Many of these devoted more attention to non-labor goals than to program goals because they needed to act quickly before losing access to sources of wealth.

The great majority of union heads who assumed office between 1957 and 1960 under the New Structure had little to show, financially, for their long association with unionism. Undoubtedly, some of these men saw the sudden affluence of the labor movement as a reward for their previous struggles for recognition and respectability. As soon as the initial installment of government funds was paid to the Congress, new and greatly increased salary scales were implemented for the TUC's top six officers. When 22 Ghanaian unionists, led by John Tettegah, visited Lagos for a 1958 conference, "almost every one of the visitors came in a brand-new car, and showed no restraint in advertising the wealth and influence of the new unionism in Ghana."[2] Foreign travel further encouraged a taste for gracious living.

Union general secretaries were invited to lavish parties at which they mingled with the political elite. The unionists felt comfortable in this company because they did not view personal austerity as an important indicator of serious commitment to socialism. Material display remained an indicator of success. The socialist Tettegah, "born of a working class parentage in the humble fishing town of Ada," earned over 5,000 pounds a year.[3]

However, the attacks which the party directed at the affluence of some unionists beginning in 1960, and the government's antipathy toward the Congress, which surfaced after the 1961 strike, served as warnings that leaders might be removed from their positions. Some of these eligible for foreign trips were passed over; some of the Mercedes-Benz cars were taken back by the party. Finally, the number of national unions was arbitrarily reduced from sixteen to ten.

The extreme political interference of the period 1962-66 increased insecurity among the senior leadership. Program goals received low priority, and the desire for personal aggrandizement was widespread. Some union executives began to feather their own nests by "cooperating" with the ministries which employed their members. Then, when the government decided that it needed to save money by dismissing employees, the retrenchment exercises were often accomplished without union protest. When Kwaw Ampah became Secretary-General of the TUC, he announced that he had came with a broom to sweep away corruption. But he and another official, G.A. Balogun, immediately had their salaries raised and purchased coveted Mercedes-Benz automobiles. At this point, during 1964-65, intraparty intrigue was so intense that the new officers installed as a result of the purge realized that their own tenure was likely to be brief.

Evidence from the period 1960-66 supports the findings in other studies of leadership behavior which have noted the "sell-out" syndrome and the "multiple interest" syndrome. The group primarily responsible for senior leaders' income and status was not the TUC, but the Convention People's Party. Thus, many men failed to perform their official duties. They tried to gain support from the party by reducing their own institution's "innovative thrust."[4]

Pleas by Marxists within the party for more union autonomy, genuine election of officials, and eventual control of the TUC by manual laborers, were rejected. Instead, the government was ensuring the reliability of officers by neglecting its obligation, under law, to oversee TUC finances. Bookkeeping was either lax or non-existent, and a variety of union-run business enterprises were unproductive, lost money, or acted as funnels for depositing funds in the pockets of labor executives. Ironically, however, the CPP did not obtain the loyalty of a large portion of these leaders because it was unwilling, or unable, to absorb most of them. It encouraged corrupt behavior because it expected the unions to be a testing ground for only a few political leaders, and a dead-end for most. It wanted the majority to be satisfied with the management of their own domains.[5]

If, in addition to tending to their own needs, the officers had been able to create a "machine" for the distribution of bounty to subordinates, corrupt or inefficient leadership might have become institutionalized. This did not happen; the government, at party direction, remained the source of funds and favors. Lesser functionaries' loyalty toward the co-opted senior officials was mitigated by the realization that the party could reduce the flow of resources to its ancillary organizations at will. For example, it was common knowledge that Kwaw Ampah was initially provided with a slush fund used to bribe junior officers; but, by the end of 1965, he was being accused of plotting the overthrow of Nkrumah. He had become one of the losers in the intra-party power struggle. Thus, although he had acted as a distributor of funds, few of the recipients would have tried to prevent his removal from office.

## Honesty

As leaders perceived that their participation in labor affairs was not a ticket into the upper echelon of the party and greater personal power, many became disillusioned. The increasing use of labor organization by the CPP as a mechanism for deflecting the ambitions of labor executives led these men to abandon hope of directly influencing or challenging the political apparatus. They became oriented, instead, toward the achievement of better wages and working conditions for union members. The party could do little to stem this tide, even with the outright replacement of senior officers which began in 1964. The antigovernment position which some leaders took during the late Nkrumah years was particularly strong among the younger, deputy and junior officers who, after 1966, became the second generation of union heads. Those observers who dismiss the genuine effort of these leaders to attain program goals have, as William Friedland points out, mistaken "the co-optation of the top ranks of the unions for a capture of the entire system of unionism."[6]

Nkrumah could never obtain the unqualified support of union officials, at any level. Most on national staff were willing to participate in the popularization of the CPP, but they resented interference in their career advancement, and their exclusion from national decision-making. Many local officers, whose personal goals were more modest but who also benefitted less from the party-dominated machine for reward distribution, found ways of coping with the CPP "study groups" in their factories. Their branches became loci of anti-Nkrumah sentiment.

Since 1966 corruption has not been endemic in the Trades Union Congress. Most incidents of illegal, personal aggrandizement have occurred at the branch level, where the stakes are relatively small and the matter can be handled by the national executive. The significant decline in the pursuit of non-labor goals is primarily the result of increased job security, combined with the continuing motivation of leaders to hold onto their positions. The "iron law of oligarchy" may hold today, and it was no less valid before 1966. However, the impact of politics on leadership tenure is now much less. Therefore, there is much less motivation to engage in corrupt practices, which injure the reputation of the movement and which threaten the Congress's unity by involving the leaders in competition for wealth and favors.

Leaders whose positions are secure and whose status has been amply confirmed have an increased opportunity, and motivation, to spend most of their time in pursuit of program objectives. Indeed, the present-day labor executives who are most influential within the Congress head unions which, regardless of size, exhibit the following characteristics:

high stability of top officers since 1966;

large percentage of workers covered by collective agreements;

well-publicized attempts at "welfare unionism";

consistent contact between leaders and workers.

Nonetheless, these general secretaries also have large automobiles and enjoy the foreign trips and a relatively comfortable lifestyle. Thus, there is a compatibility between doing well personally and helping one's union. They reinforce each other and both are legitimate.

## NORMS WHICH REDUCE CONFLICT

Integration of leadership has been important to the longevity and strength of Ghanaian unions because it makes possible the orderly conduct of TUC business; it permits a flexible and united response to challenges from the environment; and it reduces the likelihood that viable, rival national trade union centers will appear. Jealousy, rivalry, and intrigue have been typical, even among the second generation of labor officials in many African countries. However, in Ghana, conflict among the leaders has been minimized. The high level of integration is not the result of a common ethnic identification, nor because of unanimity with regard to program goals. It is, rather, the outgrowth of the leaders' mutual dependence and accountability within a bureaucratic context.

## The Impact of Ethnicity

Prior to 1966, the tribal heterogeneity of leaders was indeed responsible for conflict among them, but primarily because it was unwittingly exploited by the British and, more consciously, by the CPP. In ignoring the militant unionists from the Western Region when they reconstituted the Congress in 1950-51, the British came to support moderates who were Ewe and Ga, from the Eastern Region and Accra. The leaderships of the Gold Coast TUC and its short-lived rival, the Ghana TUC, were also split along ethnic lines. The moderates' initial acceptance of the "stalwart" John Tettegah may be explained by noting that he was Ga-Adangme. His ethnic background allayed fears of CPP domination of the Congress, at least prior to 1956, and it may have encouraged the moderates to believe that Tettegah would hold the militants in check.[7] It should be noted, however, that ethnic differences did not prevent the subsequent alliance of militants and moderates against the ascendant "stalwarts." Common ethnic ties between the moderates and many of the stalwart leaders did not reduce the anxiety that "political influence" was being used to tarnish the reputation of the unions which would not join the New Structure. Leaders' tribal affiliation was irrelevant to the exercise of creating natonal labor organization. It was inevitable that some officers from all of the major ethnic groups would suffer the loss of their positions within the smaller, house unions.

Because outside interference in Congress affairs declined after 1966, there was less chance for politicians to exploit the ethnic differences among the leaders in a way which would provoke conflict among them. The removal of John Tettegah in 1964 may have been prompted in part by Nkrumah's fears of a Ga-Ewe political conspiracy; the new secretary-general, Kwaaw Ampah, was, like Nkrumah, a member of the Nzima tribe. But, by 1972, the impact of ethnicity on leadership integration was minimal. In the contest for office between the northerner, A.M. Issifu, and Tettegah, Ewe general secretaries were divided in their loyalty.

## Mutual Dependence

Unions vary in their size and strength, so that, for some leaders, financial survival is the most immediate priority. For others, increasing welfare services to members is most important. These and other differences of circumstances between the 17 national unions create the potential for dissension among the leaders. However, their mutual dependence reduces this potential. No individual leader can obtain all he needs for his union without the cooperation of others; many of the leaders' duties require synchronized effort.

At the center of this mutual dependence is the Executive Board of the TUC composed of the general secretaries and chairmen of the unions. The board functions via the committee system; a working committee handles day-to-day business. Composition of the committees is scrupulously balanced so that no single union or group of unions may predominate. Therefore, general secretaries are often required to make decisions and undertake investigations not directly related to their own union. In addition to the board, less formal federations of unions, for example, those containing government employees or those involved in transport, meet regularly. Mutual dependence may also be documented by examining the composition of the union contingents appointed to speak for the Congress on national committees and commissions. Here again, there is a balance among unions represented, and union officers perform duties which have an impact on their peers who do not participate.

But unions share more than the time and energy of their chief executives. Junior officers have occasionally been seconded from one union in order to help another. This was the case in 1967-68 when the Public Utility Workers Union was established, with the help of personnel from the Industrial and Commercial Workers. In addition, "intellectuals" — professional labor experts — in the secretariat are shared by all of the national unions. The dependence of the general secretaries on the economic and bargaining advice of these experts aids the integration of appointed leaders with those who have been elected by their unions, and prevents the occasional jealousy of less-educated officials from erupting into open conflict. In turn, the secretariat personnel cannot be effective without help from the unions. For example, the educational programs of the congress would be severely crippled if elected officers failed to participate.

This mutually dependent behavior first became formalized after the implementation of the New Structure and the Industrial Relations Act of 1958. It may be thought that statutory recognition of the Congress has been the major constraint on dissension among the leaders. Indeed, one reason for the refusal of the NRC to change the labor law was the fear that splinter groups, led by disaffected unionists, would be encouraged if the TUC no longer enjoyed special legal status. In fact, however, the two most viable breakaways since 1966, MACAWU and the Railway and Harbor Workers, were founded by junior officers because of grievances with their parent unions, and not because of any desire to escape obligations to the TUC. Both splinters sought affiliation to the Congress and would have preferred it to the establishment of a rival national center.

Mutual dependence has been legislated to some extent, but it is also a norm which has been internalized by the general secretaries. The burdens which collective action places upon the individual are balanced by the benefits obtained. National officers of the 17 unions do not need to compete with each other in order to obtain status and power; indeed, cooperation, rather than competition, has become the accepted strategy for obtaining both personal and organizational goals.

*Mutual Accountability*

We have pointed out, above, that lessened political interference in the affairs of the Congress after 1966 reduced the leaders' opportunities for, and the temptation to engage in, corrupt behavior. It must be noted, however, that corruption and inefficiency have also been discouraged in recent years because leaders are more often held accountable for performance of their assigned roles. Accountability contributes to integraton in this case because it is mutual; the major sources of negative sanctions are each leader's own union and the Executive Board of the Congress. The men take their self-policing duties seriously, because to ignore the transgressions of their peers is to invite the imposition of punishment from the outside. The government probe of TUC assets in 1966-67, in which several former and current unionists were implicated previous abuses, is viewed with considerable cynicism by the present leaders. They respect each other as judges of their own behavior more than they do a government commission, because they feel that any criticism from outside the Congress is inevitably biased or politically motivated.

Since 1966, at least four general secretaries and one national chairman have been removed because of improper behavior, and several other officers have been accused and either exonerated or disciplined. In some cases it was alleged that peculation occurred when payments were made from the union chest in cash, rather than by check, and when dummy invoices were signed by the leaders. But sanctions were also applied against officials who violated norms of truthfulness. For example, the chairman of the union and his deputy were suspended indefinitely by the union's national executive council when they were challenged to support accusations made against their general secretary, and could not.

The Executive Board of the Congress does have the power to expel one of its members, but it has been exercised only two or three times. More often, the board has, in effect, encouraged unions to remove leaders who were found to be dishonest, inept, or politically tainted. A committee is appointed to examine disputes between officers and their unions. Its purpose is to gather evidence and to provide a forum for the accused to defend himself. If his explanation for wrongdoing is weak, or if he cannot supply financial records, the resolve of his subordinates to oust him may be strengthened.

For example, after one hearing in 1967, it was reported that the general secretary under investigatio was contemptuous of the committee and "could not lay his hands on a single document requested." It was found that his union contained too many officials, considering its low membership, and that they lacked administrative expertise. The committee concluded that the union would do better to get another general secretary, and the accused was removed from office by his own union soon thereafter. In another case the committee discovered mistrust, personal animosity, and the existence of a powerful clique among the senior officials of a union. The leaders had, it appeared, "virtually rampaged the treasury by way of taking loans for themselves." However, the committee, in its recommendations, made allowances for the brief tenure of the officers and the short time the union had existed: "We would be playing to the gallery if we pronounced judgment in a case of such magnitude, especially considering the fact that the reputation and livelihood of Secretaries were involved on the one hand, and the possible fragmentation or dissolution of an affiliated national union on the other."

Maladministration is a serious offense, but leaders are likely to be given the benefit of the doubt, or encouraged, privately, to mend their ways, unless their actions endanger the labor movement as a whole. The most glaring transgression is, therefore, to allow one's union to be manipulated by politicians. One general secretary allegedly permitted a needless strike to occur, and then offered to reveal its organizers to government, in return for the reinstatement of 260 workers who had been dismissed.[8] Two branch officers had resigned in protest, and the leader had publicly condemned another general secretary, but it was not until he identified himself with the Progress Party that he was removed, after restoration of the Congress, in 1972.

These examples illustrate that there is mutual accountability among the senior officials of the TUC, but that justice is carried out deliberately and without vindictiveness. Maturity in the application of sanctions is, perhaps, best shown by the treatment accorded the leader of one splinter group, the MACAWU. He was treated as an outcast by his parent union, the ICU, and was criticized severely at its 1970 conference. Nonetheless, in part because he was able to avoid political taint, he was offered a position with his old union when the MACAWU was dissolved. By 1973 he was general secretary of the National Union of Seamen and accepted by his colleagues on the Executive Board of the TUC. Because he was recognized as a talented leader who enjoyed genuine support from workers, he had been able to challenge some of the most influential secretaries without having his career as a unionist destroyed.

*Testing Leadership Unity*

Prior to 1966 it was difficult to maintain norms of mutual dependence and accountability when the Congress was challenged from the outside. It was unwise, and often dangerous, for labor executives to commit themselves to their peers because the government could remove most officials whom it thought to be unreliable. In 1953, for example, the allegation that he was a communist was enough to accomplish the ouster of Turkson-Ocran as secretary-general. By 1964, even John Tettegah found himself similarly isolated:

> . . . I have no role again to play in Ghana as some of the new-comers seem to infer by making me look like a social outcast, in my own country, and even amongst the Ghanaian Trade Unions . . . .It is difficult for some of us to see today, that people who but only yesterday were the arch enemies of the C.P.P. . . . are being regarded as the faithful and most loyal of the Nkrumahist socialist revolution . . . The cadres today I am told are being poisoned against some Party Comrades, and we seem to be creating and nurturing our own executioners . . .[9]

Being active in party work did not guarantee labor leaders' immunity. In one case, a deputy executive who served on a regional working committee of the CPP was denied promotion by Kwaw Ampah in favor of a man from the Workers' Brigade. Officers who had an independent following among workers or other general secretaries were suspect. B.A. Bentum, although he was the spokesman for the "right wing" of the CPP, was dismissed by Ampah and eventually became minister of forestry. Other formerly prominent CPP men who were well-integrated into Congress leadership were shunted "upstairs" to harmless ambassadorships or positions in the All African Trade Union Federation.

By contrast, over the past fourteen years the favorable reputation of leaders has depended more on their adherence to norms of unity within the Congress than on political connections to an outside government or party. Increasingly, labor officials have been able to use their reputation within the movement to minimize external threats.

Norms of mutual dependence and accountability aided a leader's survival in 1967, when General Ankrah, chairman of the National Liberation Council, replaced W.B. Otoo, head of the Ghana Motor Union, with a man of his own choosing. The NLC feared a CPP-inspired counter-coup and wanted to set an example by removing the only general secretary to retain his post from the Nkrumah period. The appointee lasted for only one year before losing to Otoo in a union election. The government had miscalculated his internal legitimacy. He was welcomed back to the TUC Executive Board in 1968, and the other general secretaries accepted their former colleague without fear of government retaliation against them.

In another case, intra-union squabbling was more important in the removal of senior union officials than was government hostility toward them. The national executives of the Railway and Ports Workers were, nominally, civil servants on leave to perform union duties. In 1970 they were dismissed from government employment. The contention that their termination was purely a civil service matter was, in effect, contradicted by a notice, sent to the men by the manager of the Railway Authority, saying that they were no longer recognized as union officials for the purposes of negotiation, from the day following their dismissal. B.A. Bentum sent a letter of protest to the manager, with copies to government officials, denouncing the tactic of victimization and noting that only the union had the power to remove the officers: "We will resist to the bitterest end, any attempts by Managements or Government to interfer (sic) either openly or covertly as to who would be elected to the post of a General Secretary of Chairman of any of the National Unions affiliated to the Trades Union Congress of Ghana." The significance of this episode is that the dismissals remained in force, and the protest fizzled, only because the constituency of the ousted men refused to reelect them. Their rivals saw the victimization as a chance to remove unpopular leadership. One of the ex-officers was appointed to a position in the TUC secretariat as a reward for years of service and as a signal to government that the Congress retained the right to judge its own leaders.

## Responding to Challenges

Since 1966 conflict among general secretaries has been lowest when they have been threatened, individually or collectively, from the outside. The 1970 congress at Winneba provides evidence for this generalization. B.A. Bentum was opposed by Mr. K.A. Ossei-Mensah, head of the Transport and Petroleum Workers, who accused him of being too much the bureaucrat, violating the rights of the national unions, and doing nothing to protest the replacement of labor executives by CPP appointees, prior to 1966. He waged an active campaign and gave the impression that his candidacy was favored by the Progress Party. It was widely believed that there had been a blatant attempt by the government to influence the results of the election. Rumors of bribery and threats of violence circulated around the conference hall. Following his defeat, Ossei-Mensah issued a statement of support for Bentum.[10] Norms of accountability and mutual dependence among the leaders were strong enough that he felt obligated to omprove his credibility with his colleagues on the Executive Board.

After the 1970 congress, Prime Minister Busia visited the TUC hall. It was a courtesy call, designed to mend fences after the acrimony surrounding Bentum's election. As the opposition paper, the *Spokesman,* put it: "If you can't beat them, join them." But, the thaw in relations which Busia initiated appears, in retrospect, to have been a tactic to ensure worker discipline by the granting of a few favors. The regime did not dampen its efforts to reduce or eliminate the power of individual union officials whom it distrusted. A "list of enemies" was compiled, and bargaining certificates were denied to some of the unions led by these "enemies," in order to embarrass the leadership and, perhaps, to force their subordinates to remove them.

But neither these tactics nor the threats against unionists led labor leaders to abandon their aggressive advocacy of the rights of workers. In fact, during 1971 government hostility actually increased mutual dependence and accountability of leadership. For example, the general secretary of the Railway and Ports Workers was jailed when he refused to allow members of his union to drive trains during a strike by another group, the Railway Enginmen. In addition, when the speaking tour was organized in August, all general secretaries, including those with Progress Party connections, participated. They spoke to groups of workers who were not exclusively members of their own unions. Even labor executives who had differences with Bentum rallied to his support when he was being vilified in the party press.

The political "smear campaign" was ineffective compared to those waged against Turkson-Orcan and Tettegah in years past. In spite of the dissatisfaction which some unionists expressed concerning Bentum's occasional flirtations with politics, his authority remained trusted and accepted by the great majority of secretaries. They recognized that he had been instrumental in delaying open conflict with the government for almost two years, an achievement which probably prevented the detention of many leaders of the labor movement.

After the sissolution in September 1971, the Congress was reconstituted with the same officials as before. This action, though technically legal, was an obvious challenge to the government, which refused to recognize the new group. All general secretaries continued to work at reduced pay, or for no pay. The Labor College, an educational branch of the TUC's Education and Research Department, became a focal point of multi-union activity, and daily consultations and planning of strategy occurred in the Hall of Trade Unions. The patterns of mutual dependence and accountability were so well established that no TUC general secretary joined the rival national labor center encouraged by the Progress Party, nor did any of the men resign.

The party tried to obtain the support of the labor leaders by telling them that if the PP government should fall, they would lose their positions also. Few of the men believed this argument. Not only did union leaders correctly assess their own appeal to junior officers and workers, but they also felt that they would be able to face an uncertain future by depending on each other.

## Leadership Unity and Congress Autonomy

After the official restoration of the TUC, Colonel Acheampong, the new head of state, addressed the general secretaries. He noted that neither he nor his colleagues on the National Redemption Council would "attempt to dictate to you who (your) leaders would be or where they may be found." This, he said, "we will leave to your own good sense of judgment as the tried and seasoned trade Unionists that you are."[11] In individual unions, this statement was proven technically inaccurate in only one case, the ouster of the executive of the General Transport and Petroleum Workers. However, there were numerous examples of interference in union elections, for example in the Railway and Ports Workers, and criticism of officials in other unions. Prior to every instance of government intervention against an elected leader, his internal legitimacy had been challenged. The degree of his accountability to other union heads, and the extent to which they could depend on him, had been called into question. Thus, whereas outside interference before 1966 contributed to malintegration among the leaders, today the pattern is reversed. A leader with a low reputation among his peers, or the membership, may attract the attention of the government and invite intervention in the union's affairs.

By contrast, the general secretary who is both dependable and accountable may use his high legitimacy within organized labor to discourage government attack. One such official spent several weeks in 1972-73 speaking to workers and criticizing the government's freeze on negotiated wage rates. He noted that the regime would not be angry with him, since he was merely explaining the implications of a regulation which is no secret. In fact, workers in his union and fellow general secretaries would have reacted instantly to any attempt to muzzle him. The commissioner for labor condemned senior Congress officials to their faces, saying that they were behaving irresponsibly, and the government announced that those who encouraged strikes would be tried under NRC Decree 90, an antisubversion measure, with judgment pronounced by military court. But, in spite of threatening language directed against "antisocial practices" by union officials, none was arrested or detained.

Unity among the leaders of the Congress is now at an all-time high and has been sustained since restoration. There has been a decided shift from external to internal support for leadrs' political viability. At the same time, the recent military regimes have been no more effective than their prodecessors in determining the standards by which general secretaries evaluate the performance of their peers.

## LEADERSHIP IDEOLOGY

Over the past 25 years, the ideology of union officials has been influenced by values extant in the larger environment, but it has manifested a distinct pattern of its own, that is, it has always been flexible and oriented toward self defense.

### Political Realism

Unionist ideology in Ghana has never prescribed a naive, "bread-and-butter" posture, opting for better wages and working conditions in ignorance of political realities. Neither, however, has it been synonymous with ideologies of the various parties which have ruled Ghana. The "good union leader" has not been so impressed with political rhetoric that he has ignored his own interests or those of the membership. This leadership orientation was apparent as early as the 1950's, when the alliances which militants, moderates, and "stalwarts" made with their political patrons resulted from more pragmatic considerations than from genuine ideological affinity.

The militant unionists' support of the conservative National Liberation Movement in the 1956 election shows that they were willing to abandon their radical principles in order to gain political advantage. But their earlier ties to the Convention People's Party also reflected ideological flexibility. We have noted that Pobee Biney and the other militants pushed the CPP into the "positive action" campaign in 1950 by declaring a general strike. Yet the militants later supported Nkrumah in part because Biney was assured that his union, the Railway Enginemen, would be recognized by the government, should the CPP come to power.

Just as the militants' initiation of the strike did not reflect co-optation by the CPP, neither did the refusal of the moderates to join it indicate an identity of values with the British. "Apolitical unionism" was not a very attractive ideology for these leaders because the colonial government has given notice that it would not tolerate the independent exercise of union power. The rewards for remaining aloof from politics were few, and the dangers of failing to secure political patrons were many. Therefore, the moderates allied themselves with the British and accepted their aid. They understood, better than their mentors did, that "there is no such thing as a non-political trade union. The question is *whose politics* shall the union follow."[12]

The ideology of the moderates was influenced more by the realities of the union movement in Ghana than by their "western training." The Mineworkers, for example, had already obtained the official recognition required to serve its members, and so felt less need than other unions to ally itself with the CPP. In addition, because the majority of miners were northerners and not particularly interested in southern politics, their leaders were perceptive enough to see that the 1950 strike would be unpopular among them. But, as subsequent events showed, the moderates were not ideologically opposed to political alliances or strikes. They supported a National Labor Party in the 1951 elections in order to avoid the rivalry between the CPP and the UGCC. This left them free to make a post-election alliance with the CPP if one was needed.

There was obviously an ideological affinity between the "stalwarts" and the CPP, but it was apparent as early as 1955, when initial proposals for the New Structure were made, that the "stalwarts' " ideological proclivities were balanced by their pragmatic interests. Labor had to maintain a wing in Parliament "to ensure its views being heard. The political set-up determines the freedom under which the Trade Unions operate," argued Tettegah. The CPP was to be the most important forum for decision making; therefore, the New Structure was essential to develop labor officials of stature and influende, "to take their place in the national leadership of the Convention People's Party."[13] Leaders who were not ideologically committed to the blend of labor organization and party were, nonetheless, anticipating the "financial" status of the larger, national unions. Similarly, much of the opposition to amalgamation wwas more practical than ideological; officers of the larger house unions were already salaried, and they feared losing their positions.

By 1958 a number of unionists were openly identifying themselves with the United Party, the CPP's opposition. But this alliance occurred because of the lessening influence which these leaders were enjoying within the Congress. The ideology of the UP with regard to labor was individualistic; it opposed the New Structure by denying that the collective interests of the unions was legitimate. This point of view was rejected by the leaders of all factions. Militants and moderates were wary of the New Structure and appreciated UP attempts to prevent its implementation. But they realized, especially after 1961, that the ideology of individualism did not dissuade the UP from trying to infiltrate the labor movement, just as the CPP had done. When the Progress Party began to espouse the same ideology in 1968, it was similarly rejected.

We have already noted that, after 1966, leaders concentrated more on administrative than political roles. However, a continuity of leadership ideology between the first and second generations is expressed in the remark of the present-day leader: "Trade unionism is the highest form of politics." Of the 17 present general secretaries, only three were committed CPP activists after the 1961 strike. Ten of the men had no connection with the party when they were junior officers, and four were only marginally, or reluctantly, active in party affairs. Yet 13 of these labor executives believed that the New Structure was a positive advance in presenting the collective interests of workers, in spite of the CPP manipulation between 1961 and 1966.[14] There is a consensus among union leaders that the present strength of the Congress owes much to the marriage of unions and party. In evaluating the progress of their institution, the leaders can make the distinction between the benefits of the New structure and the harm done to the movement by self-seekers and uncritical allegiance to Nkrumahist orthodoxy.

## Political Independence and Socialism

When the present leaders were asked if they subscribed to a particular ideology, 6 of the 17 replied, that they did not. Only three men mentioned socialism explicitly; One said that the strike was a legitimate weapon on the workers' struggle; another summed up his ideology as, "one for all and all for one." Eight general secretaries, by contrast, stated that their unions were primarily (though not exclusively) con-sumption-oriented. Their "ideology" was the advancement of workers' rights through bargaining, and the increased awareness of these rights through education. It is clear that cynicism with regard to political dogma is the legacy of the pre-1966 period. These leaders remember the bonfire of "communist books" following the NLC coup, and the sudden, humiliating change of political loyalty which party-appointed officers affected in a vain attempt to save their careers.

Yet this second generation of Ghanaian unionists is actually no less socialist than the first was. It is aware of the benefits of a labor-political party connection but reluctant to identify itself as socialist, if this means the loss of autonomy to a political party, or a reduced ability of the Congress to defend itself. The "good leader," between 1966 and 1978, kept his union out of politics because there simply were too many dangers in allying with the parties which actually appeared. Over the past fourteen years, unions have not needed a political patron in order to survive, and leaders have had the freedom to develop a flexible ideology of political independence which, in effect, outlined the circumstances under which a political connection could be reestablished.

When the National Liberation Council came to power in 1966 it suspended politics and banned all parties, but the TUC, anticipating a return to civilian rule, proscribed its top officers from becoming officials in any party, in its 1966 constitution. The secretary-general, heads of secretariat departments, secretaries and chairman of national unions, and industrial relations officers were specifically prohibited from taking such positions. Subsequently, however, several junior officers and ex-unionists became active politically, and a number of senior leaders violated the spirit of the constitutional provision, and a few, the letter.

The political resocialization of trade union leaders proceeded slowly; parties were not officially permitted to operate until 1969. However, unionists were approached informally by would-be politicians, operating within the non-partisan yet intensely political environment created by the NLC. For example, in December 1968, nine leaders were selected by the TUC Executive Board to serve as labor's representatives in the national Constituent Assembly, which was charged with drafting the new national constitution.

Between 1967 and 1969, many warnings against political activism appeared in the TUC press; the contacts made with civilian politicos had clearly not convinced the more prominent unionists that they were any more reliable or virtuous than their CPP predecessors. As early as January 1967 it was asserted: "It would be laboring the obvious to say that politics is not the proper calling of a trade union movement," but, the editorial in the *Ghana Workers' Bulletin* went on to say: "it does not follow that politics is of no concern to trade unions or workers." During 1968, additional articles reminded the workers that they were their own best friend. Gullible members could be "tricked" by the promises of politicians, it was argued. The politician "ascends the platform only to sympathise with the worker in his poor conditions of service," but his sympathy and promises would evaporate, it was implied, if workers allowed themselves to be lulled into complacency.[15]

By September 1968, pre-election fever had set in; the warnings became more direct and strident. "Workers must beware and wary of the political wolves! We cannot be fooled again!" Some unnamed "armchair politicians" were said to be goading other "amateur and sponeless politicians" to infiltrate the labor movement. Organizers, the labor press claimed, were posing as TUC men, trying to recruit workers into a so-called "workers political party."[16]

After official campaigning had begun, B.A. Bentum, who had been approached by Busia in the hopes that he would become an active PP supporter, called on workers to be vigilant and to avoid being used again for selfish political ends. In May 1969, the columnist, Labour Owl, wanted to know "whether post-coup politicians realise they are making far too many wild and sugar coated promises?" Do they realize, asked the writer, "that the next civilian government is going to have the unenviable task of solving the problems left by its predecessors?"

Against this background, the TUC convened a conference at Kumasi in July 1969. The purpose of the meeting was to determine the political posture of the unions in the coming election. Three alternatives were presented to the delegates. They could support an existing party, they could form their own party, or they could remain politically neutral. Of the 110 delegates, 108 voted for no alliance with any party.[17] The notion of the workers' political organization was dismissed. Although the great majority of junior and senior officers could support the outcome, it is probable that the lopsided vote reflected the degree to which the general secretaries influenced the delegates from their unions. By the time the conference had convened, the opinion-makers had made such a convincing case that even some general secretaries who had become party officials were reluctant to press their point of view before the delegates.

In spite of these results, the Kumasi conference did not affirm that it had been a mistake to "sell out" to the CPP. Nor had the movement passed from "political" trade unionism to "bread-and-butter" unionism.[18] It is true that a number of general secretaries had been enemies of the CPP and were ideologically opposed to any union-party connection. But a larger group opted for political neutrality on practical, rather than ideological, grounds. Many of these men had been party supporters when they were junior officers, before 1966. They had been watching the campaign, looking for a party whose aims were consonant with labor's, and which also had a reasonable chance to win. Because no party met these criteria, they decided to remain neutral.

In August 1968, the NLC removed its ban on political activity by unionists who had held office before the coup. Only one former official, John Alex Hamah, indicated his intention to form a political party sympathetic to labor. But, as the election neared, his Ghana Democratic Party failed to attract many voters. Hamah had previously failed to unseat B.A. Bentum as secretary-general of the TUC. Now, many union leaders refused to support him as a politician because they believed that a party which limited its appeal to wage-earners would possess too narrow a base to be victorious. A few general secretaries actually favored a labor party with direct connection to the TUC, but they did not attempt to organize one. It was felt that Busia's Progress Party already enjoyed too great an advantage, having been permitted to begin organizing under the aegis of the Centre for Civic Education, a semi-official body charged by the NLC with preparing the country for civilian rule.

Thus, the political neutrality which was proclaimed at Kumasi did not reflect a lack of interest in politics or possible involvement in party organization. A committee of leaders representing the various points of view was appointed to advise the Executive Board concerning the programs and campaigns of existing parties. The leaders had attempted to clarify the relationship between the TUC and politics so that the National Liberation Council would not suspect that they had been co-opted whenever they took a controversial position, and so that their disagreements with the NLC would not be politicized in the national election. However, they also realized that their official neutrality was an imperfect shield against the politicians' attempts to capture the labor movement.

In the following year, 1970, a change in TUC rules was passed, designed to keep B.A. Bentum in office until 1974, rather than 1972, the date of the next scheduled biennial congress. Quadrennial meetings were less expensive, but the delegates acknowledged that the primary motive for the rule change was political, not financial. A 1974 congress would take place *after* the forthcoming national elections. Thus, the rule change was intended to isolate the TUC even further from political campaigning.

In spite of the ideology of political independence, and the military coup which eliminated the possibility of holding national elections in 1973, the issue of a workers' party was actively discussed among the current general secretaries. When questioned about the desirability of an alliance between labor and a political party, all but one of the labor executives had definite opinions, although the NRC had then given no timetable for a return to civilian rule. The men were evenly divided; eight believed that a workers' party was a good idea, and an equal number opposed it. More significant than these raw figures, however, were the reasons given for supporting or rejecting the idea. There was a common perception among the leaders that a political connection can be dangerous for the labor movement. But in view of some, the benefits seemed to outweigh the dangers. Their opinions reflected pragmatism and an absence of ideological rigidity.

Those in opposition noted that workers would make too many demands if a labor party were victorious. It would be even more difficult to convince the membership to follow authorized grievance procedures and to be realistic in their expectations for collective bargaining. Workers, it was claimed, would take the rhetoric of the party too seriously, which would not only provoke hostility from government and business, but lead to presurre to remove labor executives. Unionists who became politicians would lose touch with their peers in the Congress, because the interests of even a labor government and the unions are different enough that it would be impossible to administer the affairs of state without saying "no" to the unions from time to time.

The proponents of a workers' party shared these concerns.

Several remarked that the TUC should not officially support the party, so that labor leaders might be free to criticize it, and so the Congress would not be blamed by the public for the failures of the politicians. The party, they argued, should be financially weaker than organized labor, so that the resources of the unions would support the politicians. This would minimize the kind of corruption that existed during the CPP era. A few general secretaries warned that the TUC could be crippled if it supported a party which could not, or did not, win. The victorious party, they said, would show labor no mercy.

There is no apparent relationship between union leaders' support for a workers' party and their pre-1966 political activities. Some of the men who were opposed to the CPP now believe that a workers' party is desirable, and there are as many former activists who want nothing to do with politics as there are those who remember the "old days" with fondness.

The great majority of leaders did not dismiss the possibility that unions could again become involved in politics. Indeed, because the major objections were practical rather than ideological, there was the likelihood that increasing numbers of unionists could support such a connection, so long as the dangers perceived by all could be reduced. By the end of 1976, the Executive Board, meeting in emergency session, had committed the TUC to socialism, and articulated the place of organized labor in the NRC regime's proposed transition to civilian rule. It noted that the Congress would "only be interested in supporting the formation of *and participation in* a form of government that is dedicated and unalterably committed to the welfare and progress of the masses of people."[19] It called for a "mass movement" to act as the "watchdog of the socialist philosophy," and noted that the mobilization of the people must not be left to the bureaucracy. The Congress proposed a house of representatives, some of whose members would be drawn from "identifiable organizations with effective membership," e.g., the unions.

It will be noted that the idea of a single, mass movement precludes the competition among parties which union leaders have found to be damaging to the interests of labor. In addition, the government, although avowedly socialist, is not identified with the unions, *per se*. Worker demands, as voiced by representatives from the unions, would compete with the demands of other groups, so that rank-and-file discontent with their leaders would not inevitably be encouraged, should the government fail to be convinced. The Congress would not bear sole responsibility for the shortcomings of the government. In effect, these proposals reflect a consensus among the general secretaries in embracing not only socialist ideology, but the ideology of political independence and self defense as well.[20]

## CONTINUITY WITH THE PAST

In 1972, shortly after the restoration of the TUC, a struggle took place between supporters of the acting secretary-general and head of the Argicultural Workers, A.M. Issifu, and backers of John Tettegah. This episode is unique in the history of the Congress; no other challenge to incumbent leadership has been so serious. This division among the union executives appears to contradict the consensus in leadership ideology which we have documented above. Actually, it was not evidence of an ideological split. It was, in fact, a sign that many of the second-generation leaders were not ready to repudiate the history of the labor movement. Tettegah's appeal was more romantic than ideological.

Based on the government's assurance that the 1965 labor law would be repealed, and that thus the TUC would become a purely voluntary organization with no special status under law, all the general secretaries agreed, early in 1972, that there would be a need to reconstitute the TUC and that a new election for secretary-general had to be held. B.A. Bentum had left the country to take a position with the International Labor Organization. The Executive Board issued an invitation for him to return. At the same time, a few union heads made overtures to John Tettegah, who had been in voluntary exile, asking him to come home and compete with Bentum. Later these men were to claim that the offer to Tettegah was extended half-heartedly, but it is likely that they were reluctant to see Bentum retain his position because they blamed him, in some measure, for the dissolution. The fact that he had left the country was also a point against him; Bentum had not been present to bolster the low morale of the union executives at the end of 1971.

Bentum decided not to return. As soon as his decision became known, some of Tettegah's backers asserted that Acting Secretary-General Issifu himself had asked Tettegah to contest the election. Resistance to Tettegah began to coalesce. There was considerable sentiment that the new top officer should come from the ranks of the general secretaries, and that they should show confidence in each other by electing one of their peers. At an Executive Board meeting one leader argued that Tettegah was ineligible to run because the TUC constitution barred him. Opposition speakers retorted that he had fled the country under duress and that he had never resigned from the movement. Tettegah himself cleared the air somewhat by announcing that no one had invited him either to return to the country or to be secretary-general, and that he had merely decided to come home because of the change in government occasioned by the NRC coup. The opinion of the majority of the Board was that, as both Tettegah and Issifu were interested in contesting the election, they should be allowed to do so.

"After this meeting," one unionist reported, "the struggle for the Secretary-Generalship became tense. The general secretaries were divided into two groups." Leaders attempted to determine where each group stood on the issue of the election. Active campaigning took place. Superficially, there were ideological differences between the candidates. It was assumed that Tettegah would be more activist and militant in his role as head of the TUC, less likely to shrink from confrontation with employers or government. It was felt that he would use his influence among the rank and file to convince them that they should take part in Ghana's next civilian regime. By contrast, it was felt that Issifu would oppose direct labor participation in government.

However, there is evidence that the supposed ideological differences were not so important in the struggle as Tettegah's veteran status, the personalities of the candidates, and the tactics which the two sides adopted. Issifu, after all, had worked with Tettegah in the All-African Trade Union

Federation; he was not lacking in socialist credentials. The main argument against him was his comparative inexperience. His supporters were upset because opponents had spread rumors about his character which were found to be baseless. Issifu's supporters thought that Tettegah and his backers were being financed by "outside sources," but no one could discover their identity. Personal loyalty was the basis for the support of Tettegah by the six union heads who favored his candidacy at the start of the campaign. No significant relationship was found between leaders' degree of commitment to socialist ideology and their decision to back Tettegah.

When, as the result of lobbying, three additional general secretaries were persuaded to support Tettegah (making a total of nine), even some Issifu supporters believed that the reconstituted Congress would defeat Issifu. The NRC, desiring continuity in national labor leadership and aware of Tettegah's reputation for mobilizing workers against unpopular government decisions, decided that the election should not take place. By refusing to alter the 1965 labor law, it eliminated the necessity for the campaign.[21] Tettegah's support began to erode, in part because it had not been based on a hard-line ideological split. By the middle of 1973, one source estimated that a majority once again favored Issifu. The minority which switched allegiance were not automatically reacting to government pressure. They had changed their opinion of Issifu, who "had done all that could be done" to lead the movement after the restoration.

At an Executive Board meeting, the chairman "expressed his inability to settle the matter of the election as it should be, owing to subsequent developments." But the members contended that "there appeared to be unity among them and that disunity had died a natural death." After agreeing to educate their rank and file accordingly, the board enjoyed "light refreshment" and a libation was poured. No recriminations occurred as a result of the campaign. The great majority of officers were genuinely relieved that the election had not taken place, although the government's *de facto* interference was resented. When Tettegah was subsequently arrested and detained, none of the general secretaries was implicated by association with him. Loyalty to Tettegah, and to the memory of political activism which he represented, had not prevented a unified response to NRC rule or inhibited the attainment of unionist objectives.

## CONCLUSION

The mutual trust which Congress leaders show today is the result, not only of commonly held norms, but common values as well. Officers do share duties and responsibilities, but also an ideology of unionism and political independence which has been shaped over the past 25 years, particularly since 1966. Pragmatic ideology serves to reduce leaders' suspicion of each other because it legitimates, and encourages, compromise. The avoidance of ideological splits within the Congress is one of the major sources of its institutional strength. Because there has not been a battle for the supremacy of a particular set of political ideas, there has been a minimum of frustration and resentment which have, in other African countries, caused self-seeking and disloyal behavior. Officers' positive valuation of the labor movement is not maintained by dogma, but by the unions' capacity to provide program and personal goal attainment, and by their past success in meeting challenges from the environment.

## CHAPTER VII

# The Reaction of Workers
# and a Wider Public

In Chapter III we noted that the Trades Union Congress has facilitated conflict resolution in Ghanaian society, resulting in confidence being placed in the unions by business and government. This chapter examines the reputation of the TUC among workers, and among those who are not its immediate clientele. The commitment of members to unions has always been a function of the personality and skill of leadership, combined with the actual performance of organized labor in negotiations. However, over the past fourteen years, union members' overall commitment has increased because the unions' bargaining position vis-a-vis employers and the state has improved, and because TUC leaders are no longer obligated to share credit for their achievements with politicians. Similarly, public opinion of the labor movement has become more favorable since 1966. It has helped to assure the permanence of unions and the consistency of TUC ideology. Unions have been able to draw on a reservoir of public support when they have come under attack from business or government. In fact, many of the basic performances and priorities of Ghanaian society have become identified with the TUC, and the public expects that the Congress will articulate these values.

## WORKER ALLEGIANCE TO LEADERS

Rank-and-file opinion of labor executives has not depended on the leadership roles they have emphasized. The "labor fighters" certainly earned the respect of their membership.

Similarly, many "stalwart" politician-unionists were popular, at least within the confines of house unions. The concentration on administrative roles, especially since 1966, has not discouraged worker support. What, then, are the sources of worker allegiance? We shall examine four potential answers: exploitation of leaders' ethnic identity; personal contact with membership; demonstrations of courage; and effectiveness in obtaining wage and fringe benefits.

*Ethnicity*

Tribalism has permeated modern political, religious, and voluntary organizations throughout Africa, so it is logical to look for its effects on the appeal of leaders to workers. In some countries, trade unions have been little more than extensions of tribal organizations transplanted to an urban environment, where leaders of the same ethnic background, in effect, replace village chiefs. Workers accept direction, and a place at the bottom of a representative structure which appears modern, only because of common ethnic ties with the unionists.

In Ghana, tribal consciousness is strong, reflecting marked differences in primary socialization, but this has not led to the violent confrontations apparent in other countries. Regional loyalties among the Ewe of the Volta Region or the Ashanti of the Kumasi area have not led to institutionalized, intertribal conflict in modern times. Explanations for the accommodations which the larger tribes have made to each other are many. Nationalism has proven more significant than separatist movements, which have appeared from time to time among the Ga, Ewe, and Ashanti. Relatively good communication and transportation have prevented regional isolation. And a number of national organizations, including the Convention People's Party and the TUC itself, have been used by many tribal groups as vehicles for self-improvement.

The earliest unions in Ghana were regionally based and therefore largely homogeneous, ethnically. In Accra and Kumasi, leaders of house unions frequently had to rely on tribal loyalty to attract and hold membership. However, the larger unions prior to the New Structure — those in the mines, railways, public works, and utilities — contained a substantial ethnic mix from the beginning. After 1958, ethnicity was no longer a factor in the composition of industrial, national unions.

Because of cultural differences and varying degrees of exposure to western education, the Ghanaian labor force has been differentiated by tribal affiliation to a significant degree. The Ewe became craftsmen and artisans. The northern peoples were attracted to day labor and largely unskilled positions, and the Fanti and Ashanti, being the most highly educated, have dominated the clerical ranks. But Ghana's unions, organized primarily by industry rather than trade, have combined all of these ethnic groups. In such a situation, if any preference is shown by officers, it is as — or more likely — to be based on members' educational differences as on their tribal differences. Blue collar workers may feel that their leaders, drawn from the white collar membership, are neglecting their needs. But this sentiment has appeared only occasionally, and has been related to inter-ethnic hostility only at the branch level, where tribal minorities are more visible and where officials are tempted to use their ethnicity to reinforce inadequate organizational skills.

At the national level, the impact of ethnicity on securing worker support for leaders has been negligible. The secretary-general of the Congress is a northerner. There are Ga, Ewe, and Fanti union leaders. Many general secretaries have subordinates of different ethnic backgrounds, and there has been no significant identification of any one union with a particular tribe. Membership and branch leadership is too heterogenious, and spread over too wide a geographic area, for worker loyalty to a union to be based on tribe. In addition, there are several other criteria which workers use to determine the worth of their leaders, each of which, if not met, has been more important than ethnicity in provoking discontent.

## Personal Contact with Workers

There have been few reliable surveys of worker opinion, but fragmentary evidence suggests that workers place a high value on personal, consistent contact with national labor leaders, and that they would like to see more of it. Part of this positive valuation is cultural in nature. The leader appears as the "wise father," giving advice and answering questions. The illiterate worker may not understand all of what is said, or at least not its wider implications, but he is impressed by the aura of power which surrounds the national leaders and which is consciously cultivated by some. If the leader has come from Accra, his reputation is enhanced; many workers still believe that Accra men are the best educated. If they discover that the speaker has been abroad, they may be even more impressed.

A commissioner for labor under the NRC told a gathering of unionists: "The expensive cars . . . which you ride in and which most employees cannot afford to buy can only help to alienate the rank and file . . . (workers) complain of your extravagance and ostentation."[1]

But for the great majority of workers the new class position of the officers has merely reflected the dignity of the union. There are, of course, a few celebrated episodes of local-level resentment against national union leadership, and some of these have been violent.[2] However, protest, when it has occurred, invariably has been dirchted against officials who were blatantly inept, corrupt, or lacking in personal courage.

Branch leaders rarely receive the deferential treatment accorded their superiors. Their contact with workers may be intimate, but they are less able to manipulate the trappings of wisdom and authority. In most unions the blue-collar membership accepts the direction of its better-educated local officials but does not confer celebrity status upon them. On the other hand, workers may be genuinely flattered by the appearance of union leaders or secretariat officials. The chairman of one national union told his audience, "we are not gods," and he encouraged workers to question the advice of their superiors. Then the meeting was adjourned and the senior officerrs took refreshment, symbolically, at a single table set high on a dais, overlooking the participants.

It is apparent that the national leaders whose attention to administrative duties precludes frequent visits to the shop floor may benefit nonetheless from the prestige of office. A modicum of popularity may result from only limited attention to internal, "grass-roots" politics. In many African countries, a leader's political position within his union has been so precarious that, if he has left the country, he has been immediately replaced. This has never happened in Ghana.

However, the image of "wise father" must be carefully cultivated. The "parent" cannot neglect his "children" for long without losing some respect. Workers become impatient with union leaders who consistently talk above their heads. Culturally, in Ghana, obedience to those in positions of authority is tempered by norms which legitimate action against them if they fail to work in the interests of "the people." Thus, the universal demand by general secretaries for reliable automobiles stems not merely from a desire to affect the trappings of high office. Trappings are useful, but not sufficient to maintain the loyalty of the membership. The automobile is essential because it also allows frequent contact with many workers. If substantive two-way communication takes place as a result, this is more important than a few more formal visits, marked by their ceremony and novelty.

*Demonstrated Courage*

Ghanaian workers have shown consistently that they respond positively to demonstrations of courage on the part of labor officials. It was the fortitude of Tettegah and Bentum, rather than any extensive and persistent contact with the rank and file, which earned these secretary-generals their reputations. The "big man" of wealth, power, and influence within government has been revered in Ghana, but even more important to his popularity is whether he risked his reputation or personal safety to attain his high position. Those union officials who were appointed, rather than elected, during 1964-65 were unpopular not only because they were foisted on the membership by the CPP, but because they were seen as "stooges" who had advanced to the top at little risk. Their positions were safe so long as they mouthed the appropriate slogans.

Respect for courage was apparent in the days of nationalist agitation. Nkrumah's display of his "prison graduate" cap was political dynamite. The jailing of the militants Biney, Woode, and Ocran also aided their reputations. However, even moderate officials, who were not imprisoned, saw value in risking the government's displeasure. In 1955, for example, leaders of the Mineworkers refused to submit grievances to a government tribunal voluntarily. Unity within the union was increased when, after resisting, they submitted only when ordered.[3]

John Tettegah stated that if leaders' views did not reflect those of workers, the latter would lose confidence in their officers, and the TUC would disappear. But workers' confidence in Tettegah was not based exclusively on their perception that his views were identical to their own. In fact, between 1960 and 1964, Tettegah wavered between the position of articulate spokesman for the rank and file, and party apologist. For example, he actually denounced the 1961 strike. His reputation was, however, based on the recognition that when he did challenge the CPP he did so at considerable personal risk. "We would expect reasonable demands submitted by us to be put into practice without being whittled down," he argued.[4] The removal of Tettegah was mandated by his refusal to be intimidated by the party watchdogs who had been assigned to the secretariat.

Tettegah's ouster was accomplished without arrest or trial, which would have turned his case into a *cause celebre* and further enhanced his reputation as a man of courage. Tettegah was detained following the coup, and again in 1974, although he had not held an official position in the TUC for ten years. Each arrest has merely added to his credentials and given him legendary status in some quarters.

The rank and file's suspicion appears to be aroused when senior union officials begin to echo government consistently. General secretaries lost credibility during the 1961 strike; junior officers disobeyed their superiors, partly out of principle, but also because they too would have been accused of "selling out" had they not led the strike. A union which cannot oppose the government is considered impotent. During 1967-68, the wildcat strikes led by local leadrs served to maintain the loyalty of many workers. For them, courage and action were synonymous. Few members appreciated the degree to which the general secretaries, by following regulations and refusing to sanction illegal strikes, were aiding their welfare.

Under the Progress Party regime, many top leaders found themselves in an adversary role vis-a-vis government; predictably, worker morale was high. Resistance culminated with the speaking tour in August 1971. Many leaders suspected that the government would be displeased and would take drastic action against the Congress. "But, it had to be done anyway," said one union leader, "or else we no longer would be enjoying the respect of the workers." The PP attempted to discredit B.A. Bentum by asking: "How can somebody who commands a fleet of cars, owns a super-modern restaurant and supervises over a fat bank account have the cheek to talk of the plight of workers unless he is a brazen-faced hypocrite and power drunk?"[5] But workers, in refusing to support the party's position, showed that they believed the amount of Bentum's assets was not associated with corrupt behavior and that they believed him when he claimed that he had not "sold out" to the politicians.

Several contemporary leaders have shown that they are in touch with the historic appeal of men of courage by averring that, as they have told their wives and families, they are prepared for arrest at any time. But personal charisma among officers has been absent in recent years. In a relatively benign political environment, opportunities for demonstrating fortitude are rare. More significant in predicting the longevity of the Congress is the fact that the primary standard which workers use to evaluate their leaders seems to be universal, and that is success in winning concessions from management.

## Achieving Unionist Objectives

The record of TUC officials in obtaining higher salaries and improved working conditions, and in influencing government to adopt policies favorable to labor, is vital to their popularity. Branch leaders may win votes temporarily by making excessive demands of management and promising workers more than they can deliver. But worker allegiance to today's national officers has depended on making steady progress toward more modest goals.

1948-1966.    Before an explicit connection was established between the Convention People's Party and the unions, worker evaluation of union leaders was a direct process, unfiltered by the agitation for independence and the expected "promised land." However, in the decade after 1948, attention was focused away from wages and working conditions. Much of the reputation of labor leaders was based on their influence within the CPP or their courageous defiance of the British. Prior to 1961, it was undoubtedly the popularity of Nkrumah that sustained the enthusiasm of many workers, even more than the popularity of the unionists themselves.

The New Structure enhanced the power of the unions, but the legitimacy of many senior officials depended more on the party than on the people they were representing. Moreover, before 1966, the program of the Congress was politicized. Unionist objectives were identified closely with those of the party. The overlapping official policies make it difficult to measure the impact of management concessions on the popularity of labor leaders. When the needs of workers were served by unionists, the CPP absorbed much of the credit.

During the CPP era, TUC officials tried to maintain program integrity, but they found that obligatory participation in political mobilization and the inculcation of worker discipline often conflicted with the goals of rationalizing industrial relations and bettering wages and working conditions. For example, Africans replaced expatriates on the staff of the Workers' College for the training of labor cadets as early as 1959, but, subsequently, officials were required by the party to take courses at the Winneba Ideological Institute. In addition, although the CPP initially embraced Congress objectives, it showed, after 1961, that it was also free to ignore workers' economic grievances. It made use of the workers' demands to criple its political opposition. But it also crushed the 1961 strike without considering seriously the "gut issues" which had inspired it.

It is impossible to accurately measure the appeal of general secretaries whose organizations workers were compelled to join in the early 1960's. Many members, the TUC admitted subsequently, "did not enjoy any benefits by their association" with it.[6] Yet these leaders changed the consciousness of their workers; they emphasized the important role of labor in national development, and they preached the fundamentals of unionism along with the socialist rhetoric. Workers who were inactive in union affairs, or who had not chosen to be union members, nonetheless participated in patterned behavior, payment of dues, occasional strikes, demonstrations and rallies. Through these experiences workers learned what they had the right to expect from their leaders, even if the expectation was not always fulfilled.

John Tettegah symbolizes the difficulties faced by labor executives in pursuing unionist goals within the context of the TUC-CPP alliance. He was active in CPP affairs and an ambassador extraordinary and minister plenipotentiary, but he was perhaps the only nationally prominent figure whose position owed as much to the support of his clients as to the CPP. Enjoying greater internal union support than most other "stalwart" leaders, he was thus insulated from government attacks until 1964. But his intimate connection with the regime sometimes forced him to compromise program objectives. Even when the government showed blatant disrespect and disregard for labor matters, he claimed, it was best for unions to show "seasoned restraint and tacit patience."[7] Unionists still remain divided on the issue of where Tettegah's primary loyalty lay, since he made frequent attempts to maneuver within the CPP, using the TUC as the vehicle.

The major accomplishments of Tettegah and his colleagues were obtaining the power for unions to bargain collectively, to receive dues by check-off, and to force recalcitrant groups to join the Congress. But these successes did not, in themselves, inspire positive valuation of TUC leadership. In fact, many workers (as well as junior union officers and businessmen) viewed the attainment of these goals primarily as a means for the CPP to consolidate its control, rather than as an advance for organized labor as a counterweight to government. Leaders' independent power was most evident in negotiations over fringe benefits, instead of the sizable wage increases which the membership desired.

Therefore, the survival of the Congress after the National Liberation Council coup should not be attributed to the attainment of unionist objectives by the first generation of TUC leaders. Rather, as we have suggested, it was the result of the supportive legal environment, which remained

unchanged, and patterns of exchange of resources which had
been established previously. In addition, survival was
predicated on the availability of experienced junior officers,
who were promoted beginning in 1966. Although many
workers left the unions, the great majority remained. This is,
in part, evidence for the respect earned by middle-level
leaders which could not have been elicited by compulsory
unionism alone.

1966-1978. One of the objectives of the second generation
of Ghanaian union heads was to fight for the TUC's priorities
while maintaining its integrity.[8] This goal has, in large
measure, been attained. The Congress has been able to resist
politicization of its program and to prevent politicians from
exploiting strikes. The power of the unions has been
enhanced. Credit for these achievements has devolved on the
new officers. Labor leaders are, after all, "organization men,"
changing as the character of their institution changes. In its
beginnings, the Congress was, perhaps, a more effective
means to upward mobility for its leaders than an effective
representative of workers' economic interests. By 1970, those
days were gone. Workers expected their leaders to be honest
and efficient because these qualities increased the likelihood
that their needs would be met. As C. Wright Mills noted:
"regardless of autocracy in the unions, in the long run the
members will either destroy the leader or they will get some
leadership out of him."[9]

The angry response of many of the rank and file to the
dissolution of the TUC in September 1971, even more than the
favorable reception of the speaking tour, indicates that they
believed they would be worse off without a strong union
center and without their current leadership. In Takoradi,
there was a general strike led by the Railway and Ports orkers
and Enginemen. More than four thousand workers marched in
a demonstration in defiance of a police order. The port was at
a standstill for five days. Omnibus Services employees
stopped work in Accra. But, in the face of depleted union
treasuries and military protection given strikebreakers, the
disturbances ceased. Three thousand workers jeered
representatives of the Takoradi Council of Labor when the
settlement was announced.[10]

Another test of workers' confidence in their leaders' ability to reach unionist goals was provided by the post-dissolution exercise of signing up members for continued dues deduction. The process was slow in the majority of unions, although several general secretaries reported branches which proudly submitted 100 percent membership rolls. There is evidence that the sluggish response of workers was caused, not by dissatisfaction with leadership, but because it was thought to be politically imprudent to identify oneself as an "active" unionist. After restoration all union executives decided to ask memebers to sign check-off forms, although legally, with the repeal of Act 383, they were not required to do so. Their faith in their own appeal was well placed. After only one year, even with seriously depleted staffs, almost all unions reported recouping their lost members.

Approximately 35 percent of unionized workers are not currently covered by collective agreements. It is difficult to assess the degree to which these members, in particular, respect the ability of their officers. There have been many worker complaints and appeals to the commissioners for labor under the military governments of the 1970's, bypassing union channels. Perhaps workers merely think the government is more approachable than their unions, or perhaps labor executives are perceived as ineffectual by some members. But it is undeniable that a great proportion of the rank and file recognizes the goal-attaining potential of its leaders.

## COMMITMENT OF MEMBERS TO UNIONS

Many workers who have joined labor organizations since 1958 have not done so because of real, personal commitment. However, as they have participated in the activities of their groups for an extended period, they have come to have a more favorable opinion of them. The proportion of veteran members is rising, and, in some families, a tradition of trade unionism has been initiated. Workers have learned that they have the right to expect from their *unions* as well as from their leaders. They have reacted positively when the general principles of

TUC ideology were actualized in the program of the labor movement.

We have seen that union leaders have developed codes of fairness and truthfulness in their dealings with each other, withut which their groups could not function so effectively. Similarly, there are standards for workers' conduct. Merely telling them that the union stands for what is "right, fair and just" and opposes what is "unfair, unjust and wrong" has not effected a change in consciousness. Rather, values and action continually reinforce each other. Workers follow a unionist code of behavior because they are rewarded for doing so; what is good for the union is also good for them. For example, the union bureaucracy supports the utilization of the chain of command in voicing complaints. Officials are reluctant to help members of their grievances are unnustified and cannot protect them if they violate the terms of the collective agreement.

Although Ghanaian unions are not "life-embracing," their welfare functions affect workers away from the work place. This also encourages a positive valuation of the labor movement. Unions, and the TUC itself, sponsor social gatherings, visits, dances, and sporting events. Opportunities for making friends, as well as obtaining job training and medical care, are part of the benefits of union membership which workers have enjoyed.

*Assimilation of Unionist Attitudes*

As worker commitment to the unions has strengthened, the rank and file has come to identify with a set of beliefs and attitudes supporting worker organization. Among these are the inherent dignity of labor; solidarity and equality; and the validity of cooperative, rather than individual, economic action.[11] In many cases, unions have secured fair treatment for workers who would otherwise have been ignored or humiliated by employers because of their youth, low level of skill, or tribal affiliation. The age of the participants is irrelevant in negotiations, as is ethnicity, and the union which protects its members from being bullied or treated in a paternalistic or patronizing manner gives them confidence and self-respect. For the worker who confronts his better-educated employer across the bargaining table, "solidarity" is more than a slogan. The right to organize has gotten him where he is. Many who have left unionized enterprises in an attempt to better their individual position have learned, first hand, the value of cooperative economic action. In one survey, all of the ex-unionists in a Ghanaian-owned company were anxious to rejoin. They complained of "the ascriptive nature of promotions, poor working conditions, (and) authoritarian management."[12]

Perhaps because survival in traditional society depended on sharing responsibilities and cooperation with one's neighbors, selfishness and egotistic, interpersonal conflict are condemned in Ghanaian culture. As a prominent trade unionist noted, "Our drive toward material and physical needs has been individualistic and has thus outstripped our search for the spiritual values of men and life itself."[13] Yet, for workers, conflict with management is justified because, through their unions, they are taking collective action as their ancestors did. In public, union leaders may exhort them to increase productivity, but, in private, they are told to make sure they get what is rightfully coming to them.

*Acceptance of Union Ideology*

Several labor leaders reported that the rank and file does not appreciate the finer points of ideology, and that it is "for officers, not workers." In their opinion, the membership does not remember much of what it was taught before 1966, except that the ideologues both in the party and in the unions became wealthy. It is hardly surprising the Nkrumahist ideology was not internalized by workers, since it contained conflicting messages. They were praised for being revolutionaries, but condemned when production lagged. They were told that employers were their enemy, except when the state paid their wages. They were exhorted "to accept some restriction of consumption," but, as a contemporary unionist argued, "the demand for 'sacrifice to builld' " was used as a "justification to make the low income workers of this country poorer."[14]

Many leaders reported that the rank and file conceives of ideology as something foreign and "not suitable" for Ghana. As one put it, "Workers are the best judges of how well off

they are, and regardless of rhetoric, they will react negatively
to high prices and poor working conditions." Other officers
indicated that rhetoric is useful in organizing, if the goals it
encourages workers to attain are general. As one said, "we
shall overcome" is an immensely popular slogan among the
rank and file, "but it doesn't mean throwing out the
bourgeoisie, just overcoming our troubles."

Formal systems of ideas have been discarded. The rank and
file does not possess the skill to resolve inconsistencies in
ideology. However, the attitudes which workers have
assimulated as a result of union membership and activity are
consistent with those of their present leaders. Moreover,
many workers have shown acceptance of specific elements in
the ideology in their persistent affirmation of the right to
strike, and in their appreciation of the history of the labor
struggle in Ghana.

Strikes in the 1940's and 1950's served as models for the
Sekondi workers in 1961. In turn, during the last decade, the
1961 strike has been "accorded the status of an heroic attempt
to maintain the genuine principles of Ghanaian unionism."[15]
indeed, the strikers had internalized important values which
were then part of TUC doctrine, namely solidarity, equality,
and one which was added only after 1966: "the right of the
workers in the last resort to withhold their labor by concerted
action."[16]

Many of these who participated in the wave of work
stoppages between 1967 and 1970 and the abortive general
strike of 1971 were veterans of prior walkouts, and adopted
the identical rationale, in consonance with TUC ideology. But
even newcomers to the labor movement learn of the heroes
and tactics of the past four decades in union folklore. A
unionist culture is perpetuated, not only by participating in
strikes, but by retelling stories of defiance and courage: the
brave engine driver who would not "sell out" as the clerks and
artisans had done; the stooges who betrayed the Railway
Union in 1947; the miners who stood watch on the first night of
their strikes "as if they were shepherds watching the flock,
waiting for the Angel of Heaven."[17]

Most unions are not so venerable as the Railwaymen and
Miners. They are products of the New Structure. But, if many

workers cannot recall much from the distant past of the labor movement, the less romantic memory of more recent occurrences is nonetheless a part of their value system. The knowledge of "how it was" before the collective agreement was signed inspires solidarity in the present. It has been noted that self-control and loyalty among members is essential if unions are to achieve "the maturity and stability that is needed to negotiate successfully and to uphold voluntary agreements on a regular and uninterrupted basis."[18] The fact that collective bargaining is a reality in Ghana is a good indication that workers can see the logic behind the codes of conduct, attitudes, and values of unionism. It is said that such self-discipline comes only with years of struggle. To this we may respond that, although the labor movement in Ghana is young, its members and their families have often struggled just to obtain the necessities of life.

## PUBLIC OPINION OF ORGANIZED LABOR

Finally, we examine a more diffuse measure of reputation, the esteem in which unions are held by those without firsthand knowledge of TUC program or ideology.

### Union Goals and Public Values

In 1971 a pamphlet published by the Centre for Civil Education noted the major concerns of a generation of Ghanaians, union members and nonmembers alike:

. . . life in the traditional setting and few years of the colonial era (has) not changed significantly for the better. Things are rather becoming more and more difficult for our generation. The cost of living continues to rise and the population increase is forcing families to spend more than they used to spend, and this in turn, stifles the desire and reduces the ability to save towards the future. Under such a situation there is always a feeling of insecurity, among workers and the whole public. Above all, the social changes taking place are making the immediate family grow more in importance than the

extended family. This means that one can no longer
be dependent on the extended family.[19]
For the preceding 25 years, the TUC had advocated policies
designed to reduce the personal insecurities associated with
rapid social change, not only by supporting a workable social
security scheme, but also by encouraging price controls and
workers' savings cooperatives. By 1971 the Congress's
position on these and other matters of direct concern to the
general public had become well known. However, this process
did not occur easily or quickly.

The historical analysis presented the previous chapters
provides much of the explanation for initial public cynicism
concerning the unions. During the twilight of the colonial era,
labor did benefit from being identified with the nationalist
movement, but the image of unionists as "strike mongers,"
reinforced by colonial government intransigence and
inexperience of some early union leaders, plagued the TUC.
Organized labor did act as a pressure group, advocating a
better standard of living for workers in the early Nkrumah
years; however, this was not widely recognized in Ghana
itself. During the 1950's the high cost of living was associated
with colonial rule; therefore, the coming of independence for
Ghana, rather than the efforts of the unions, was seen as more
valuable in bringing prices down, even by many union
members. In addition, the unions' frantic search for patrons,
both in and out of government, led to their being regarded as
mouthpieces for policies which had been decided by more
powerful organizations and individuals.

The promises which Nkrumah made to the Congress in 1960
— housing, education, leisure time, and purchasing power —
might have enhanced the reputation of the TUC as a pressure
group, were it not for the economic squeeze in which Ghana
found itself. The public saw these promises as remaining
largely unfulfilled; there was "widespread popular opposition
to the development policies of the CPP regime." Thus, the
public reputation of the TUC suffered because of the marriage
of unions and party between 1961 and 1966. It became
increasingly dependent on the acceptance of a party which had
"declared war on itself" as a popular organization.[20]

The 1961 general strike, which opposed a National

Development levy, focused attention on the favorable position of workers vis-a-vis farmers. Cocoa growers were already contributing about one-fifth of their income to the public chest in "voluntary" deductions. Therefore, the 1961 strike resulted in an unfavorable opinion of unionized workers among farmers, who saw union members as a labor aristocracy wanting to "chop" more for itself. Official union opposition to the strike was inconsistent, came too late, and was too obviously the result of government pressure, to improve the reputation of the Congress in rural areas.

However, in urban communities, particularly Sekondi-Takoradi, the strike was popular among market women, unskilled non-union members, and even some of the unemployed. There was an air of excitement and pride throughout the city; morale was high, and railway workers were heroes. "The unionized workers and other groups among the urban masses were united by a common sense of social injustice."[21] By contrast, because the TUC opposed the strike, its reputation as a national organization declined.

It is significant that the crude rhetoric and threats which showed the hostility of the government toward the strikers did little to win it the loyalty of the Ghanaian public. The party purge following the strike was merely a scapegoating exercise. No amount of venom directed against the extravagance and excess wealth of the few ministers could disguise the fact that real grievances of union members and nonmembers concerning falling real wages and rising prices had not been addressed. "Austerity," for CPP officials, meant that each was "limited" to two homes and two cars! "Workers could see that it was the party boys and not they who had gained the fruits of the political kingdom."[22] But, between 1961 and 1966, many non-unionists came to realize this as well. Farmers whose economic position continued to deteriorate joined workers in welcoming the 1966 coup with a sigh of relief. Some awareness of national, in addition to purely sectional, problems was the inevitable result of "ties of common antecedents and traditions." As John Tettegah had noted, ". . . there is hardly a worker in this country whose closest kin are not peasants."[23]

After 1966, the Congress began to identify itself as a battler against a variety of the grievances which affected nonmembers no less than unionists. These included low pay, poor transportation, inefficiency in government, and victimization of black workers by white, Levantine, or Indian superiors. Although it was trying to eliminate suspicion, during 1966-68, that it was a haven for former CPP supporters, the TUC still advocated a balanced view of the Nkrumah years, in sharp contrast to the paranoia and knee-jerk anti-CPP position of the NLC and PP governments. Its view that Nkrumah was a great world leader, that he was a courageous fighter for independence and freedom for blacks, and that pan-Africanism, for which he struggled, was a worthy aim, was undoubtedly closer to public opinion in Ghana than the position of the soldiers and politicians.

The Congress did, however, take the view that, in domestic affairs, Nkrumah's record was flawed. In particular, it emphasized Ghana's hugh foreign debt and continuing inflation. In its criticism, the TUC set a standard for national economic success, regardless of the regime in power. The Congress desired the image of an independent critic, no longer under the thumb of any government. Yes, economic conditions under Nkrumah were poor, but they had continued to be so, argued union spokesmen. Between 1970 and 1971, for example, the cost of living rose 16 percent. The cost of locally produced goods was rising even faster than imported commodities. These criticisms were not inspired exclusively by a selfish interest of workers. In fact, the consumer price index had increased more for rural than for urban consumers.[24]

*The Voice of the People*

Prior to 1966, John Tettegah had tried to impress upon union members the idea that their goals were identical to the rural majority. He noted that "the workers and peasants belong to that big group . . . who have to earn their living by their own hard work." This rhetorical appeal was rooted in Marxist ideology but was unsupported by any concrete unionist effort to compromise with farmers over economic issues. Under the CPP umbrella, unions would not have been permitted to act as spokesmen for rural interests. Before

1966, popular identification with the aims and values of unions *per se* was confined to a miniscule group of ideologues. The general public could not separate unionism from its "Siamese Twin," the CPP, with which unanimity was enforced. After 1966, however, the independent status of the TUC allowed it to build a more permanent and genuine positive image. A.M. Issifu noted that trade unionism had assumed a role far greater than any person could imagine, "within the narrow confines of a national union."[25]

Not from exclusively ideological motives, but also to avoid the criticism that it was making its demands on the basis of sectional selfishness, the Congress came to speak for a wider working class. An editorial in the *Ghana Workers' Bulletin* indicated that "trade union action with regard to wages should be governed by a supreme concern for economic development, without prejudice to the needs of workers."[26] "As members of the community with an interest in the whole society," unionists accepted responsibility for the elaboration of national planning, "as well as the distribution of its accomplishments."[27]

The Progress Party regime, as it turned out, could not live with an independent "Voice of the People" such as the TUC now represented. In September 1971, the party decided that the government itself ought to be the major channel for public grievances, spokesman for national aspirations, and allocator of rewards. A PP minister put it succinctly: "The government will not sit by and allow itself to be dictated to by the T.U.C. Either the Government will take the T.U.C. on or the T.U.C. will have to take the Government on. We have pledged to rule and will see whether it is the Government which has the power to rule or the T.U.C."[28]

Unions' claims to speak for a wider public than their members had appeared consistently since the initiation of the New Structure; these were not surprising and would not have upset PP leaders so much if they had not perceived that, perhaps for the first time in Ghanaian history, the rhetoric was close to reality. When B.A. Bentum demanded cancellation of the proposed payroll tax in the 1971 budget, he did so not only on the grounds that workers "have made and are continuing to make a lot of sacrifices." He reminded the government that, in addition, thousands were unemployed, and that the burden of feeding, clothing, and housing them fell on the wage-earner, more than the government. It was a statement with which it was difficult to argue.

## National Debate on the TUC

Is the role of national spokesman which the TUC has arrogated to itself considered legitimate? It is admittedly risky to gauge public opinion in Ghana, in the absence of reliable polls. This analysis uses two less direct measures: 1) the extent of public debate concerning the justification of the demands made by organized labor; and 2) the ability of Congress leaders to defend themselves and their unions against government attacks by evoking a public response.

It would be inaccurate to describe Ghana as a totalitarian state during 1961-66, when the TUC was subjected to control and intimidation by the CPP. Nonetheless, it is difficult to discover evidence of genuine debate or genuine unanimity during this period concerning the public issues with which the Congress later came to identify itself. The destruction of the political opposition, the muzzling of an independent press, and the "study groups" for ideological indoctrination foisted on students and workers were successful in covering legitimate disagreements on national goals and priorities with an, albeit ill-fitting, ideological blanket. Between 1966 and 1972, however, in the press, in educational institutions, and in the political arena, an exchange of ideas on these issues flowered. These years were marked by increasing, though by no means universal, public acceptance of the legitimacy of strong labor unions and, concomitantly, the development of what approaches a consensus on economic and social issues. As we shall see, the National Redemption Council, at least through 1975 a popular regime, also was most sensitive to favorable public opinion of the TUC and the values and policies with which it is identified.

Civil servants' views. Following the promulgation of NLC Decree 134, civil servants emerged as a major source of criticism of unionism. No longer required to join, they deserted by the thousands. The Congress claimed that civil servants misunderstood the decree and that they thought, mistakenly, that they were barred from membership. It is probable, however, that employees in government departments understood their rights and that their rejection of the values of unionism was genuine. In fact, although most Ghanaian unions today contain some civil servants, this group still represents the largest identifiable pocket of unfavorable opinion of the Congress.

Many civil servnats are suspicious of union leaders and believe that monthly dues are making them wealthy. They do not view the union officer as a role model, but, instead, through a process of anticipatory socialization, identify with their superiors in management. The idea that unions do not really know how government organization works is reinforced by the contracts between senior administrators and workers, specified in the General Orders. Junior personnel are concerned that a revision of the orders, as supported by the TUC, would handicap them financially, or would make cordial relations with their superiors more difficult.[29] Wage increases have brought many of them only higher taxes and burdensome responsibilities.

Today, civil service resistance to unionism remains a part of the national debate, but the impact of this resistance on public opinion is mitigated by a number of factors. First, although the dissolution resulted in a decrease in membership for those unions which are predominantly or exclusively composed of civil servants, these have been able to attract new members in recent years through the beginnings of welfare unionism. Second, union membership for civil servants, while not compulsory, is much more probable as their departments become semi-autonomous or are converted to public corporations which sign collective agreements. Finally, the Junior Civil Servants' Association, which is responsible for publicizing the views of its members, was much more active under the PP regime, when there was thought to be political advantage in resisting unionism, than it is at present.

Public impressions, 1966-72. We have already mentioned that strike activity greatly increased after 1966, and this was attributed to an absence of shared norms between the unions and some businessmen. Paradoxically, the rise in the number of work stoppages may indicate a more favorable opinion of

unions among the general public. Because the causes of strikes
were well-publicized, and the impediments to settlement
which business often presented were explained to the public,
the Congress began to outgrow its "strike monger" image.
One observer concluded that "during the N.L.C. era . . . the
strikers were no longer alone in their fight to improve wages
and working conditions."[30] It is logical to assume that union
leaders would not have encouraged, or tacitly approved of so
many strikes if they feared substantial public "backlash."

As politics were revived in Ghana during 1968, candidates
did attempt to capitalize on industrial unrest and, in effect, to
lower the reputation of the Congress by claiming that worker
militancy was ruining the country. But there is little evidence
that this rhetoric was attractive to anyone but civil servants
and businessmen with Progress Party connections. The PP
was extreme in its anti-strike position. Voters who supported
it in the election nonetheless found it difficult to believe the
PP's claim that strikes were inevitably based on a conspiracy
or a plot by the CPP to retake control of Ghana.

The Congress's firm opposition to the 1971 budget hardened
the conflict between unionists and politicians and reconfirmed
the need "to ignore the unions and appeal directly to
individual workers for cooperation."[31] But the TUC was
already too much an institution for such "direct appeals" to be
successful. The uncertainty of the regime in reacting to the
challenges it perceived, and the false promises made to
workers, contributed to the decline of the PP's image with the
public. So too did the retreat of some party leaders behind a
facade of arrogance.

Unions were not the only bodies which were subjected to
such treatment. Many PP officials were generationally and
ideologically out of tune with students and the military, as
well. By September 1971, the PP had abandoned earlier
attempts to bridge these gaps and was trying to make up a
propaganda, bombast, and intimidation what it could not win
by persuasion and assertion of its "natural right" to rule.
Many groups within the public at large could agree with the
leader of Ghana's largest union when he said, "You cannot
ensure good relationships by governmental edict."[32]

The cause of the dissolution of the TUC was not the poor

economic picture, continued industrial unrest, or even the obvious animosity between some PP officials and the secretary-general. Similar circumstances had existed before in Ghanaian history but had not provoked the government of the day to take the drastic step of making the TUC a legal nonentity. Certainly the rapid deterioration of relations between unions and government during the summer of 1971 was a result of the fading popularity of the Progress Party. It was the loss of appeal to all segments of society, including workers, which caused the regime to become increasingly defensive, to equate opposition with treason, to over-react to the issue of CPP revival, and to see B.A. Bentum as a revolutionary leader. The Congress appeared calm and competent by comparison.

The speaking tour organized by the TUC secretariat was popular precisely because the Ghanaian public possessed the political sophistication to make the connection between the unfulfilled promises, which the speakers stressed, and possible remedies, which were left to the imagination. The words of the union leaders had the ring of truth, not only for workers, but for all those who had been disappointed by the regime.

The legitimacy of the Congress as a spokesman resulted largely from its resistance to the upper-middle-class leadership of the Progress Party, which was committed to maintaining, intact, the Ghanaian system of social stratification. In a poor country there was great popular acceptance of the unions' position rejecting the existing distribution of income. The TUC had been hammering away at the theme of "bridging the gap" between the salaries of the lowest and highest paid workers. But even middle-class readers of the *Spokesman* doubtless appreciated the irony in the report of the minister for finance arriving at Parliament to announce a ban on automobile imports in a "gleaming black Mercedes 280 Super."[33]

There was much public criticism of the decision to dissolve the TUC. The opposition's shadow attorney-general stated that the government was trying to persecute the Congress for the firm stand it had taken in favor of a rise in the minimum wage. He then asked a question that was on the minds of many: If the TUC was really illegal, as the government claimed, why had it not been abolished as soon as the PP took office? Even as the new labor legislation was being drafted, the independent paper *Palaver* urged the government to "bury the hatchet" and to restrain itself. Bentum was being painted as worse than he really was, the paper said.[34] A week after the dissolution the same source noted that it was unfair to the TUC, and to Bentum, that the NLC and the PP had not corrected their "oversight" sooner, when they could have more easily molded things to their pleasure. "Now T.U.C. have been treated like squeezed oranges and contrary to what official circles think, have excited much genuine support."

Widespread resentment against the government's tactic of repressing the TUC was reported during the fall of 1971. The dissolution had not been demanded by any of the important "publics" in the country. Those who suspected that the power of the government, now unleashed against the Congress, could soon be turned on them were indeed correct. By year's end, military expenditures had been cut, the currency devalued, and transport allowances for civil servants eliminated. The Progress Party had succeeded in alienating almost all of its constituency — students, labor, bureaucracy, military, and business — except for some rural chiefs and university professors. Even the cocoa growers, in whose behalf urban workers were required to make sacrifices, did not buoy up the regime. They became at least passive allies of the workers, as they had been in 1966. Many observers, including Frantz Fanon, have predicted rural resistance to the attempts of the urban worker to better his position. But Busia's Progress Party regime could not capitalize on the farmers' resentment, if, indeed, it was there.

It is clear that many of the goals and values which comprise the doctrine of the Trades Union Congress had become so deeply ingrained, and so successfully publicized, that it was impossible to reduce their attractiveness to the public merely by eliminating, by law, the group with which they were identified. The consensus which emerged from the public debate was that the Congress's criticisms were justified. There were simply too many inequities and unfilfilled promises, which affected almost every group in society, for the regime to survive.

## Contemporary Opinion of the Unions

Of course, the "public" did not carry out the coup in January 1972, but the soldiers' action was well received and remained popular. The NRC presented a more active posture than the NLC, but its policies were more a mirror of public sentiment than they were mobilizing in intent or effect. The Charter of Redemption (the NRC's creed) and other official pronouncements reflected a broad spectrum of public opinion. The armed forces intervened, not as an ally of organized labor or any other single group with grievances against the PP regime, but as a "guardian" which attempted to reduce or eliminate social conflict. The prompt restoration of the TUC shows, however, that in industrial relations, as well as other areas of potential conflict, it wished to be the authority of "last resort." The popularity of restoration, as one of the policies of the new government, indicated general agreement that the previous regime, in dissolving Congress, had unnecessarily crippled an effective conflict-regulating mechanism.

The value positions taken by the National Redemption Council with regard to labor were greeted with satisfaction by unionists. Of these NRC positions, the most relevant follow:

A revisionist evaluation of the PP was offered, in which the chairman of the NRC noted that "the dissolved Progress Party comprised men who were completely against the working class of this country and had been so since the early days of the struggle for independence."

The "dignity of labor" was acknowledged. Ghanaians should be "first rate Africans," rather than second-rate Europeans, the chairman said. The commissioner for labor warned employers not to belittle their workers, but to treat them with the respect they deserve. "Anyone who is really familiar with the Ghanaian workers of today should have confidence in the aggregate intelligence of these people."

The goal of improving working conditions and the standard of living was embraced.

Increases in productivity and improved industrial peace were said to be dependent on improving working conditions for employees.

Some change in allocation of rewards in society was advocated. The Charter of Redemption specified, as a goal, that "the wealth of the nation should be equitably distributed, assuring every person a just return for his labour, and proper attention to his needs."[35]

If these positions appear rather dull and non-controversial, this indicates not only the extent to which the NRC was in tune with public opinion, but, more significantly, that the justice of these claims, which correlate exactly with the TUC's own, is no longer an object of disagreement with Ghanaian society.

There has been, of course, some remaining public hostility to organized labor. Striking unions still have a poor image. "Irresponsible" union leaders are often blamed for work stoppages, particularly since there has been, in recent times, less publicity in the media regarding the grievances leading to strikes or the efforts of labor leadership to prevent them. It is, however, essential to point ut that the employers' "image" is often no better than that of the militant unionist. "Most Ghanaians regard the businessman as a criminal," reported a columnist for the *Daily Graphic*.[36]

The influential journal, *Legon Observer*, which has been proscribed at times because its criticisms have embarrassed governments, noted shortly after restoration that unions in Ghana should do more than negotiate collective agreements. "They should also try to influence opinion on questions of social justice."[37] Evidently, the journal has not been institutionalized as a gadfly, but the TUC *has* been accepted as a source of opinion on social justice. It has continued to play the role of the independent critic, questioning, for example, government's sincerity in effecting a redistribution of income.

*Summary*

Primarily favorable, and at least neutral, public opinion was obviously an important factor in the survival of the TUC intact, after the dissolution. Negative opinion, especially among significant sub-groups in society, might have allowed government to be even more punitive against the Congress, or could have forced it to be so. However, there was no public outcry for the arrest and detention of union leaders; the only raids conducted on TUC headquarters or the homes of unionists were carried out by the police, not angry mobs. Only the party press provided a consistently unfavorable image of the Congress. The government-owned papers, although they did support the dissolution, continued to give coverage to the leaders who were under fire. The independent and opposition papers, of course, criticized aspects of the dissolution, and it may be assumed that this position was supported by their readership.

The TUC had become, perhaps for the majority of urbanized Ghanaians, the most important articulator of discontent. This assertion is supported by the government's numerous attempts to compromise with the group prior to August 1971. In addition, the care which was taken by PP ministers to present a rationale for a dissolution, including legalistic, red-baiting, and *ad hominem* arguments, shows that these politicians were concerned about negative public opinion of their actions.

However, the Congress was not seen merely as one of the many groups supporting policies which had been ratified by popular consensus. By 1971 a bundle of national values had become inseparably bound to TUC ideology, so that in the process of protecting, defending, and improving the welfare of their own members, the unions were also articulating many of the deepest grievances, and expressing the finest hopes, of the general public. Further, it had become expected that this voice would be heard, and the government which stifled it was itself toppled.

Thus, the TUC has become an institution which not only embodies societal values, but which reinforces them and influences their evolution. Because of the favorable reputation which the Congress enjoys, it is unlikely that civilian politicians will attempt to dismantle the TUC again — unlikely, so long as the public continues to view government as its "father," and the TUC as the legitimate spokesman for his deserving "children." As B.A. Bentum explained, "When your child asks for food, you don't give him stone."[38]

## CHAPTER VIII

# Conclusion

## FINDINGS

Trade unions in Ghana have indeed been undergoing a process of institutionaliaztion. Over the past 30 ears the attitudes and actions of labor leaders and their organizations have become accepted in Ghanaian society. The TUC has been able to demonstrate to governments, employers, its members, and the wider public the value of what it is doing. The Congress has not achieved all of its program objectives, but its accomplishments have certainly been sufficient for the initiaton and maintenance of a wide variety of patterned relationships with its environment. Ironically, the 1971 dissolution occurred, in part, because the labor movement was successful enough to have embarrassed the Busia regime. Moreover, the restoration of the Congress reflected the positive valuation of its program and the recognition that the TUC was uniquely capable of attaining the goals which its doctrine enunciated.

It is also apparent that the TUC manifests structural characteristics which enhance the probability that these strong external linkages will continue. The behavior of organized labor is patterned and expected by society because the mechanisms which the Congress has created for the satisfaction of its own internal needs are relatively permanent and predictable to workers, labor leaders, and constituent unions.

We traced the origins of worker loyalty to the labor movement and discovered evidence of respect and admiration of leaders by the rank and file, especially since 1966. This was attributed to the elimination of systematic corruption, the fulfillment of promises made, and pride in the personal courage and success of the officers.

Similarly, we attempted to explain the ability of the Congress to attract and retain leaders. We found that, like many organizations, the TUC provides its executives with financial rewards and the opportunity to manage substantial resources. However, the constellation of leadership roles which was created 20 years ago by the New Structure has remained essentially undisturbed, in spite of periodic and substantial losses of membership and income. Therefore, it is evident that the officers' commitment is also inspired by comraderie, friendship, and the ethos of a common responsibility. Role specificity and universalistic standards for performance evaluation have produced mutual dependence and accountability and have minimized problems of leadership succession.

We also attributed the cohesiveness of the TUC primarily to the desire of the 17 unions to come together for mutual gain, rahter than to legislaton or the personal appeal of individual secretary-generals. There has been a gradual centralization of authority at the top of the bureaucratic hierarchy, but this authority is now shared by general secretaries and national chairmen of unions, inhibiting the appearance of factions. Unity in the Congress today is the result of strategic compromises on program content, effectiveness of cooperative rule-making and enforcement, and the development of a usable ideology to which all unions may relate.

We have shown that the program goals which the labor movement now sets for itself are practically identical to those expressed in the 1940's. These have been but marginally affected by "even revolutionary upheavals in its basic political situation."[1] This remarkable consistency may be attributed to the institutional culture which has been created to validate and inspire unions' achievements, a culture which has evolved independently of external ideologies, and in which workers, as well as leaders, have participated. We can see the wisdom in the observation that the labor movement in Ghana "survived in Nkrumah regime with its trade union values and attitudes largely intact."[2] In spite of the cooptation of the unions, the effectiveness of cooperative economic action and collective bargaining, as well as the futility of involving the TUC in the cold-war international rivalry, had been amply demonstrated by 1966. Similarly, a tradition of struggle had been established which survives today, and which expresses, for unionists in Ghana, the continuity between past and present.

## TUC AUTONOMY IN THE FUTURE

Can the process of institutionalization be reversed? As the TUC exchanges resources and ideas with its environment, it may become vulnerable. How much power does the Congress now possess to maintain its own autonomy and distinctiveness?

Today, the TUC does not rely on government or other groups in Ghanaian society for money, leaders, or doctrine. The unionist ideology of its officers is, therefore, a practical guide to action, not idealistic rhetoric. Over time, the Congress has obtained the authority to make its own contacts with the business community and the wider public. Collective bargaining is no longer politicized, and even the dissolution could not alter the acceptability of the TUC as a "voice of the people." As government has lost its ability to prevent labor's external alliances, its power to use the movement for purposes other than its own has been reduced. In fact, the many favors which the National Redemption Council bestowed on the Congress did not automatically qualify the regime as a "friend of labor" in the opinion of most senior union officials. In relation to the NRC, as well as subsequent regimes, TUC officials could afford, in every sense, to adopt a "wait-and-see" attitude.

However, Congress autonomy involves more than freedom from outside control and manipulation. Perhaps more important is its ability to intervene in the environment, to "export" its own norms and values in Ghanaian society, thereby minimizing the chances for a reassertion of government authority over its affairs. For example, labor executives have developed their own standard for peer evaluation. It is these which have come to determine the viability of TUC leadership in the larger environment, not the standards imposed by business or government. Similarly, the Congress has assumed authority over the jurisdiction of its own unions, and over the granting of legitimacy to splinter groups and breakaways. The government no longer enjoys a monopoly of organization sanctioning power, and it recognizes the TUC's views concerning which unions should be representatives of the workers.

The Congress also influences its own environment via the collective bargaining process, in which its internal norms of justice and orderly adjudication of grievances have become a part of the labor contract, transforming industrial relations in Ghana. Moreover, in its role as a "voice of the people," the TUC does more than echo public sentiment; it also inspires and channels it for its own purposes. Because it is able to intervene in its environment in these ways, the power of the Congress to influence national policy in the coming years is likely to be much greater than when its secretary-general was a minister plenipotentiary in the government.

## SOCIOLOGICAL IMPLICATIONS

In Chapter I we suggested that this research may provide a model to help explain the relationship between organized labor and the development of poor countries. It is now time to assess Ghana's experience in theoretical terms. Neither major intellectual system, modernization theory nor its dependency critique, fits the data exactly. Elements of each perspective are confirmed, but there is also evidence to challenge both. Our research corroborates Marxist and neo-Marxist analyses of colonialism which have demonstrated that organizational forms transplanted to the Third World serve primarily the interests of the metropole.[3] Ghanaian trade unions were useful to Britain in its attempt to maintain authority and "law and order." At the same time, however, it is important to realize that they were helping to propagate the values of modernism.[4] Our data sustain the idea that trade unions are a major source of universalistic and achievement values in developing countries, and that labor organizations may effectively resist forces of tribalism and traditionalism. We found that ethnicity was relatively unimportant in explaining the internal dynamics of Ghanaian unionism or industrial relations, supporting previous studies doen in Tanganyika and Nigeria.[5]

There is additional evidence that Ghanaian unions have performed some of the other manifest functions posited by "modernization" studies of organized labor, but it is not unequivocal. Wages and working conditions have been improved, at least for those union members covered by collective agreements, but the remainder of the wage labor force continues to battle inflation with limited success. Labor commitment has been increased, but some workers have not internalized unionist values or TUC ideology, and a substantial portion of the non-agricultural labor force remains unorganized. Conversely, there is indirect support for the dependency thesis, in that the relatively stable industrial relations environment which the unions seek to maintain makes Ghana more attractive to international capitalism and lending agencies, such as the World Bank. Clearly, the Ghana case illustrates that neither theoretical point of view is superior to the other, but that there is a need to transcend them both. In sum, these perspectives each deserve more criticism than support.

Our findings challenge widely-held "modernization" notions about the weaknesses of formal, complex organizations in the Third World. A variety of groups has been pictured as "circumscribed and controlled." Labor unions, in particular, are described as "dominated by the government and/or the party," and as "little more than ciphers in the development of African society." One observer concluded that "society wide institutions, other than the state, are scant."[6] These judgments were, perhaps, accurate for the immediate post-independence period in many nations, but they need to be reexamined in light of the present work, and other studies of functioning organizations.

Moreover, the examination of TUC/government relations, particularly under Ghana's first two military regimes, shows that western and African trade unions may not be as divergent in their evolution as modernization theorists have supposed. American unions, for example, provide relatively uncritical support to the government on issues most removed from their immediate economic interests. The same may be said for Ghanaian labor organizations. However, in both cases there is sometimes extreme hostility to official policy directly affecting workers, and a purposive indifference to pleas for cooperation. It is significant that the Ghana TUC could not now adopt this independent posture were it not for the strength it amassed under government tutelage, prior to 1966. Actually, official support for unions is not untypical in the west. As Walter Galenson has noted: "Organizational progress is usually feasible only when the government steps in to provide protection; after all, it required the Wagner Act to pave the way for the unionization of heavy industry in the United States."[7]

Second, this study shows that institutional structures of foreign origin do not inevitably work to preserve Africa's subordinate status in the post-independence era. Unions in Ghana have transcended their original *raison d'etre*. They have not deterred working class consciousness. Even the most militant of the rank and file are convinced of the benefits of unionism. They do not want unions to disappear; they want to make them more efficient and responsive. To claim, as some proponents of the dependency argument do, that this is "false consciousness" ignores the issues of the real achievements of Ghana's labor movement. Nor does it give the Ghanaian worker credit for recognizing what is in his/her own interest. It is evident that the unions are more a benefit than a hindrance to autonomous national development, in that they have eschewed external ideologies, supported the growth of indigenous (public and private) business, and have served as spokesman for the unemployed. This is, admittedly, not the "image" of labor organizations posited by the dependency critique, but it exists in Ghana nonetheless.


## THE GHANA MODEL


On the assumption that the flaws in the dependency critique as well as modernization theory keep us from seeing Ghanaian unions as they are, not as some may wish or believe them to be, the following model is offered as an alternative explanation for the behavior of trade unions and their leaders which I observed in the field. I have tried to let the theory emerge from the data, inductively, as much as possible,[8] so as to avoid the mistake of imposing problems as well as solutions on a country which has already suffered enough from mismanagement and imperialism.

The Ghana model sensitizes us to three major possibilities for developing countries. These are: 1) the uneven evolution of important social institutions; 2) the likelihood that institutions will perform multiple, latent functions, some in their own self-interest, some in the interests of the nation; and 3) the potential for one-coopted institutions to change, to acquire autonomy over time, and to resist cultural and economic domination, whether domestic or foreign.

Contrary to the classic analyses of modernization, not all social institutions evolve at the same pace, or in equilibrium.[9] For example, industrial relations structures (trade unions, employers' groups, and their supporting legal framework) may become more accepted, and their behavior more expectable and patterned, than political structures (parties, elections, government executives). Our findings call into question the capacity of the state to dominate institutional life in developing countries. Ghana is perhaps the best example in black Africa, though by no means the only one, in which a nascent institution has proven to be more resilient than the government which attempted to co-opt it. Where state authority is precarious, workers will not assume an inevitably passive role in industrial relations, nor in a nation's unofficial political life. They can create and utilize their own vehicles for expressing discontent, and otherwise servicing their needs.

We have shown that unions may outgrow their role as mere adjuncts to political mobilization and inspire new associational sentiments. Thus, the Ghana model may be particularly useful for the comparative analysis of post-coup regimes in less developed countries. Under military rule, the unions may fill the void left by the proscription of parties. They are among the few remaining groups which have the potential to induce members' participation in modern-sector economic activity. It is this potential which most of the coup-makers lack, yet it is essential to the development effort. Subsequent studies may reveal the crucial position of unions in contributing to the dynamism of military regimes, and in helping to ensure that "praetorian" societies do not become more prevalent.[10]

It is apparent that Ghanaian unions, like their counterparts in other less developed countries, have enjoyed only limited success in performing the functions which foreign observers have assigned to them. It is not this ambiguous record, alone, which accounts for their vitality and survival. This study has shown the value of the labor movement for the people who actually participate in it, and interact with it. Unions in Ghana have become institutions because they are a means of career advancement and status rise for their leaders, but also because they have helped to rationalize industrial relations. They have helped to govern the country when politics declined and the military assumed power. The unions regulate political demands and translate them into concrete policy recommendations. Furthermore, they have made the urban wage worker a part of the debate on national priorities and have served as a channel through which the nation articulates its hopes for the future to its own citizens and to the world. The absence of a variety of other groups which could perform these latent functions has resulted in a commitment to keep unions alive. regardless of their specific impact on the national economy.

# Appendices

Appendix 1

## *Abbreviations*

AATUF   All-Africa Trade Union Federation
AFL-CIO   American Federation of Labor and Congress of Industrial Organizations
CPP   Convention People's Party (1949-1966; in power 1957-1966)
GEA   Ghana Employers Association
GCL   Ghana Confederation of Labor (1969-1972)
GCTUC   Gold Coast Trades Union Congress (1945-56)
GTUC   Ghana Trades Union Congress (1951-53)
ICFTU   International Confederation of Free Trade Unions
ICU   Industrial and Commercial Workers Union
ILO   International Labor Organization
ITS   International Trade Secretariat
JCSA   Junior Civil Servants Association
LAC   Labor Advisory Council
MACAWU   Manufacturing, Commercial and Allied Workers Union
NLC   National Liberation Council (1966-1969)
NLM   National Liberation Movement (1956)
NRC   National Redemption Council (1972-1976)
OATUU   Organization of African Trade Union Unity
PP   Progress Party (in power 1969-1972)
RHWU   Railway and Harbor Workers Union
SMC   Supreme Military Council (1976-1979)
TUC   Trades Union Congress
UAC   United Africa Company
UGCC   United Gold Coast Convention
UP   United Party (1957-1962)
WFTU   World Federation of Trade Unions

Appendix 2

*Official Rates for Ghanaian Currency*

Before July 1965     1 Ghanaian pound = 1 pound sterling
                          = US $2.80
July 1965-Feb 1967 Ghanaian currency changes to the cedi (C)
                          C2.40 = 1 Ghanaian pound
                          C1.00 = US$1.17
Feb 1967-July 1967 Currency changes to the *new cedi* (NC)
                          NC1.00 = C1.20 = US$1.40
July 1967-Dec 1970 NC1.00 = US$ .98
Dec 1970-Jan 1971  NC1.00 = US$ .54
Jan 1971-Feb 1972  Currency changes back to cedi
                          C1.00 = US$ .78
Feb 1972               C1.00 = US $ .87

— — — —

After Peter C. Garlick, *African Traders and Economic
Development in Ghana* (Oxford: Clarendon Press, 1971), p. 8.

Appendix 3

*Number of Unions, Membership, and Strikes, 1945 - 73*

| Year | # of Unions[a] | Members Claimed | # of Work Stoppages | # of Workers Involved | Man-Days Lost |
|---|---|---|---|---|---|
| 1945 | 14 | 6,030 | 2 | 700 | n.d. |
| 1946 | 24 | 10,976 | 3 | 7,750 | 96,650 |
| 1947 | 28 | 30,548 | 7 | 946 | 3,823 |
| 1948 | 37 | 32,000 | 37 | 46,865 | 1,350,108 |
| 1949 | 61 | 38,135 | 27 | 7,650 | 44,779 |
| 1950 | 62 | 17,985 | 55 | 72,257 | 585,345 |
| 1951 | 83 | 25,000 | 19 | 5,482 | 11,017 |
| 1952 | 58 | 32,908 | 39 | 15,504 | 38,185 |
| 1953 | 65 | 35,129 | 83 | 32,548 | 129,676 |
| 1954 | 75 | 46,309 | 65 | 20,529 | 125,927 |
| 1955 | 66 | 44,902 | 35 | 8,263 | 29,207 |
| 1956 | 87 | 67,173 | 25 | 33,319[b] | 2,479,224 |
| 1957 | 95 | 128,000 | 45 | 11,858 | 33,005 |
| 1958 | 95 | 135,615 | 64 | 27,837 | 41,020 |
| 1959 | 24 | 230,000 | 49 | 8,875 | 21,673 |
| 1960 | 16 | 201,991 | 50 | 10,101 | 12,788 |
| 1961 | 16 | 320,248 | 40 | 12,259 | 132,483[e] |
| 1962 | 16 | 380,295 | 4 | 1,690 | 2,800 |
| 1963 | 16 | 324,648[c] | 8 | 940 | 1,372 |
| 1964 | 16 | 351,711 | 13 | 2,844 | 2,888 |
| 1965 | 10 | 386,750 | 13 | 7,100 | 66,507 |
| 1966 | 16 | n.d. | 32 | 15,027 | 20,427 |
| 1967 | 16 | 338,154 | 27 | 6,326 | 6,738 |
| 1968 | 17 | 270,149 | 36 | 52,419 | 156,171 |
| 1969 | 17 | 333,800 | 51 | 30,988 | 165,570 |
| 1970 | 17 | 342,480 | 58 | 21,467 | 145,107 |
| 1971 | 17 | 362,839 | 71 | 46,715 | 133,096 |
| 1972 | 17 | n.d. | 14 | 3,711 | 5,281 |
| 1973 | 17 | 340,658 | 14 | 4,443 | 4,307 |
| 1974 | 17 | n.d. | 38 | 31,020 | 43,628 |
| 1975 | 17 | n.d. | 27 | 12,575 | 36,078 |
| 1976[d] | 17 | 375,000[f] | 25 | 19,732 | 16,600 |

Sources: Dennis Austin, *Politics in Ghana.*
    *Colonial Reports,* London: H.M.S.O., 1949-54.
    U.G. Damachi, *The Role of Trade Unions in the Development Process.*
    *Directory of Labor Organizations,* Washington, D.C.: United States Department of Labor, 1958, 1962, 1966.
    Ghana, *Annual Reports of the Labour Department,* Accra, 1948, 1968.
    Jon Kraus, "Labor Organization and Labor Protest in Ghana Under Colonial Rule, 1945-51."
    J. Roper, *Labour Problems in West Africa.*
    TUC, *Reports of Biennial Congresses* (mimeos), 1968, 1970.
    Unpublished Figs., Ghana Labor Department.
    Interview data.

Many of these sources conflict for given years. In such cases we have picked the numbers cited by the majority of sources.

[a]Functioning unions which had not been amalgamated.

[b]Miners comprised 24,000 of total.

[c]Decline in members the result of Parliamentary action exempting nurses from unions, and a loss of 24,000 in Public Utilities.

[d]Figures are for the first eight months.

[e]Includes data from the 1961 general strike.

[f]Estimate.

Appendix 4

*Map of Ghana*

# Notes

## Chapter I

1. The methodoligical strategies and techniques employed in this study are summarized in my article "Exchange and Access in Field Work," *Urban Life,* October 1980.

2. See Robert Dubin, *Working Union-Management Relations.*

3. These are summarized in Jon Kraus, "African Trade Unions: Progress or Poverty?"

4. See Robert H. Bates, "Approaches to the Study of Unions and Development." A refreshing exception is Richard Jeffries, *Class, Power and Ideology in Ghana: The Railwaymen of Sekondi.* Of the works cited by Kraus, the most sophisticated, theoretically, are Robin Cohen, *Labour and Politics in Nigeria* and Richard Sandbrook, *Proletarians and African Capitalism: The Kenyan Case, 1960-1972.*

5. See papers by E.M. Kassalow, and D.G. Lazorchick and C.R. Hare in *The Role of Labor in African Nation Building,* ed. Willard A. Beling; Walter Galenson, ed., *Labor in Developing Economies;* and Bruce H. Millen, *The Political Role of Labor in Developing Countries.*

6. See George C. Lodge, *Spearheads of Democracy.*

7. Wilbert E. Moore and Arnold S. Feldman, eds., *Labor Commitment and Social Change in Developing Areas.*

8. Clark Kerr *et al., Industrialism and Industrial Man.*

9. See., e.g., Arnold Rivkin, ed., *Nations by Design: Institution Building in Africa.*

10. See., e.g., Giovanni Arrighi and John S. Saul, "Socialism and Economic Development in Tropical Africa"; and Peter Kilby, "Industrial Relations and Wage Determination: Failure of the Anglo-Saxon Model." These provide critiques of African unions from the Left and Right of the political spectrum, respectively.

11. See Jeffries, *Class, Power and Ideology,* p. 170.

12. John S. Saul, "The 'Labor Aristocracy' Thesis Reconsidered," in *The Development of an African Working Class*, ed. **Richard Sandbrook and Robin Cohen**, p. 303.

13. Seymour Martin Lipset, Martin Trow, and James Coleman, *Union Democracy*, p. 7ff.

14. Philip Selznick, *Leadership in Administration*, p.5.

15. See, e.g., Arnold M. Rose, ed., *The Institutions of Advanced Societies*, p. 32ff.

16. Everett Charrington Hughes, "Institutions," in *New Outline of the Principles of Sociology*, ed. Alfred McClung Lee, p. 231.

17. Melvin G. Blase, ed., *Institution-Building: A Source Book*, p. 256.

18. For a similar definition, see Arthur L. Stinchcombe, *Constructing Social Theories*, pp. 9-10.

# Chapter II

1. See, e.g., Barbara Callaway and Emily Card, "Political Constraints on Economic Development in Ghana," in *The State of the Nations*, ed. Michael F. Lofchie.

2. See International Monetary Fund, *Surveys of African Economies*, Vol. 6.

3. These and following figures are from The World Bank, *World Development Report, 1978;* and *Washington Post*, July 1, 1977.

4. Ioan Davies, *African Trade Unions*, p. 41.

5. Michael Lofchie and Carl Rosberg, "The Political Status of African Trade Unions," in *The Role of Labor in African Nation Building*, ed. Willard A. Beling, p. 4.

6. Dennis Austin, *Politics in Ghana*, pp. 74-75.

7. Gold Coast Colony, *Report on the Labour Department for the Year 1947-48*, p.9.

8. Rolf Gerritsen, "Pressure Group and Political System: The Case of the Ghana Trades Union Congress" (unpublished master's dissertation), p. 66.

9. E.A. Cowan, *Evolution of Trade Unionism in Ghana*, p. 25.

10. See Aristide Zolberg, *Creating Political Order.*

11. Kwame Nkrumah, *Ghana: The Autobiography of Kwame Nkrumah*, p. 117.

12. Roger Scott, in noting that the identification of African trade unions with the nationalist effort has often been exaggerated, points to the fact that the most solidly entrenched unions were the least political. See Scott, "Are Trade Unions Still Necessary in Africa?," p. 27. This generalization certainly applies to the Ghana Mines Employees Union.

13. Austin, *Politics in Ghana*, p. 89.

14. Gold Coast Colony, *Report on the Labour Department for the Year 1949-50*, p. 8.

15. See Great Britain, *The Colonial Territories* [*1950-51*]; and Ghana Mineworkers Union, *Brief History*, p. 32.

16. See Austin, *Politics in Ghana*, p. 141ff.

17. Trades Union Congress, *Correspondence Course*, Part 1, p. 74.

18. Nkrumah, *Ghana*, p. 178.

19. See G.E. Lynd, *The Politics of African Trade Unionism*, p. 40.

20. See B.D.G. Folson, "The Development of Socialist Ideology in Ghana," p. 10.

21. See Cowan, *Evolution of Trade Unionism*, p. 24; and Trades Union Congress, *Correspondence Course*, p. 74.

22. Jon Kraus, "The Political Economy of Trade Union-Government Relations in Ghana Under Four Regimes" (mimeographed), p. 38.

23. Douglas Rimmer, 'The Industrial Relations Act, 1958," p. 14.

24. J.L. Roper and R.B. Davison, eds., *The Labour and Trade Union Ordinances of the Gold Coast*, p. 19.

25. John Tettegah, *A New Chapter for Ghana Labour*, p. 13.

26. Many of the 95 unions listed in 1957 were inactive. See Appendix 3.

27. Douglas Rimmer, "The New Industrial Relations in Ghana," p. 219.

28. *West Africa*, February 1, 1958.

29. See Ghana, *Parliamentary Debates*, Official Report, First Series, XII, col. 632ff.

30. Ibid., col. 545-46.

31. Tettegah, *A New Chapter for Ghana Labour*, p. 8.

32. See Chas. III and V below.

33. Ghana, *Annual Report on the Labour Department for the Year 1963-64*, p. 30.

34. *Ghana Workers' Bulletin*, III, I (1969).

35. *Light*, March 31, 1971.

36. *West Africa*, August 20, 1971.

37. *Ibid*, October 1, 1971.

## Chapter III

1. See Jon Kraus, "The Political Economy of Trade Union - Government Relations in Ghana Under Four Regimes" (mimeographed), pp. 28-29.

2. Ghana, *Parliamentary Debates*, Official Report, First Series, XII, col. 578.

3. John Tettegah, *A New Chapter for Ghana Labour*, p. 45.

4. Lester N. Trachtman, "Ghanaian Labor Relations Since Independence," p. 548.

5. See Ghana, *Report of the Commission of Enquiry into the Funds of the Ghana Trades Union Congress.*

6. Kraus, "Political Economy" (mimeographed), pp. 37-40.

7. Ghana, *Economic Survey, 1963.*

8. Kraus, "Political Economy" (mimeographed), p. 40.

9. Cf. Elliot Berg, "Urban Real Wages and the Nigerian Trade Union Movement, 1939-60: A Comment."

10. See *Ghana Workers' Bulletin*, III, 6 (1969).

11. See Rolf Gerritsen, "Pressure Group and Political System: The Case of the Ghana Trades Union Congress" (unpublished master's dissertation), p. 99; and Trades Union Congress, "Report on the Activities of the T.U.C. (Ghana) to the Second Biennial Congress Held at Tamale" (mimeographed). In 1966-67, one new cedi equalled US $1.40. See Appendix 2.

12. *Ghana Workers' Bulletin*, II, 7 (1968).

13. *Ibid.* II, 9 (1968), p. 2.

14. See *Daily Graphic*, August 23, 1973.

15. See John D. Esseks, "Government and Indigenous Private Enterprise in Ghana."

16. Ghana, *Annual Report on the Department of Labour for the Year 1959-60.*

17. *West Africa*, September 24, 1971.

18. Quoted in Frank T. deVyver, "The Transplantation of Trade Unions to British Africa," *The Transfer of Institutions*, ed William B. Hamilton, p. 231.

19. Kraus, "Political Economy" (mimeographed), p. 48.

20. *Ghana Workers' Bulletin*, II, 7 (1968).

21. General Agricultural Workers Union of TUC (Ghana), "Report of the National Executive Council" (mimeographed), August 1970.

22. Naomi Chazan and Victor T. Le Vine, "Politics in a 'Non-Political' System: The March 30, 1978 Referendum in Ghana."

23. V.L. Allen, "Management and Labour in Africa," p. 225.

24. See Paul Fisher, "The Economic Role of Unions in Less-Developed Areas," p. 955.

## Chapter IV

1. See Robert Dubin, *Working Union-Management Relations.*

2. Ioan Davies, *African Trade Unions*, p. 35.

3. E.A. Cowan, *Evolution of Trade Unionism in Ghana*, p. 31.

4. J.L. Roper, *Labour Problems in West Africa*, p. 86.

5. Jack Woddis, *The Lion Awakes*, pp. 54-55.

6. Either side of the negotiating committee, management or union, has the right to request a meeting. Once proper notice of the desire to meet has been given, it must be honored.

7. See Douglas Rimmer, "The New Industrial Relations in Ghana," p. 225.

8. Cited in Kwame Afreh, "The Role of Trade Unions in Ghana," p. 259.

9. Benjamin M. Selekman, *Labor Relations and Human Relations*, p. 27.

10. Most unions in Ghana employ special personnel for this purpose. Industrial relations officers do not risk victimization since they are not employed by management.

11. Trades Union Congress, *Protecting and Defending Our Members*, p. 14.

12. *Light*, March 31, 1971.

13. U.G. Damachi, *The Role of Trade Unions in the Development Process*, p. 113.

14. See *West Africa*, April 14, 1972; and *Daily Graphic* April 14 and March 24, 1973.

15. "Address by the Commissioner for Labour, Social Welfare and Co-Operatives, at the Annual General Meeting of the Ghana Employers' Association on 26th January, 1973" (mimeographed).

16. Address by Mr. Akumiah, principal labor officer, to branch officials, March 1973.

17. Such permanent consultative machinery was in place by 1979.

18. *Ghanaian Times*, June 8, 1973.

19. See., e.g., *West Africa*, September 23, 1974.

20. A revised discussion of these themes appears in Paul S. Gray, "Collective Bargaining in Ghana."

21. Ghana, *Annual Report on the Labour Department for the Year 1963-64*, p. 14.

22. See *In the Cause of Ghana Workers;* and B.C. Roberts, *Labour in the Tropical Territories of the Commonwealth.*

23. There are six such "groups" within the GEA, in the civil engineering, timber, garment trade, furniture, insurance, and general manufacturing industries.

24. See Ghana, *Report of the Commission on the Structure and Remuneration of the Public Services in Ghana, 1967;* and Kodwo Ewusi, *The Distribution of Monetary Incomes in Ghana.*

24. Roper, *Labour Problems in West Africa*, p. 83.

26. Dubin, *Working Union-Management Relations*, p. 214.

27. Woddis, *The Lion Awakes*, pp. 54-55.

28. See St. Clair Drake and Leslie Alexander Lacey, "The Sekondi-Takoradi Strike — 1961," in *Politics in Africa: Seven Cases*, ed Gwendolyn M. Carter.

29. See Ghana, *Report of the Committee of Enquiry into the Recent Disturbances at Prestea;* and Ghana, *Report of the Commission of Enquiry into Obuasi Disturbances, 1969.*

30. *Light*, March 31, 1971.

31. Trades Union Congress, *Correspondence Course*, Part III.

32. See Gold Coast Colony, *Award of Arbitrator.*

33. *Evening News* (Accra), April 13, 1961.

34. Quoted in *West Africa*, September 3, 1960.

35. Damachi, *The Role of Trade Unions*, p. 87.

36. *Ghana Workers' Bulletin*, II, 7 and II, 11 (1968); and "Report on the Activities of the T.U.C. (Ghana) to the Second Biennial Congress Held at Tamale" (mimeographed).

37. Ghana, *Report of the Commission on the Structure and Remuneration of the Public Services*, p. 26.

38. See *Daily Graphic*, July 27, 1970; and *Africa Confidential*, August 20, 1971.

39. *Star*, August 11, 1971.

40. Quoted in Damachi, *The Role of Trade Unions*, p. 141.

## Chapter V

1. The national chairman is the titular head of the union. He acts as advisor to the general secretary and is responsible for convening union conferences.

2. Bernard Barber, "Participation and Mass Apathy in Associations" in *Studies in Leadership*, ed. Alvin W. Gouldner, p. 487.

3. Cf. Delbert C. Miller and William H. Form, *Industrial Sociology*, p. 251.

4. Victor L. Allen, *The Sociology of Industrial Relations*, p. 243.

5. Trades Union Congress, *Correspondence Course*, Part I, p. 75.

6. See R. Dowse, *Modernization in Ghana and the U.S.S.R.*, p. 29.

7. Allen, *The Sociology of Industrial Relations*, p. 270.

8. Ghana, *Parliamentary Debates*, Official Report, First Series, XII, col 565.

9. Everett C. Hughes, "Institutions," in *New Outline of the Principles of Sociology*, ed. Alfred McClung Lee, p. 243.

10. See *Daily Graphic*, March 27, 1968.

## Chapter VI

1. U.G. Damachi, "The Internal Dynamics of Trade Unions in Ghana," *The Development of an African Working Class*, ed. Richard Sandbrook and Robin Cohen, p. 181.

2. See Ghana, *Report of the Commission of Enquiry into the Funds of the Ghana Trades Union Congress*, p. 13; and Wogu Ananaba, *The Trade Union Movement in Nigeria*, p. 177.

3. See *Labour* I, 1 (1960); and *Ashanti Pioneer*, August 13, 1960.

4. Melvin G. Blase, ed., *Institution-Building: A Source Book*, p. 22.

5. See Martin Kilson, "Tensions and Dynamics of African Single-Party Systems: Case of the Erstwhile Convention People's Party" (mimeographed).

6. William H. Friedland, "African Trade Unions: Analysis of Two Decades" (mimeographed), p. 12.

7. Cf. G.E. Lynd, *The Politics of African Trade Unionism*, pp. 38 and 41.

8. See *Daily Graphic*, July 29, 1970.

9. Quoted in B.A. Bentum, *Trade Unions in Chains*, p. 30.

10. See *Daily Graphic*, July 25 and August 3, 1970.

11. Ghana, "Address by Colonel I.K. Acheampong, Head of State and Chairman of the N.R.C. to the Workers of Ghana at the Hall of Trade Unions on Saturday, 2nd September, 1972," *Speeches and Interviews by Colonel I.K. Acheampong*, I.

12. Jack Woddis, "Role of the African Working Class in the African Liberation Movement," *World Marxist Review*, V, 7 (1962), p. 47.

13. E.A. Cowan, *Evolution of Trade Unionism in Ghana*, pp. 93-94.

14. It is significant to note, in addition, that the four general secretaries who believed the New Structure to have been a mistake opposed it not merely on ideological grounds. Their unions benefitted least from the framework of large, national organizations mandated in 1958, because they contained mostly civil servants, many of whom deserted the movement in 1967.

These and the following opinions of present general secretaries were expressed in personal interviews which I conducted in 1973.

15. *Ghana Workers' Bulletin* II, 3 (1968).

16. *Ghana Workers' Bulletin*, II, 14 (1968).

17. Rolf Gerritsen, "Pressure Group and Political System: The Case of the Ghana Trades Union Congress" (unpublished master's dissertation), p. 113.

18. Cf. U.G. Damachi, *The Role of Trade Unions in the Development Process*, p. 75.

19. *TUC Newsletter*, V, 1 (1977). Italics mine.

20. This ideological position was further demonstrated during 1977-78, when the TUC supported the military regime's proposals for a return to civilian rule, *not* because it was intimidated into doing so, but because it distrusted the professionals who were opposing the government. See Naomi Chazan and Victor T. LeVine, "Politics in a 'Non-Political' System: The March 30, 1978 Referendum in Ghana," p. 190. In the 1979 campaign, the TUC. co-sponsored a full-fledged party, the Social Democratic Front.

21. See *Daily Graphic*, April 15, 1973. The government's statement read, in part: "With the formal meeting of the Executive Board and the appointment of an Acting Secretary-General in accordance with the constitution of the present congress, it is now time for the present congress to streamline its affairs before the Constituent Trade Unions think of setting a new congress."

## Chapter VII

1. "Address by Major Kwame Asante, Commissioner for Labour, Social Welfare & Co-Operatives to the Executive Board of the T.U.C. — 20/10/72" (mimeographed).

2. See, e.g., Jeff Crisp, "Union Atrophy and Worker Revolt: Labour Protest at Tarkwa Goldfields, Ghana, 1968-69" (unpublished paper).

3. Ghana Mineworkers Union, *Brief History*, p. 46.

4. John K. Tettegah, *Towards Nkrumahism: The Building of Socialist Ghana*, p. 46.

5. *Star*, August 25, 1971.

6. *Ghana Workers' Bulletin*, II, 11 (1968).

7. John Tettegah, "The African Proletariat," p. 11.

8. See Rolf Gerritsen, "Pressure Group and Political System: The Case of the Ghana Trades Union Congress" (unpublished master's dissertation), p. 124.

9. C. Wright Mills, *The New Men of Power*, p. 290.

10. See *Africa and the World*, December 1971; and *West Africa*, October 1, 1971.

11. Cf. Delbert C. Miller and William H. Form, *Industrial Sociology*, p. 237.

12. See U.G. Damachi, *The Role of Trade Unions in the Development Process*, p. 183.

13. B.A. Bentum, addressing the Tamale Congress, 1968, *Ghana Workers' Bulletin*, II, 12 (1968).

14. See St. Clair Drake and Leslie Alexander Lacey, "The Sekondi-Takoradi Strike — 1961" in *Politics in Africa: Seven Cases*, ed. Gwendolyn M. Carter, p. 114; and *Ghana Workers' Bulletin*, II, 7 (1968).

15. Richard D. Jeffries, "Populist Tendencies in the Ghanaian Trade Union Movement," in *The Development of an African Working Class*, ed. Richard Sandbrook and Robin Cohen, p. 273.

16. B.A. Bentum, *Trade Unions in Chains*, p. 66.

17. J.B. Blay, *The Gold Coast Mines Employees Union*, p. 33.

18. Peter Kilby, "Industrial Relations and Wage Determination: Failure of the Anglo-Saxon Model."

19. Centre for Civic Education, *Social Security Scheme and Your Future*.

20. Basil Davidson, *Black Star*, p. 177.

21. St. Clair Drake and L.A. Lacey, cited in Jeffries, "Populist Tendencies," pp. 269-270.

22. Selwyn Ryan, "Socialism and the Party System in Ghana: 1947-1966," pp. 82-83.

23. Tettegah, *Towards Nkrumahism*, p. 62.

24. Ghana, *Newsletter*, 1973.

25. *Ghana Workers' Bulletin*, II, 14 (1968).

26. *Ibid*, II, 6 (1968).

27. John Alex Hamah, "Observations and Conclusions by the Ghana Delegate to the I.L.O. Workers' Education Programme African Seminar on the Role of Trade Unions in Development Planning, Dakar, 28 November — 10 December, 1966" (mimeographed).

28. Quoted by Maxwell Owusu, "The Search for Solvency: Background to the Fall of Ghana's Second Republic," p. 59.

29. See Robert M. Price, "Organizational Commitment and Organizational Character in the Ghanaian Civil Service" (unpublished paper).

30. Damachi, *The Role of Trade Unions*, p. 130.

31. *Ibid*, p. 119.

32. Ben Edjah, "Report on the Activities of the I.C.U. of T.U.C. (Ghana) to the 3rd Biennial Delegates Conference Held at Cape Coast from the 4th-6th of September '70" (mimeographed), p. 16.

33. *West Africa*, July 27, 1971.

34. See *Daily Graphic*, September 10, 1971; and *Palaver*, September 9, 1971.

35. For further discussion of these and other NRC positions, see Paul S. Gray, "Developing Political Relations Between the Ghana Trades Union Congress and the National Redemption Council—1972-74" (unpublished paper).

36. Kofi Quaye, "Business and the Revolution."

37. Kwame Afreh, "The Role of Trade Unions in Ghana."

38. Quoted in Damachi, *The Role of Trade Unions*, p. 101.

## Conclusion

1. Rolf Gerritsen, "Pressure Group and Political System: The Case of the Ghana Trades Union Congress" (unpublished master's dissertation), p. iv.

2. G.E. Lynd, *The Politics of African Trade Unionism*, p. 46.

3. See, e.g., Samir Amin, "Underdevelopment and Dependence."

4. Cf. Alex Inkeles and David Horton Smith, *Becoming Modern* (Cambridge, Mass.: Harvard University Press, 1974).

5. See the review of ethnicity in William H. Friedland, "African Trade Union Studies: Analysis of Two Decades" (mimeographed), pp. 21-23.

6. See Arnold Rivkin, ed., *Nations by Design: Institution Building in Africa*, p. 17; Friedland, "African Trade Union Studies," p. 15; and Edward Shils, "On the Comparative Study of the New States," in *Old Societies and New States*, ed. Clifford Geertz, p. 22.

7. Walter Galenson, ed., Labor in Developing Economies, p. 3.

8. See Barney G. Glaser and Anselm L. Strauss, *The Discovery of Grounded Theory*.

9. Cf. Wilbert Moore, *Social Change*, Ch. 5; and Neil J. Smelser, "Toward a Theory of Modernization, in *Social Change*, ed. Amitai and Eva Etzioni.

10. See Samuel P. Huntington, *Political Order in Changing Societies*.

# Bibliography

## Books

Allen, Victor L. *The Sociology of Industrial Relations*. London: Longman, 1971.

Ananaba, Wogu. *The Trade Union Movement in Nigeria*. New York: Africana Publishing Co., 1970.

Austin, Dennis. *Politics in Ghana*. Oxford: Oxford University Press, 1964.

Beling, Willard A., ed. *The Role of Labor in African National Building*. New York: Praeger, 1968.

Bentum, B.A. *Trade Unions in Chains*. Accra: Trades Union Congress, 1966.

Blase, Melvin G., ed. *Institution-Building: A Source Book*. Beverly Hills, Calif.: Sage, 1973.

Blay, J.B. *The Gold Coast Mines Employees Union*. Devon: Arthur H. Stockwell, 1950.

Carter, Gwendolyn N., ed. *Politics in Africa: Seven Cases*. New York: Harcourt, Brace & World, 1966.

Centre for Civic Education. *Social Security Scheme and Your Future*. Accra: Ghana Publishing Corporation, 1971.

Cohen, Robin. *Labour and Politics in Nigeria*. London: Heineman, 1974.

Cowan, E.A. *Evolution of Trade Unionism in Ghana*. Accra?: T.U.C. Ghana, n.d.

Damachi, U.G. *The Role of Trade Unions in the Development Process*. New York: Praeger, 1974.

Davidson, Basil. *Black Star*. London: Allen Lane, 1973.

Davies, Ioan. *African Trade Unions*. Baltimore: Penguin, 1966.

Dowse, R. *Modernization in Ghana and the U.S.S.R.* London: Routledge & Kegan Paul, 1969.

Dubin, Robert. *Working Union-Management Relations*. Englewood Cliffs, N.J.: Prentice-Hall, 1958.

Etzioni, Amitai, and Etzioni, Eva, eds. *Social Change*. New York: Basic Books, 1964.

Ewusi, Kodwo. *The Distribution of Monetary Incomes in Ghana*. Legon: Institute of Statistical, Social and Economic Research, University of Ghana, 1971.

Galenson, Walter, ed. *Labor in Developing Economies*. Berkeley and Los Angeles: University of California Press, 1962.

Geertz, Clifford, ed. *Old Societies and New States*. New York: Free Press of Glencoe, 1963.

Ghana Mineworkers Union. *Brief History*. Accra: The Secretariat, 1963.

Glaser, Barney G., and Strauss, Anselm L. *The Discovery of Grounded Theory*. Chicago: Aldine, 1973.

Gouldner, Alvin W., ed. *Studies in Leadership*. New York: Russell & Russell, 1950.

Hamilton, William B., ed. *The Transfer of Institutions*. Durham, N.C.: Duke University Press, 1964.

Huntington, Samuel P. *Political Order in Changing Societies*. New Haven and London: Yale University Press, 1968.

International Monetary Fund, *Surveys of African Economies*, Vol. 6. Washington, D.C.: I.M.F., 1975.

*In the Cause of Ghana Workers*. Berlin, East Germany: Ghana T.U.C., 1961.

Jeffries, Richard. *Class, Power and Ideology in Ghana: The Railwaymen of Sekondi*. London: Cambridge University Press, 1978.

Kerr, Clark; Dunlop, John T.; Harbison, Frederick H.; and Myers, Charles A. *Industrialism and Industrial Man*. London: Heinemann, 1962.

Lee, Alfred McClung, ed. *New Outline of the Principles of Sociology*. New York: Barnes & Noble, 1946.

Lipset, Seymour Martin; Trow, Martin; and Coleman, James. *Union Democracy*. Garden City, N.Y.: Doubleday, 1956.

Lodge, George C. *Spearheads of Democracy*. New York: Harper & Row, 1962.

Lofchie, Michael F., ed. *The State of the Nations*. Berkeley and Los Angeles: University of California Press, 1971.

Lynd, G.E. *The Politics of African Trade Unionism*. New York: Praeger, 1968.

Millen, Bruce H. *The Political Role of Labor in Developing Countries*. Washington, D.C.: Brookings Institution, 1963.

Miller, Delbert C., and Form, William H. *Industrial Sociology*. New York: Harper & Bros., 1951.

Mills, C. Wright. *The New Men of Power*. New York: Harcourt, Brace & Co., 1948.

Moore, Wilbert E. *Social Change.* Englewood Cliffs, N.J.: Prentice-Hall, 1963.

Moore, and Feldman, Arnold S., eds. *Labor Commitment and Social Change in Developing Areas.* New York: Social Science Research Council, 1960.

Nkrumah, Kwame. *Ghana: The Autobiography of Kwame Nkrumah.* New York: International Publishers, 1967.

Rivkin, Arnold, ed. *Nations by Design: Institution Building in Africa.* Garden City, N.Y.: Doubleday, 1968.

Roberts, B.C. *Labour in the Tropical Territories of the Commonwealth.* London: G. Bell & Sons, 1964.

Roper, J.L. *Labour Problems in West Africa.* London: Penguin, 1958.

Roper, and Davison, R.B., eds. *The Labour and Trade Union Ordinances of the Gold Coast.* London: Staples, n.d.

Rose, Arnold M., ed. *The Institutions of Advanced Societies.* Minneapolis: University of Minnesota Press, 1958.

Sandbrook, Richard. *Proletarians and African Capitalism: The Kenyan Case, 1960-1972.* Geneva: International Labor Office, 1972.

Sandbrook, and Cohen, Robin, eds. *The Development of an African Working Class.* Toronto and Buffalo: University of Toronto Press, 1975.

Selekman, Benjamin M. *Labor Relations and Human Relations.* New York & London: McGraw-Hill, 1947.

Selznick, Philip. *Leadership in Administration.* Evanston, Ill. & White Plains, N.Y.: Row, Peterson & Co., 1957.

Stinchcombe, Arthur L. *Constructing Social Theories.* New York: Harcourt, Brace & World, 1968.

Tettegah, John K. *A New Chapter for Ghana Labour.* Accra: Ghana T.U.C., 1958.

Tettegah, John K. *Towards Nkrumahism: The Building of Socialist Ghana.* Accra: Education and Publicity Department of TUC, 1962.

Trades Union Congress [Ghana]. *Correspondence Course.* Accra: Ghana Labour College, n.d.

Trades Union Congress [Ghana]. *Protecting and Defending Our Members.* Accra: Ghana Labour College, 1969?

Woddis, Jack. *The Lion Awakes.* London: Lawrence & Wishart, 1961.

The World Bank. *World Development Report, 1978.* Washington, D.C.: World Bank, 1978.

Zolberg, Aristide. *Creating Political Order.* Chicago: Rand McNally, 1966.

Articles and Periodicals

Afreh, Kwame, "The Role of Trade Unions in Ghana." *Legon Observer*, VII, 1 (June 2, 1972).

*Africa and the World.* December 1971.

*Africa Confidential*, August 20, 1971.

Allen, V.L. "Management and Labour in Africa." *The Listener*, August 15, 1963.

Amin, Samir. "Underdevelopment and Dependence." *Journal of Modern African Studies*, X, 4 (1972).

Arrighi, Giovanni, and Saul, John S. "Socialism and Economic Development in Tropical Africa," *Journal of Modern African Studies*, VI, 2 (1968).

*Ashanti Pioneer*, August 13, 1960.

Bates, Robert H. "Approaches to the Study of Unions and Development." *Industrial Relations*, IX, 4 (1970).

Berg, Elliot. "Urban Real Wages and the Nigerian Trade Union Movement, 1939-60: A Comment." *Economic Development and Cultural Change*, XVII, 4 (1969).

Chazan, Naomi, and Le Vine, Victor T. "Politics in a 'Non-Political' System: The March 30, 1978 Referendum in Ghana." *African Studies Review*, XXII, 1 (April 1979).

*Daily Graphic*, 1968-73.

Esseks, John D. "Government and Indigenous Private Enterprise in Ghana." *Journal of Modern African Studies*, IX, 1 (1971).

*Evening News* (Accra), April 13, 1961.

Fisher, Paul. "The Economic Role of Unions in Less-Developed Areas." *Monthly Labor Review*, September 1961.

Folson, B.D.G. "The Development of Sociolist Ideology in Ghana." *Ghana Social Science Journal*, I, 1 (1971).

*Ghanaian Times*, 1968-73.

*Ghana Workers' Bulletin*, 1967-69.

Gray, Paul S. "Exchange and Access in Field Work." *Urban Life*, October 1980.

Gray, Paul S. "Collective Bargaining in Ghana." *Industrial Relations* XIX, 2 (1980).

Kilby, Peter. "Industrial Relations and Wage Determination: Failure of the Anglo-Saxon Model." *Journal of Developing Areas*, I, 4 (1967).

Kraus, Jon. "African Trade Unions: Progress or Poverty?" *African Studies Review*, XIX, 3 (1976).

*Labour*, 1960-61.

*Light*, March 31, 1971.

Owusu, Maxwell. "The Search for Solvency: Background to the Fall of Ghana's Second Republic." *Africa Today*, XIX, 1 (1972).

*Palaver*, September 9, 1971.

Quaye, Kofi. "Business and the Revolution." *Daily Graphic*, February 5, 1973.

Rimmer, Douglas. "The Industrial Relations Act, 1958." *Economic Bulletin of Ghana*, III, 4 (1959).

Rimmer, Douglas. "The New Industrial Relations in Ghana." *Industrial and Labor Relations Review*, XIV, 2 (1961).

Ryan, Selwyn, "Socialism and the Party System in Ghana: 1947-1966." *Pan-African Journal*, III, 1 (1970).

Scott, Roger. "Are Trade Unions Still Necessary in Africa?" *Transition*, 33 (1967).

*Spokesman*, August 22, 1970.

*Star*, August 11, 1971 and August 28, 1971.

Tettegah, John. "The African Proletariat." *Spearhead*, January 1962.

Trachtman, Lester N. "Ghanaian Labor Legislation Since Independence." *Labor Law Journal*, XII, 6 (1961).

*TUC Newsletter, 1973-77.*

*West Africa*, 1958-74.

Woddis, Jack. "Role of the African Working Class in the African Liberation Movement." *World Marxist Review*, V, 7 (1962).

## Government Publications

Ghana. *Annual Report on the Department of Labour for the Year 1959-60.* Accra: State Publishing Corporation, 1962.

Ghana. *Annual Report on the Labour Department for the Year 1962-63.* Accra: State Publishing Corporation, 1966.

Ghana. *Annual Report on the Labour Department for the Year 1963-64.* Accra: State Publishing Corporation, 1966.

Ghana. *Annual Report on the Labour Division of the Ministry of Trade and Labour for the Year 1956-57.* Accra: Government Printing Department, 1959.

Ghana. *The Civil Service Act, 1960.* Accra-Tema: Ghana Publishing Corporation, 1971.

Ghana. *Economic Survey, 1963.* Accra: Central Bureau of Statistics, 1964.

Ghana. *Industrial Relations Act, 1958.* Accra: Government Printing Department, 1964.

Ghana. *Industrial Relations [Amendment] Act, 1971 — Act 383.* Accra-Tema: Ghana Publishing Corporation, 1971.

Ghana. *Newsletter.* Accra: Central Bureau of Statistics, 1973.

Ghana. *Parliamentary Debates* (Official Report, First Series). Accra: Government Printing Department, 1959.

Ghana. *Prices and Incomes Board Decree, 1972.* Accra-Tema: Ghana Publishing Corporation, 1972. ·

Ghana. *Report of the Commission of Enquiry into Obuasi Disturbances, 1969.* Accra-Terma: Ghana Publishing Corporation, 1970.

Ghana. *Report of the Commission of Enquiry into the Funds of the Ghana Trades Union Congress.* Accra-Tema: Ghana Publishing Corporation, 1968.

Ghana. *Report of the Commission on the Structure and Remuneration of the Public Services in Ghana, 1967.* Accra-Tema: Ghana Publishing Corporation, 1970.

Ghana. *Report of the Committee of Enquiry into the Recent Disturbances at Prestea.* Accra-Tema: Ghana Publishing Corporation, 1968.

Ghana. *Report of the Salary Review Committee.* Accra-Tema: Ghana Publishing Corporation, 1974.

Ghana. *Speeches and Intervals by Colonel I.K. Acheampong,* I Accra-Tema: Information Services Department, 1973.

Ghana. *White Paper on the Report of the Salary Review Committee.* Accra-Tema: Ghana Publishing Corporation, 1974.

Gold Coast Colony. *Annual Report on the Labour Department for the Year 1939-40.* Accra: Government Printing Department, 1940.

Gold Coast Colony. *Annual Report on the Labour Department for the Year 1941-42.* Accra: Government Printing Department, 1942.

Gold Coast Colony. *Annual Report on the Labour Department for the Year 1942-43.* Accra: Government Printing Department, 1943.

Gold Coast Colony. *Award of Arbitrator.* (In the Matter of the Trades Disputes [Arbitration and Inquiry] Ordinance, 1941 and in the Matter of a Trade Dispute between the Gold Coast Mines Employees Union and the Gold Coast Chamber of Mines). Accra: Government Printing Department, 1947.

Gold Coast Colony. *Report on the Labour Department for the Year 1938-39.* Accra: Government Printing Department, 1939.

Gold Coast Colony. *Report on the Labour Department for the Year 1947-48.* Accra: Government Printing Department, 1949.

Gold Coast Colony. *Report on the Labour Department for the Year 1948-49.* Accra: Government Printing Department, 1950.

Gold Coast Colony. *Report on the Labour Department for the Year 1949-50.* Accra: Government Printing Department, 1951.

Great Britain. *Colonial Reports,* 1949-54. London: H.M.S.O.

Great Britain. *The Colonial Territories — 1950-51.* Cmd. 8243.

United States. *Directory of Labor Organizations,* 1958; 1962; 1966. Washington, D.C.: U.S. Department of Labor.


## Reports and Documents


"Address by the Commissioner for Labour, Social Welfare and Co-Operatives, at the Annual General Meeting of the Ghana Employers' Association on 26th January, 1973." Mimeographed.

General Agricultural Workers Union of T.U.C. (Ghana). "Report of the National Executive Council." Mimeographed. August 1970.

Trades Union Congress. "Report on the Activities of the TUC [Ghana] to the Second Biennial Congress Held at Tamale." Mimeographed. July 1968.

Trades Union Congress. "Report on the Activities of the TUC [Ghana] to the Third Biennial Congress Held at the Advanced Teacher Training College — Winneba." Mimeographed. July-August 1970.


## Unpublished Papers and Dissertations


Crisp, Jeff. "Union Atrophy and Worker Revolt: Labour Protest at Tarkwa Goldfields, Ghana, 1968-69." Paper presented at the Annual Meeting of the African Studies Association, Baltimore, 1978.

Friedland, William H. "African Trade Union Studies: Analysis of Two Decades." Mimeographed. Paper prepared for the meeting of the African Studies Association, New York, November 1972.

Gerritsen, Rolf. "Pressure Group and Political System: The Case of the Ghana Trades Union Congress." Unpublished master's dissertation, Institute of African Studies, University of Ghana, Legon, May 1972.

Gray, Paul S. "Developing Political Relations Between the Ghana Trades Union Congress and the National Redemption Council — 1972-74."

Paper presented at the Seventeenth Annual Meeting of the African Studies Association, Chicago, 1974.

Kilson, Martin. "Tensions and Dynamics of African Single-Party Systems: Case of the Erstwhile Convention People's Party." Mimeographed. Paper presented at the Annual Meeting of the American Political Science Association, Washington, D.C., September 2-7, 1968.

Kraus, Jon. "Labor Organization and Labor Protest in Ghana Under Colonial Rule." Unpublished paper. Fredonia, N.Y.: State University College of New York at Fredonia, 1978.

Kraus, Jon. "The Political Economy of Trade Union-Government Relations in Ghana Under Four Regimes." Mimeographed. Fredonia, N.Y.: State University College of New York at Fredonia, 1972.

Price, Robert M. "Organizational Commitment and Organizational Character in the Ghanaian Civil Service." Paper presented at the Seventeenth Annual Meeting of the African Studies Association, Chicago, 1974.

# Index

AATUF (All African Trade Union
Federation), 69
Acheampong, Col. Ignatius (Kutu),
12, 13, 92, 152
Adjei, Ako, 36
AFL-CIO, 70
Akuffo, Lt. Gen. F.W.K., 13
Ampah, Kwaw, 42, 140-141, 144, 149
Amponsah, R.R., 35, 37, 157

Baako, Kofi, 57
Balogun, G.A., 140
Bentum, B.A., 44, 51, 60, 87, 91,
113-115, 130, 133-134, 150, 158,
162, 171, 173, 185, 189-190
Biney, Pobee, 24, 27, 124-126, 154,
171
British Trades Union Congress,
14-15, 35, 70
Brice-Konuah, Dr. A., 89-90
Busia, Dr. Kofi, 12, 46, 51, 54, 114,
150

Chamber of Mines, 65, 111
Charter of Redemption, 191-192
Civil servants, 186-187 (see also
Trade unions, containing civil
servants)
Cocoa trade, 11-12
Collective bargaining, 58, 96-107
content of agreements, 100, 104
extension orders, 97, 101
group agreements, 101

tactics, 101-102
and worker discipline, 76, 181
Colonial Development Act (1940), 14
Congress of Free Trade Unions
(1956), 28, 71
Cooperative Distillers' Workers
Union, 49
Corruption, 138-142, 146-147, 183
CPP (Convention People's Party),
17, 19, 23, 65, 84, 140, 186
relations with Trades Union
Congress, 20, 22, 24-25, 27,
34-35, 38-43, 60, 112, 140-141,
174-175
Danquah, Dr. J.B., 18
Dependency critique, 2, 4-6, 198-201
Dowuona-Hammond, A.J., 35

Employers' associations, 65-67
Ethnicity, 143-144, 168-169

GCL (Ghana Confederation of
Labor), 48 49, 51-52, 71
GEA (Ghana Employers' Association, 66, 67, 84, 94-95, 101,
116-117
Gold Coast Unemployed Association, 125
GTUC (Ghana Trades Union Congress, 1951-53), 24, 125

Hamah, John Alex, 159
"house unions," 15, 56

ICFTU (International Confederation
  of Free Trade Unions), 24, 27,
  32, 35, 68, 120
ICU (Industrial and Commercial
  Workers Union), 47-48, 53, 104,
  145
ILO (International Labor Organization), 69
Industrial relations
  colonial environment for, 79-82,
    111
  grievance handling, 82-83, 85-86
  norms, 79
  under CPP, 97, 111
  under NLC, 88, 112-114
  under NRC, 92-95, 105, 152-153
  under PP, 89-92, 102-103, 109,
    151
  and violence, 107-110
Industrial Relations Act (1958), 30,
  35-38, 40, 82-83
  impact on bargaining, 96-98
  impact on employers, 84-85
Industrial Relations Act (1965),
  42-44, 53
Industrial Relations (Amendment)
  Act, 1971, 50-51
Inflation, 12
"institutional transfer," 7-8
International Trade Secretariats, 69
Issifu, A.M., 134, 144, 162-164,
  185

JCSA (Junior Civil Servants Associ-
  ation), 71-72, 187
Jones, I.G., 14-15
Justice Party, 68

Kitching, Oswald, 15
Kumah, I.K., 26, 125

Labor aristocracy, 5-6
LAC (Labor Advisory Council), 67
Leadership
  corruption, 138-142, 146-147,
    173
  courage, 171-173

ideology, 153ff.
  norms, 142-143ff.
  roles, 122-123 ff., 167-168
  social status, 137-138, 170-171
Lidbury Commission, 56
Limann, Hilla, 13
Local Government Workers Union,
  49

MACAWU (Manufacturing, Com-
  mercial and Allied Workers
  Union), 47-49, 52-53, 145, 148
Maritime and Dockworkers Union,
  32, 104
Mensah, J.H., 49, 102, 114-115
Methodology. See Research method-
  ology
Mills-Odoi Commission, 72, 105,
  113-114
Mines Employees Union (Mine-
  workers), 21, 23, 24, 31, 172,
  180
Modernization theory, 2, 3-4,
  198-201
Moffatt, A.A., 19, 24

Nationalism, 16-17, 42
"New Structure," 29-32, 34, 40,
  57-58
  impact on employers, 66
Nkrumah, Kwame, 12, 18-19, 21-22,
  24, 34-35, 38, 43, 174, 184
NLC (National Liberation Council),
  12, 44, 60-61, 87-88, 157
NLM (National Liberation Movement, 1956), 28, 68, 154
NRC (National Redemption Council), 12, 53, 61, 63-65, 116,
  152-153, 191-192
Nyamitei, H.P., 20

OATUU (Organization of African
  Trade Union Unity), 70
Ossei-Mensah, K.A., 150
Otoo, W.B., 149

"Positive Action," 20-21, 37, 125

Posts and Telecommunication
Workers Union, 80, 105
PP (Progress Party) regime, 46-50,
52, 61, 89, 114, 151, 155, 185,
188-190
Prices and Incomes Board, 93-94,
105-106
Public opinion, 181 ff.
Public Transport Workers Union,
52
Public Utilities Workers Union, 145

Railway Enginemen's Union, 53, 90,
105, 151, 154, 176
Railwaymen (Railway and Ports
Workers Union), 14, 16, 30-31,
46-47, 53, 105, 149, 151, 176
Rawlings, Lt. Jerry, 13
Research methodology, 1, 209n
RHWU (Railway and Harbor
Workers Union), 46-47, 49, 53,
145

Salary Review Committee, 106
Scott, Sir Robert, 18
SMC (Supreme Military Council),
12-13
Strikes, 74-75, 83, 108, 110
and nationalism, 17-18
1950 general strike, 20-23
1961 general strike, 42, 108-109,
129, 172, 174, 182-183
after 1966, 187-188
1971 strikes, 176
pre-1941, 14
tradition of, 180
wildcat strikes, 110
Tachie-Menson, C.W., 19, 125
Tachie-Menson, F.E., 26-27
Tettegah, John K., 26-27, 30-35, 38,
40, 42, 57, 59, 68, 111, 126-127,
133, 139, 143-144, 148, 155,
162-165, 171-172, 175, 183-184
Tevie, A.K., 47
Timber and Woodworks Union, 104
Trade Union Ordinance (1941), 14,
16

Trade unions
administrative skills in, 15,
125-127, 130
branch leadership, 129-130
breakaways, 34, 46-49, 52
colonial environment for, 11,
13-14, 22, 28-29
containing civil servants, 39, 41,
44, 60, 71, 87, 97
culture, 180-181
democracy in, 131
early leadership styles, 123-124
institutionalization, 1, 7, 8-9
and modernization, 2
western, 2
TUC (Trades Union Congress of
Ghana)
amalgamation in, 30-31, 33,
40-42
dissolution of, 49-52, 61,
151-152, 188-189
doctrine, 182, 184, 189-190
Executive Board, 144, 146-147
foreign assistance, 70
innaguration, 15
leaders' career patterns,
121-122
leadership education, 120
member unions, 45
membership, 58, 60, 177
militants in, 19, 24-28, 31,
124-126, 154
moderates in, 19, 23-27, 31, 127,
154
and political alliances, 156ff.,
216n
pre-1948, 16
relations with chiefs, 18, 21
relations with Convention
People's Party (CPP), 20, 22,
24, 27, 38-43, 76, 112, 155, 174,
182-183
relations with post-CPP
regimes, 176
representation on boards and
commissions, 63-64
restoration, 53

230

"stalwarts" in, 26, 126-127, 155
Turkson-Ocran, E.C., 26-27,
124-126, 171

UAC (United African Company)
Employees Union, 24, 27, 31-32,
41
UGCC (United Gold Coast Conven-
tion), 17-19
Unfair labor practices, 83
UP (United Party), 35, 37, 41, 68,
155

Wage rates, 56, 59, 72, 82, 105, 117
Watson Commission, 19
Webb, Sidney (Lord Passfield), 14
Welbeck, N., 33-34
WFTU (World Federation of Trade
Unions), 26-27
Woode, Anthony, 24, 26-28, 124-126,
171
Woode, Frank, 19
Workers
commitment to unions, 167ff.
ideology, 179-180
reaction to 1971 dissolution,
176-177
socialization of, 76, 174-175,
177-178

## ABOUT THE AUTHOR

Paul S. Gray is a member of the faculty of the Department of Sociology at Boston College. He received his doctorate from Yale, where he was awarded a University Fellowship and an NIMH comparative sociology traineeship. He has also earned degrees from Princeton and Stanford universities. Dr. Gray's previous publications include *Economics for Ghanaian Trade Unions* (Ghana Labour College, 1973) and numerous articles on voluntary organizations, unions, collective bargaining, and sociological research methods. Unions and Leaders in Ghana is the result of fourteen months of intensive field research.

# CONCH MAGAZINE, LIMITED

## BOOK CATALOGS

**Conch Magazine, Limited** publishes books on every aspect of African affairs, including African culture, literature, history, law, politics, economics, military affairs, children's literature, sociology, anthropology, education, religion and philosophy.

**Trado-Medic Books**, a division of Conch Magazine, Limited, specializes in books about traditional healing, health, behavioral sciences and psychiatry in the Third World, Africa in particular.

Conch catalogs and seasonal announcements are designed to give you an opportunity to build your own private library at considerable savings. If you would like to receive news of forthcoming Conch and Trado-Medic books, just send us your name and address, plus 50 cents to help defray postage and handling costs.

---

### CONCH MAGAZINE, LIMITED

102 Normal Avenue
Buffalo, New York 14213
USA

P.O. Box 573
Owerri, Omo State
Nigeria

Please send me news of ☐ **Conch** ☐ **Trado-Medic** books.

Name _____

Profession _____

Address _____

_____
City                State                Zip Code

Do you know someone who would like to find out about Conch and Trado-Medic Books?

Please send news of ☐ **Conch** ☐ **Trado-Medic** books to:

Name _____

Profession _____

Address _____

_____
City                State                Zip Code

r